THE EFFECTIVE MANAGER

THE EFFECTIVE MANAGER

Being the Best in Financial Sales Management

Karl F. Gretz

and

Steven R. Drozdeck

The New York Institute of Finance

New York   London   Toronto   Sydney   Tokyo   Singapore

Library of Congress Cataloging-in-Publication Data

Gretz, Karl F.
   The effective manager : being the best in financial sales
management / Karl F. Gretz and Steven R. Drozdeck.
      p.   cm.
   ISBN (invalid) 0-13-173881-6
   1. Financial services industry—Management.   2. Brokers.   3. Sales
management.   I. Drozdeck, Steven R.   II. Title.
HG173.G75   1991
332.1″068″8—dc20   90-24712
                                                            CIP

This publication is designed to provide accurate and authoritative information in regard to the subject matter covered. It is sold with the understanding that the publisher is not engaged in rendering legal, accounting, or other professional service. If legal advice or other expert assistance is required, the services of a competent professional person should be sought.

From a Declaration of Principles
Jointly Adopted by
a Committee of the American Bar Association
and a Committee of Publishers and Associations

Printed in the United States of America

10   9   8   7   6   5   4   3   2   1

Dedication

This book is dedicated to the authors' parents and families, without whose support no manager can succeed: William, Janis, Inge, Michael, Anna, Maria, and Sara Gretz; and Jane, Sandy, and Nicholas Drozdeck.

Preface

The Effective Manager has been written in response to requests from the many managers we have trained in all areas of the financial services industry. Today, more and more managers are recognizing the need for communications, leadership, motivational coaching, and counseling skills in their day-to-day work. Unfortunately, while there are many exciting motivational speakers and a host of communications training available, they provide a wide variety of philosophies as well as techniques. As a result, senior and branch managers often appear to provide inconsistent messages which confuse their employees and lower instead of raise morale.

This book provides techniques for managing and motivating people based on the simple philosophy that your personnel and customers are your most important assets. If you place your employees' development before the "bottom line," instead of after it, you will increase not only your profits, but also employee production and job satisfaction, while reducing stress and litigation. Hence, the principles and techniques of *The Effective Manager* are not limited to the financial services industry.

We would like to thank the many individuals who helped us in preparing this book: our fine contributing authors; S. Randolph Gretz who provided a wealth of useful insights and advice; Philip Ruppel, associate publisher at the New York Institute of Finance, and Tim McManus whose insights into branch manager training were extremely helpful.

About the Authors

Karl F. Gretz, Ph.D. is a Managing Partner in Training Groups Inc. and President of Gretz Associates, Corporate Consulting and has over 12 years experience in training professionals in the financial services industry, medicine, education, and the military. Prior to establishing Gretz Associates, Dr. Gretz was associated with Merrill Lynch, first as a successful financial consultant and then as a senior training consultant. Working with corporations in the brokerage, banking, and insurance industries, he has trained over 6,000 sales professionals and their managers in the psychology of sales, management, and leadership. He has also helped them to increase sales productivity and lower staff turnover by providing easy, effective methods for managing stress.

Steven R. Drozdeck is a Managing Partner and the President of Training Groups Inc., and has over ten years experience in training. Prior to assuming the position of president of Training Groups, he worked for Merrill Lynch for 16 years, most recently as Manager of Professional Development. During his ten years with Merrill Lynch training, Mr. Drozdeck instructed over 18,000 stockbrokers in sales and stock selection techniques. Prior to his position with the training department, he was a financial consultant for six years. Mr. Drozdeck is a Certified NLP (Neuro Linguistic Programming) Trainer and a consultant/speaker for various training groups. He is also listed in numerous Who's Who... publications.

About the Contributors

Robert Clark, CLU, CPCU, CHFC, is the General Manager of the Greater Princeton Agency of Prudential Insurance of America. During his 20 years of work in the insurance industry, Mr. Clark has also been the Manager of Training for Prudential and has acted as an internal consultant on training. He has trained over 3,000 domestic and international sales and management professionals for Prudential throughout the world. In addition, he has been a multiple winner of the *General Agents and Managers National Management Award* and has also been awarded Prudential's *President's Citation* in seven of the last nine years.

Victor T. Ehre, Jr. is Regional Manager for the Merchants Insurance Group in Buffalo, New York. Mr. Ehre has over 15 years of management experience in the insurance industry. He has also been a casualty facultative reinsurance underwriter and in 1978, he started Uni-Service Excess Facilities (an excess and surplus lines wholesale insurance agency), a division of Utica National Insurance. He holds a Masters of Insurance degree from Georgia State University.

E. Noel Gouldin is Vice President of Programming of the Dallas, Texas-based Financial Satellite Network. He is responsible for the development, production, and overall quality of the network's programming which is aimed at the financial, insurance, and banking industries. This includes a wide variety of programming dedicated to sales training, product knowledge, motivation, and management skills. Prior to joining FSN, Mr. Gouldin was a registered representative with Dean Witter Reynolds, where he also developed marketing campaigns and literature adopted by Dean Witter nationally.

James G. Miller is a Vice President of Merrill Lynch Capital Markets, and Manager of Merrill Lynch International Sales and Management Training, of the International Private Client Sales and Marketing Division. Mr. Miller has been with Merrill Lynch for ten years, first as a commodity futures and retail financial consultant and later as a senior training specialist. He has trained over 5,000 domestic and international financial consultants and managers.

Glen W. Mitchell is a producer with the Dallas, Texas-based Financial Satellite Network. He is also the host of two FSN programs, "Managed Money" and "FSN Magazine." Mr. Mitchell's diverse background includes business reporting, anchoring an all-business news television station, and running a commercial writing company. He is also a freelance contributor to Voice of America and National Public Radio.

James D. McLean is Manager of Marketing Training for the Davis & Geck Division of American Cyanamid Company. Prior to that he was Manager of International Sales Training for American Cyanamid. Mr. McLean has been with his current company for 14 years and has trained over 1,000 sales and management professionals from over 30 countries. He has also been a sales representative for Procter and Gamble and has managed several political campaigns for state offices.

Robert J. Miesionczek has been an Assistant Vice President and Manager of Management Training and Development in Operations, Systems for Merrill Lynch for the last four years. He has also been a management consultant for six years. Mr. Miesionczek has trained over 1,000 managers in financial services operations and management skills.

Marilyn Pearson is an Assistant Vice President and Marketing Manager, Business Financial Services for Merrill Lynch. She was previously Manager of Special Training and Development and a Senior Training Consultant as well as a very successful financial consultant with the same firm. She has trained over 5,000 sales professionals. In addition, she developed and implemented programs for minority recruitment and trained numerous sales and branch managers in minority awareness programs.

Joseph Ross, Ph.D., is a Vice-President at Merrill Lynch, where he started in 1960 as a sales trainer. He is the co-author of three works: *Words of Wall Street, More Words of Wall Street,* and *Still More Words of Wall Street* (Business One—Irwin). He has been a faculty member of the New York Institute of Finance for more than 20 years.

Michael Saggese is the Senior Management Consultant with Human Concepts, Inc., providing human resources consulting services to Fortune 1000 companies. Prior to this, Mr. Saggese was the director of Training for Midlantic National Bank, and trained over 3,000 sales and management professionals. He is also a Certified Trainer in NLP (Neuro Linguistic Programming), specializing in business applications.

Introduction

Characteristics of Star Managers

Over the last ten years, the financial services industry has changed significantly. Areas once clearly dominated by either banks, insurance agencies, or brokerage firms are now being intermingled as each arm of the financial services industry expands its products and services to include those of the other two. Today, banks are moving into both brokerage and insurance services while brokerage firms offer banking and insurance services, and insurance companies, not to be left behind, are expanding into the banking and brokerage industries. The result is a growing need for branch managers in all three areas to increase their understanding of not only all areas of this expanding marketplace, but also how to help their sales and operational professionals cope with changes in both clientele and sales techniques.

When you think about it, we all know branch managers who are real "STARS" among their peers. They always seem able to get the most out of their people while maintaining a low rate of personnel turnover. How do they do it? What are the characteristics of these super successes? Throughout this book, we will explore and teach those characteristics and skills which separate the good from the really great sales managers.

Trait 1: Great Branch Managers Can Manage Themselves

- They have developed a set of principles that they live by and they are continually improving on those principles.
- They effectively manage the myriad of events that take up their valuable time. As such, they are particularly effective in establishing effective goals and setting priorities.
- They have developed ways to manage the tremendous stress associated with the job of managing a branch.
- They are self-motivating.
- They can manage their personal lives so that they complement rather than compete with their profession.
- They maintain balance in their lives and activities.
- They genuinely *like* people!
- They can make decisions and accept responsibility for the outcomes of those decisions.
- They lead by personal example.

Trait 2: Great Branch Managers Are Great Communicators

- They can quickly size up the emotional needs of the people with whom they speak (e.g., employees, customers, peers, and superiors) and communicate to those needs.
- They are able to quickly establish rapport with those to whom they are speaking. They realize the barriers that are created when their listeners do not feel kinship with them.
- They *listen* to people, and are able to effectively communicate genuine interest in and understanding of their needs.

- They are able to organize their sales presentations in ways that are motivating and easy to understand. This also makes it easy for their sales personnel to explain new products and services to clients.
- They know how to run effective sales and planning meetings; how to set an agenda; and how to modify the meeting to fit the desired outcome (e.g., motivational, product specific, etc.).

Trait 3: Great Branch Managers Know How to Manage and Work Well with Others

- They know how to determine what motivates their personnel, especially sales personnel. With this information, they keep personnel excited about both work and customers.
- They know how to build a sales team, getting their people to work effectively together.
- They know how to conduct an effective hiring interview or termination interview. They can fully explain their expectations and the requirements of a job to a new employee, and they follow-up to make sure that they have been understood.
- They coach and counsel their personnel as it becomes necessary, and before serious problems occur.
- They know how to effectively negotiate with others (e.g., customers, peers, etc.) to obtain cooperation in achieving their goals.

These traits have been universally recognized as the factors that separate the outstanding from the merely good branch managers in every area of the financial services industry. In the chapters that follow, we will teach you how to develop or strengthen these traits in yourself.

This book has been written for the benefit of branch and sales managers in banking, insurance, and the securities industries. However, since, of the three, the larger securities firms appear to have most fully integrated the full range of financial services available from all three areas, the book is written most often from the point of view of a securities branch manager.

Note that certain portions of this book may appear similar to the authors' previous volume, *Consultative Selling Techniques for Financial Professionals* (New York Institute of Finance, 1990). Because this volume was written for the branch and sales managers who work with financial sales professionals, we have purposely used a similar structure and examples wherever possible to aid the manager when discussing the concepts provided with his sales personnel.

The authors realize that some financial professionals refer to their clientele as clients while others refer to them as customers, hence the words "customer" and "client" may be used interchangeably throughout the book. Since financial service sales personnel are referred to by various titles (e.g., insurance agents, account executives, brokers, etc.) throughout the industry, but all act in the role of providing financial consultation to their clients, the authors will refer to all sales personnel as financial consultants (FCs). Finally, for the sake of ease of reading the male gender predominates in the book. The authors recognize that a significant number of women are also found in the ranks of "star" managers within the banking, insurance, and securities industries.

Contents

**SECTION II
MANAGERS, EMPLOYEES, AND CUSTOMERS:
A PSYCHOLOGICAL MODEL, 49**

CHAPTER 6
Who Are We? General Personality Traits, 51

CHAPTER 7
Manager Types and Styles, 59

CHAPTER 8
FC and Customer Personality Types, 67

xxviii

SECTION I

Creating a Successful Branch

Today's branch manager in the financial services industry is unique. He is effectively president and chief operating officer of his own company with full authority to hire and fire employees, negotiate problems with customers, and establish standards for excellence and productivity. Ironically, he is expected to do this without the benefit of a graduate degree in business management. In fact, most branch managers were previously sales managers and financial consultants (FCs) themselves. Despite this, branch managers are expected to run a branch efficiently with only a minimum of training from their respective corporations. The characteristics that made them successful FCs are *not* necessarily the same characteristics needed to be a successful branch or sales manager. In fact, some of the attributes that made them successful FCs (e.g., high drive and the ability to ignore everything and everyone around them as *they* do *their* work) may actually be counterproductive to a manager who needs to be responsive to the needs of individual staff members.

This section will deal with two important traits of successful branch managers:

1. Great branch managers can manage themselves and;

2. They can effectively administer an office.

As a result of these two primary traits, a host of other benefits is derived:

- They recognize changes in the markets they serve and adjust to those changes before their competition.
- They have developed a set of principles that they live by and they are continually improving themselves.
- They effectively manage the myriad of events that compete for their valuable time. As such, they are particularly effective in establishing effective goals and setting priorities.
- They have developed ways to manage the tremendous stress associated with the job of managing a branch.
- They are self-motivated.
- They can manage their personal lives so that they complement instead of compete with their profession. They maintain balance in their lives and activities.
- They genuinely *like* people!
- They can make decisions and accept responsibility for the outcomes of those decisions.
- They lead by personal example.

CHAPTER 1

How to Prosper in a Client-Centered Market

Within the financial services industry, today's branch manager faces three major challenges: the changing competition, FCs, and the changing nature of the market. At the same time, while a manager is effectively the CEO of his branch, being a successful FC is hardly adequate preparation for running a company. After all, most company managers have at least a Masters of Business Administration from schools such as Wharton or Harvard. This chapter discusses each of the manager's three challenges and how to deal with them. This book will help you to develop the leadership and management skills needed to create and maintain a smoothly functioning and profitable branch.

Challenge One: The Changing Competition

Your first challenge is the changing competition. With the slow demise of federal regulation, banks are beginning to offer products and services once considered to be the exclusive realm of the brokerage and insurance industries. At the same time, brokerage houses are selling insurance and offering banking services. Finally, insurance companies are selling mutual funds and stock and bonds, as well as other products which could be considered alternatives to bank CDs.

Gone are the days when a branch manager only had to deal with a limited number of products and the relatively few firms available to supply those products. Today, each arm of the financial services industry can provide almost total financial coverage of every customer's needs. As a result, unless a customer has all of his eggs in *your* basket, you may lose him to whichever firm handles the rest of his assets. When you think about it, that's quite a threat.

Challenge Two: The "Independent" FC

Your second challenge is the fact that every FC who works for you is really a semi-independent business that can move to another location and take his customers with him. The growth of proprietary products and central asset accounts has done a lot to make that more difficult, but it is still very common for FCs to switch. In addition, with the shrinking compensation offered at some major firms, it may become even more common as various financial services companies compete by trying to lure their competitor's FCs and their clients with more lucrative offers.

We all know what prima donnas some successful FCs can be, and how hard they can be to deal with. In addition, as a branch manager you are in the position of potentially being put out of business by a single major error on the part of just one of these "semi-independent businessmen." One major compliance problems and you may find yourself unemployed, or even in court. After all, as the "CEO" of your branch, you are technically responsible for everything that happens or fails to happen in your branch.

How do you keep your FCs and their support personnel happy and efficient while maintaining profitability? How do you deal with upset FCs or customers? How do you motivate your personnel and obtain their very best work at all times?

Challenge Three: The Customer

Some branch managers we know think that things were easier in "the old days" when customers just took their broker's advice and bought and sold when they were told to. Maybe they were "good old days," but those days are gone forever. Today's customer is far better informed than his predecessor and wants to be treated as an equal, not manipulated into buying products that he doesn't understand. And, he is willing to go to court in ever-increasing instances in order to make his point.

Summary

The role of today's branch manager is rapidly changing, requiring that a host of skills be brought to play. This book is designed to provide you with those skills.

CHAPTER *2*

Reflections of You: Developing Star Traits

You are already a success, or you wouldn't be a branch manager. You've worked hard and it's paid off. In addition, you've already developed a series of excellent work habits that have brought you to where you are today. Then why begin the book with a chapter on character? For four reasons:

1. In the same way that a ship and its crew are a reflection of their captain, your branch is a reflection of you, your attitudes, and character. If you want a successful branch that is based on consultative selling and client service, you must look beyond the sales techniques that helped you to succeed as an individual and consider the overall message you unconsciously communicate to your staff and customers.

2. Even if *you* are already perfect, you must help your sales personnel to develop winning characters if they are to succeed as you have and as you would like them to.

3. No matter how successful we are (financially, socially, in our career, etc.), there isn't one of us who wouldn't benefit by trying to improve.

4. Finally, our interviews with sales personnel and managers have clearly demonstrated that the single greatest factor separating the outstanding from the merely good is their character.

In this chapter, we'll not only discuss how to strengthen your own character, but also point out ways that you can help your FCs and other employees to develop character traits of success.

Reflections of You

As an FC you undoubtedly were an influence in the lives of your customers, your sales assistant, and some of the other FCs around you. This is especially true if you acted as a mentor to any of them. Now, as a branch manager, your personality, character, and partialities will influence *all* of your employees to some extent. In addition, through your employees, you will influence your branch's customers.

If you genuinely believe that the only way to gain accounts and penetrate their assets is to put customer service first, you will communicate that to your employees in all that you do, and they will sell accordingly. You will even select employees with that criteria in mind, unconsciously, if not consciously. You will reward and be friendlier toward those who embody your attitudes and you will be emulated. However, if moving product and production figures are the only things that matter, you will communicate that just as clearly, regardless of stated company policy. Unfortunately, this can confuse employees and lose customers.

One of the biggest problems faced by many firms in the insurance and securities industries has been a perceived tendency to place immediate sales before the long-term needs of the customer. This has resulted in much negative press and is disadvantageous to the public. Now, most firms are strongly re-emphasizing the need to develop long-term customer relations through increased service. To do this, firms are increasing the emphasis of their training programs toward increased service. Unfortunately, many FCs report that when they start at a new branch after training, they are told to forget what they were taught and to concentrate on immediate commissions and new accounts by managers who have not made the same transition as the company's upper executives.

What are your primary objectives—service or short-term profit? Whichever you choose will be reflected in your employees.

The Character of Greatness

During the last few years, the news·media have been full of accounts of "successful leaders" in the financial services industry who have been indicted and convicted for various crimes. Lack of character has been the cause. In every case, the individual involved decided to cut corners and make a name for himself by making himself a superstar at the expense of his character. Unfortunately, any list of such individuals would be too long for this publication.

Contrast these individuals with some of the really great men and women of history: Thomas Jefferson, Betsy Ross, George Washington, Thomas Edison, George Washington Carver, Susan B. Anthony, Theodore Roosevelt, Eleanor Roosevelt, Benjamin Franklin, Simon Bolivar, and Marie Curie. What was it that made them great? Was it intelligence coupled with opportunity? Hardly. Some of the world's most famous losers were intelligent. At the same time, while all these people were intelligent, many had little opportunity when they began. Many came from very poor backgrounds and, by all accounts, should have failed. The single common denominator of their greatness was their character. They became great men and women because of their characters. Essentially, while both intelligence and character are two key ingredients to success, intelligence without character can eventually lead to failure.

But what of our character? Most of us have achieved what we have thus far through a series of accidents. That may sound pretty strong, but think about it. An accident of birth placed us in the homes where we were nurtured. Our character is the result of the accidents of whom we have met and their influence on us (family in the beginning, then friends, teachers, television, etc.). In a sense, we have developed our characters through a process of osmosis, absorbing bits of experience from our associates. Yet, despite the extreme importance of character, very few people consciously try to develop it. Amazing, isn't it? During a period of five years, we asked over 5,000 people if they had ever consciously worked to develop their characters. Only six said yes!

One of the greatest causes of failure in the financial services industry is the lack of character of many individuals. Most who fail simply give up and quit because it requires more work than they had planned. Many others fail because they lack the self-discipline to organize their time and goals and to stick with the tasks required for success. A few fail because their greed overwhelms their character and they place immediate profits ahead of their integrity and concern for their customer's welfare.

As you think about the personnel in your branch, what kind of character does each of them have? Are they totally honest, or just in the areas where compliance is watching, now? Do they have the strength of character to keep cold calling in a down market? Do they put the customer's needs ahead of immediate commission? There's no doubt about it; it's hard work!

Many studies have indicated that most employees work at only 30% of their capacity. Yet they expect to be paid for 100% of their time! Consider the mental, emotional, and work ethic differences between the superstars you have known and the numerous runners up. The stars had *character*. This word has various meanings, but it would certainly include, to one degree or another, such attributes as:

- Persistence
- Determination
- Integrity
- Honesty
- Loyalty
- Kindness
- Courage
- Self-discipline
- Belief in a higher good
- Concern for others.

The chances are that virtually everyone that you know has a few of these attributes to some degree. A useful mental experiment might be to compare your perceptions of the people in your office with some of these criteria (as well as any you wish to add). Use any rating scale that you wish, but compare and contrast your best, average, and worst employees. Who do you really want working for you?

If some of these traits stand out as being highly desirable, keep them in mind as you interview potential new hires. Although these traits are not easily and precisely identified, you will certainly get a feel for them during the hiring interview. You'll also obtain a more precise understanding of each new hire as you observe them during their probationary period (whether you have a formal probationary period or not is immaterial to the following points). Remember:

- While virtually all new employees are on their best behavior during the first month or so, they usually show their true colors shortly thereafter.

- Since most people do not have highly defined characters, they are most easily influenced by their co-workers and "the way things are done around here" during the first two or three months of employment. As the branch manager, you have your best opportunity to set the stage in terms of your desires when employees are first hired. Have absolutely no doubt that they will obtain this information from someone. Would you rather it came from you, or one of the coffee crowd.

- Your personal example will probably be your most powerful influence. What do people perceive when they observe you? What do they think about what you say or fail to say? What do you reward, punish, tolerate? Almost everybody in your office already knows from the informal networks that exist everywhere.

- Consider reviewing the list of character attributes that were provided. Where are you strong? Where would you like to develop greater strength? What are you proud of? What personally meaningful attributes would you add to the list?

- Remember, "people don't plan to fail, they just fail to plan." While this is true of goalsetting and time management, it is even more true of character development (something that effects your success in *all* areas).

In Chapter 3, we will discuss the need to set individual and branch goals, and then to determine what resources you will need to attain those goals. We'll also discuss how to help your FCs set and attain realistic production and character goals. After all, since the single most important resource to any real success is character, it is important to set character development goals as well as material goals with yourself and your FCs if you are to succeed. As you do, you will not only build a materially successful branch, you will also be proud of the people who accomplished that success.

Character and Habit

Benjamin Franklin is generally considered to be one of the greatest men who ever lived. He helped frame the Declaration of Independence and the Constitution, was the first Ambassador to both England and France, established the first fire department and post office, discovered electricity, and invented bifocals and the Franklin Stove. Not bad when you consider that, at age 20, he was a printer's apprentice with few or no prospects.

What happened to him? How did someone with so little going for him achieve such greatness? When he was a young man, Franklin realized that if he were ever to amount to anything, he must work to develop his character. Here's how he set about it: First, he determined 13 character traits that he thought were critical to greatness. The traits that you or your employees choose may be different from his, but think of some that you feel are appropriate for you. Perhaps integrity, empathy, promptness, temperance, and so on can be selected.

Second, Franklin wrote his character goals in a notebook and defined what each meant to him. To be effective, your definitions of character traits need to include observable behavior. If you achieve a given trait, would someone else be able to tell from observing your behavior? If you counsel an FC about traits, remind him that others should be able to tell that he has developed the trait by observing his behavior.

Third, Franklin spent a week on each trait. Beginning with the first trait, he would spend a week focusing on trying to live his definition of that trait. At the end of each day, he would review his progress and rate himself: did he improve, remain the same, or fall back? At the end of the week he would review his progress for the week and then focus on the next trait.

He worked on one character trait per week for 13 weeks, then began again. He did this for over 60 years. It's easy to see how he made a *habit* of developing a winning character.

Building character requires good habits!

Remember that good habits, whether they represent ways of thinking or acting, require persistent effort to develop. They will not grow by themselves. President Coolidge made this point excellently when he said that, to succeed, you have to stick to it, and never give up. He said:

> Press on. Nothing in the world can take the place of persistence. Talent will not: Nothing is more common than unsuccessful men with talent. Genius will not: Unrewarded genius is almost a proverb. Education alone will not: The world is full of educated derelicts. Persistence and determination alone are omnipotent.

Persistence pays off!

Perserverance is not only a good character trait; we need it to develop other character traits. And, without character, the time may come when it will seem impossible to resist the "opportunity" (read, temptation) to cut corners to make an extra or a quicker profit. For example, some managers suggest that it is all right to lie to secretaries if it will enable you to get past them to prospect their boss. Here are three good reasons for ignoring such spurious advice:

- There is no way that anyone can lie 50 times a day and not have it effect his relationship with his family and with himself;
- Once a client realizes that an FC has lied once, he will never trust the FC or your company again; and,
- To tell an FC to lie to someone else and then expect him to be honest with you is unrealistic at best. It's actually asking for compliance problems.

Winning Traits and Habits

In our interviews with great branch managers, several traits and habits of character have appeared repeatedly. We've listed a few of them and their possible definitions.

- Put quality service for both the customer and employees first.
- Never compromise your integrity or tolerate an employee who does, no matter how big a producer.
- Organize your time, energy, and resources. If you can't measure something, you can't manage it.
- Listen to your employes and customers. They're the real assets you manage.
- Fight for your employees. They need to feel that you'll back them up.
- Accept responsibility for the branch's problems, but spread credit around for its successes.
- Build bridges to your community.

Summary

Choose your traits and make a habit of living them. In the end, you'll have a far more successful and productive branch, and you'll be a lot happier! Remember that everything you do or say, or fail to do or say, communicates something about you. What do you want to communicate? In Section II, we will explore effective ways to make certain that what you communicate is what you want to communicate.

CHAPTER *3*

Hitting What You Aim At: Goal Setting

What are you shooting at? Where do you want to be in 5, 10,. or 20 years? For that matter, where do you want to be in one year, six months, next month? Odds are, you didn't get where you are by accident. You established your goals and now you've attained them, or at least one of them. Now what? Where to next? And, also how many of your FCs have effective goals? After all, if they don't have effective goals, you'll never be able to achieve yours. In this chapter we'd like you to take a second look at your goals and at ways to help your FCs develop some effective, motivating goals of their own.

Someone once said, "What the mind can conceive, it can achieve." These conceptions become our goals. However, before a goal can become a motivating, dynamic source of power, it must meet several criteria:

- *Goals must be stated positively.* Concentrate on what you want to achieve, rather than what you want to avoid. For example, "I want to increase sales production by 30% in the current fiscal year." (Positive.) Rather than, "I don't want to be the second-best office in production for the third year in a row." (Negative.)

    To get where you are now, you've probably already developed the habit of stating your goals positively, but some of your FCs may not. An example for them might be, "I want to cold call 100 new contacts each day." (Positive.) Instead of, "I want to stop being so afraid of the telephone." (Negative.) Essentially, stating your goals positively gives the mind a direction to move toward, rather than merely an idea of where it doesn't wish to be. Imagine someone giving you directions by saying, "Well, don't go north." That certainly leaves a lot of other possible choices. We need a sense of positive direction if we are to fully channel our energies toward a desired goal. Now, review your current goals to be sure that they are stated in positives, and change the ones that aren't. And, the next time you review the careers and sales goals of your personnel, do the same thing for them.

- *Your goals must be within your control.* This can be particularly frustrating for a branch manager because almost all of your goals depend upon what *someone else* does. For example: Wanting to gather X millions of dollars in sales from new accounts each year for your department is dependent upon actions taken by your FCs, the market, etc., in addition to your own actions. However, the task of reviewing and updating the production goals of every FC in your office is under your control. You *can* meet with each FC who is not producing up to standards and determine whether that person needs assistance or a new career. Hence, each goal should be challenging, but also realistic.

    This is important because your fate is primarily in *your* hands. Selecting goals beyond your control is a little like saying, "I'll become rich when I win the lottery." There are certain things that you can do to ensure your success. They include time management, periodic personnel reviews, identifying and quickly solving problems, developing yourself, and so forth. There are other things that you can influence, but which you *cannot* absolutely control, such as employees making their prospecting and sales calls, and so on. Still other things, like the stock market, are totally outside your control.

    Remember, too, that goals need to be reasonable and attainable. Goals that are virtually overwhelming become discouraging and can sap your will to continue. At the other extreme, goals that are too easy are boring and quickly lose their ability to motivate. Select goals that you can achieve only by stretching. If you find that you are achieving your goals too easily, make the next one harder. If you find yourself becoming too frustrated at the difficulty of a goal, consider first if you are working efficiently toward achieving it (see Chapter 4). If you are, break it down into smaller pieces and re-examine the time frame you've established to achieve it. When you meet with your FCs to review their goals and their progress, help them set challenging but achievable goals that you can both feel good about.

- *Each goal must be testable in some objective manner.* This is true whether your goal is character development or production. For example, if your goal is to be able to afford a certain kind of new car or house, it is easy to test whether or not you have achieved it. However, if your goal is to increase your standing with your boss, that may be more difficult. Be sure to establish criteria for testing each goal. These criteria should be sufficiently objective so that an observer could tell if you have achieved your goal.

  Be sure that you really understand each goal. For example, if your goal is a certain level of income, how much production must your office develop for you to earn that income? What kinds of orders must your FCs write to attain that production? How many, and what kinds of customers must each of your FCs develop to write those tickets? How much prospecting must each of them do to obtain those customers? What *specific* steps must you take to motivate them to do the prospecting, to get the customers, to write the tickets, to increase the office production, so that you can obtain the level of income that you desire? *Note:* Remember the concept of control, again. If achievement of your goal depends on a bonus, how might the size of that bonus be affected by the overall profitability of your company this year?

- *Your goal should be worth the effort.* For example, let's say that your goal is to achieve a personal income of $1 million during the next fiscal year. You may be able to accomplish this, but it may also cost you your family, your integrity, your best employees, and/or your health. Would it be worth it? The same is true for your FCs. The number of unhappy, unhealthy, divorced, million-dollar FCs is too great to ignore.

Does all of this mean that you shouldn't develop great goals, or encourage your FCs to do the same? Of course not. There are also a great number of very happy, healthy million-dollar producers who have fully satisfying family lives. In fact, the most consistently successful branch managers and FCs are healthy, happy, and have satisfying family lives.

To avoid having it cost more than it is worth, we'd like to suggest that you ask yourself a few simple questions about each goal that you consider, then write them down. You may wish to have your FCs do the same.

- Is this *your* goal, or something that you think is expected of you by your peers or society? Granted, you must fulfill the expectations of your company to remain employed. However, trying to live up to other people's expectations has caused more stress and more burnout than almost any other factor.

- How will you know when you have achieved it? (Tests?)

- When, where, and with whom do you wish to attain your goal?

- What will change in your life if you obtain your goal? For the better? For the worse? Always remember that there is a cost that must be paid for every goal. What will happen if you don't achieve it? This is particularly important because the way that we define the results of not attaining a goal are a large factor in how stressful a goal becomes. It also determines how effective this goal will be in motivating you. And, of course, if you attain the goal, will what you receive be worth what it costs?

- Related to the above is the question: How do you know if your goal is really worth obtaining? Did someone else tell you? How do they know?

- What is stopping you, or what might stop you from obtaining your goal? What obstacles do you face?

- What resources will you require to overcome these obstacles and achieve your goals? Which of these resources are already in your possession?

- Always write your goals down. In 1950, the Ivy League colleges began a study of that year's graduating classes. They asked the graduates if they had established goals for their lives. The results: 87% said that they had not; 10% had established mental goals, but had not written them down; only 3% had developed written goals for their lives. The schools followed the progress of their graduates for 25 years. In 1975, they found the following: The 87% who had not established goals had performed in an average manner during the intervening 25 years. That is, after attending the most expensive schools in the country, they achieved **mediocrity**. The 10% who established mental goals but had not written them down outperformed the combined 87% of their classmates without goals. The 3% who developed written goals outperformed the other combined 97% of their classmates.

If You Can't Measure It, You Can't Manage It

So much of your success as a branch manager depends on factors that are outside yourself. Yet, you are expected to set and achieve goals that are affected by these factors. Consider the impact of a few of the following:

- FC turnover.
- Your "critical few;" that is, those critical items for which you will be held accountable by higher management.
- The amount of assets under management in your branch and the level of asset penetration per account.
- The number of new accounts opened each month.
- The performance of your branch compared to others in your region and the competition in sales of given products (e.g., equities, CDs, mutual funds, or whole life insurance).
- Community demographics.

How will each of these influence your success, and how will you control or deal with them? The reality is that you will be held accountable for the effects of these and many other factors upon the production of your branch. However, if you can't measure something, you can't manage it either. Once you stop managing, you are reduced to being a failure waiting to happen. You must be able to measure/test not only your goals, but also the factors that influence them.

How To/Chance To/Want To

As you set goals for yourself and for each of your FCs, it is important to answer three questions about each goal:

1. Do you or the FC know **HOW TO** achieve the goal? Do you have the technical skills necessary?

2. Do you or the FC have the **CHANCE TO** achieve the goal? If your goal is to meet privately with every FC within the next two weeks, do you have enough uncommitted time available to do so?

3. Do you or the FC really **WANT TO** achieve this goal? Is this your goal or someone else's? Does this goal motivate you enough to give it the necessary effect to achieve success?

Even before you begin, these questions will enable you to determine the feasibility of your goals. If you're going to modify, or eliminate a goal, do it before you've made a significant commitment to it.

Long-Range; Intermediate; Short-term

Most of us think primarily in terms of long-range goals. What we forget is the importance of the milestones we pass on the way to achieving those goals. For example, you may have a long-range goal of becoming the president of your company; for one of your salesmen, it may be a goal of becoming a million-dollar producer. But, right now, either goal may look almost impossible simply because it seems too big, or too far away.

Remember the old joke about how to eat an elephant? One fork full at a time. Becoming the president of the company or a million-dollar producer is no different. However, even by the forkfull, an elephant can be a bit daunting. But, how about the elephant's leg? That's only one chunk of elephant. Given enough time, it's easy to believe that anyone could eat just the leg. That's how we establish intermediate- and short-term goals; we "chunk down."

Chunking down is the process of breaking a large goal into pieces that are small enough to handle. Large pieces become milestones, or intermediate goals, which tell us that we have made significant progress toward our long-range goal. Small pieces become short-term goals and tell us that we are making progress toward our intermediate goals. Each bite could be a daily goal.

However you break a goal down, it is important to do so in a manner that will motivate you and demonstrate your ability to eventually achieve your desired result. If your chunks are too small, you risk boredom again (or the feeling that you will never reach the end). If they are too large, you can become frustrated and discouraged. At the end of each day, you should feel satisfied with what you have done. Do the same with your employees. Be sure that their goals become achievable by helping them to break the goals into manageable chunks that still require a little extra effort. Then have them ask themselves this question, "What's in it for me?"

In addition to specific chunks, remember the need to include whatever resources you need to achieve your goal. They must be included in your short-term and intermediate chunks as well. What skills and knowledge will you need to become president? What skills and knowledge will your sales representatives need if they are to become million-dollar producers? Make the obtaining of those resources (skills and knowledge) into goals in themselves. Then break them down into manageable chunks as well. Does your branch have the resources necessary to help your FCs become superstars? If not, are there steps you can take to change that? Remember, their success is your success.

Setting a Time Frame

The most effective way that we know to determine if you are on track is to monitor your progress along your road to success (i.e., achieving your goal). We've already discussed the importance of placing milestones on the road; now let's look at setting up a time frame for accomplishing each goal.

To establish a goal without setting a specific time within which to accomplish it is to give it the lowest of priorities (we'll discuss priorities in more detail in Chapter 4). After all, if you don't set a time requirement, you have "all the time in the world." How much effort do you put into something, *now*, that has no time requirement? We need that sense of urgency to help motivate us and to help us determine which tasks must be completed first.

The problems with long-range goals is that they are exactly that—

long range. They are so far in the future (at least a year, usually five or more years) that there appears little reason to put one first today. By establishing intermediate- and short-term goals, we increase not only the sense of urgency, but also the sense of accomplishment and movement toward that long-term goal. Hence, whenever you set a goal for yourself, or for an employee, establish the time frame in which you wish it to be accomplished; then follow up! Whether for yourself, or for an employee, no time frame has credibility unless someone is held accountable for the goal's attainment.

Long-term goals usually imply five to ten years, intermediate goals stretch from one to five years, and short-term goals occur within six months to one year. However, even a short-term goal can, and probably should, be broken down into monthly, weekly, and even daily chunks. Let's take a look at what a typical FC's goals might be if becoming a million-dollar producer (and all that goes along with that achievement, such as being able to afford a certain lifestyle or not having to worry about providing for one's children's education) was his five year goal.

Long-Term Goals: Million Dollar Production

Time frame: Five years. Requirements:

Sales: Figuring a commission of 1% of total sales, he needs to develop an asset base of at least $100 million.

Accounts: If his *average* account represents a sale of at least $100,000, he must obtain at least 1,000 accounts to gain the necessary sales.

Skills: To obtain and maintain 1,000 large accounts, he must have a thorough knowledge of his company's business, products and services, ways of financing those products, his competition, the appropriate laws affecting his company's business, and the economy as a whole. He must also understand how to determine what products and services will solve his customers' problems, and how to sell them.

Intermediate Goal: $700,000 in Production

Time frame: Four years.

Requirements: At least 700 accounts with sales of $100,000 or more equaling $70 million in total assets.

Intermediate Goal: $450,000 in Production

Time frame: Three years.

Requirements: At least 450 accounts with sales of $100,000 or more equaling $45 million in total assets.

Knowledge: A thorough understanding of all of his company's products and services which might have an impact on his customers.

Intermediate Goal: $250,000 in Production

Time frame: Two years.

Requirements: At least 250 accounts with sales of $100,000 or more equaling $25 million in total assets.

Knowledge: A solid understanding of the basics of his company and industry, any necessary licenses, an idea of what his competition offers, and a solid understanding of the economy and its expected effect on the financial services industry.

Intermediate Goal: $100,000 in Production

Time frame: One year.

Requirements: At least 100 accounts with sales of $100,000 or more equaling $10 million in total assets.

Knowledge: A good understanding of how his company works and where to go for information and assistance when his customer has a requirement beyond his immediate ken.

Short-Term Goal: $35,000 in Production

Time frame: Six months.

Requirements: At least 35 accounts with sales of $100,000 or more equaling $3.5 million in total assets.

Short-Term Goal: $12,000 in Production

Time Frame: Three months.

Requirements: At least 12 accounts with sales of $100,000 or more equaling $1.2 million in total assets.

The FC needs to be aware of lag time. You already know that, depending on the nature of your business, it can take an average of three weeks to three months from his first contact with a prospect to open the account. In addition, there may be an additional lag between opening the account and obtaining a substantial order, which must be built into the plan. Otherwise, frustration can result from failure to achieve unreasonable goals within an unrealistic time period.

The production numbers that we provided above are only examples. They are based on an average commission figure of 1% of total assets. The actual figures will vary with the nature of your products and services, and your specific industry.

Be sure to break down your own and your employees' goals into monthly, weekly, and daily chunks. To reach that figure of $10 million in total assets his first year, he will need to open between 200–300 new accounts, or an average of at least one a day. However, it takes time, especially for the new FC, to get into the swing of things. Some FCs try to go too fast, too soon.

Daily Focus

Set daily goals for yourself and keep track of them (this is also discussed in the chapters on managing stress). For example, make a list of FCs to meet and discuss their progress, then keep track of who you've seen and whose work needs to be followed up. Set goals of specific tasks to complete each day, then keep track of how many you accomplish. Have your FCs keep track of the number of prospecting and sales calls that they make each day, and how many of the prospecting calls result in sales. They may wish to use a "tick sheet" which will allow them and you to keep track of their progress. Exhibit 3-1 below is an example of such a sheet. You may wish to design one that meets your specific goals and then make copies of it.

Such a sheet will tell you the progress that each FC is making towards each day's goal. It will also provide information regarding the effectiveness of the prospective customer lists that the FCs are calling and the prospecting scripts that they are using.

Remember that if you don't have a goal, any direction you go is as good as another.

> Goals give direction to your drive for success!

EXHIBIT 3-1. FC's Tick Sheet.

Dials:

Contacts:

Follow-up Appointments:

New Accounts:

Overcoming Fear of Failure

In his excellent book on leadership, *The Ten Most Wanted Men*, Paul H. Dunn suggests that many of us have been raised to be so afraid of failure that we drive through life with our brakes on. Not only is this exhausting, it keeps us from reaching our fullest potential. In fact, fear of failure is the single greatest reason why so many people never even attempt to reach for their dreams. The great psychiatrist, Alfred Adler, called this, "Assumed Disability." Essentially, this means we'd rather not try than try and fail. But, what is "failure," and why are we so afraid of it? As someone who is already a success, it may be difficult for you to understand and empathize with that fear in others. However, your ability to do so will greatly enhance your ability to help your FCs overcome it in themselves.

For most of us, failure means not living up to somebody's expectations of us and being rejected as a result. For any manager, failure means producing less than is required of us. Ironically, for the FC who prospects for customers, it means that the more conscientious he is, the more he will fail and be rejected. That's terrible! Or is it?

A well-known motivational expert, Art Mortell, likes to point out that failure is the only way that we ever try something new. As long as what we've been doing works even a little bit, we will continue rather than risk trying something new which could be even better. Simply put, we need to fail if we are ever to ultimately succeed.

We're all familiar with Thomas Edison's invention of the light bulb. However, did you know that he failed 10,000 times before he finally found a filament that would last and that was economical as well. When asked how he felt about failing 9,000 times (he still hadn't "succeeded" yet), he said that he hadn't failed at all. He had succeeded in finding 9,000 ways that didn't work.

Another person who was a great failure was Henry J. Kaiser. In his later life Kaiser stated that *he failed at 75% of the things that he attempted*. However, by being willing to take a risk, and lose 75% of the time, he accomplished staggering achievements. Here are a few of them:

- During World War II, he built 1,500 merchant ships.
- His mills produced over 1 million tons of steel and 20 million pounds of magnesium.
- He was the world's largest producer of cement and the third largest producer of aluminum.
- He helped build the Hoover and Grant Coolly dams, and he played a major role in building the San Francisco-Oakland Bay Bridge.

Just imagine what he would have accomplished if he never failed at all—nothing! How do you deal with failure, both in yourself and in your FCs?

Sir Winston Churchill, one of the greatest world leaders of all time, gave the shortest speech of his political career when he left Parliament for the last time. Yet, it summarized the philosophy he exemplified in overcoming the near-impossible odds against Great Britain during World War II. It was just seven words long: "NEVER GIVE UP! NEVER, NEVER GIVE UP!" He couldn't afford to give up on Great Britain, even if it had given up on itself. As a result, he instilled in the British populace the will to continue on to success regardless of the impossibility of the task.

In the examples above, we have already shown that failure has two sides. One is instructive and even motivational, while the other is discouraging and exhausting. The following is an example of how one form of failure, common to all FCs, can be turned into a motivating force that results in success.

- In the financial services industry, the average FC may obtain only 10 good contacts and one new account from every 100 prospecting calls. New accounts usually result in a first sale with an average commission of about $500. That means that every time an FC picks up the telephone and dials a prospect, he is earning $5 whether the prospect answers the phone and accepts him, rejects him, the line is busy, or the prospect doesn't even answer. No matter how the call ends, every dial is worth a $5 bill.

With that motivating thought, how many dials can an FC make in an hour? As he improves, his level of success will increase and the value of each call will increase with it. *Note:* The actual statistics will vary with the products that your company sells and the experience of your sales force. The preceding figures have been true for the average FC.

Essentially, every time that an FC calls a prospect, you and he both succeed! He may succeed in opening a new account or in eliminating a "nonstarter" from his prospecting list; he may even succeed in improving his prospecting approach. You may succeed through the improvement in his attitude and the general atmosphere in his sales area, or through the effects that his good example has on the FCs around him. In any scenario, you both always succeed! The only way to fail is to fail to try.

> You only have to try to succeed!

Do It and Review It!

Goal setting is not to be treated as a long-term goal in itself. If you haven't already done so, begin today and write down your long-term goals for your career, your personal development (physical, intellectual, emotional, and spiritual/character), and your family. This may take some time, and you may wish to discuss it with your spouse or a close friend, but do it!

Once you have written down major goals in each of these areas and they have met the criteria discussed in this chapter, break them out into intermediate- and short-term goals, until you have a daily program to achieve each goal. Once you've accomplished this, each year have your FCs and other personnel write their goals down. People need to feel good about doing things on a daily basis so that they can go home with the satisfaction that they have made some headway toward their intermediate- or long-term goals.

Finally, remember that experience and circumstances tend to change one's outlook on things. Review your goals regularly. Short- and intermediate-term goals should be reviewed at least monthly, and long-term goals need to be reviewed quarterly. Have your personnel review theirs regularly as well. Review new FCs' goals with them monthly at first and quarterly later on. You'll find it worthwhile to review each FC's goals at least semiannually and, probably, quarterly. Keep a copy of their goals to review with them.

As you review each goal, also review your progress toward achieving it. Where you have met or exceeded expectations, congratulate yourself and keep up the good work. Where you have not met expectations, try to determine why. Then reassess your plan for achieving that goal. Ask yourself, "What have I learned?" This is particularly important when reviewing your employees' goals. Let them know how pleased you are with their progress if they have met or exceeded goals. If they haven't, review the possible causes and work with them to overcome anything that is holding them back. Reaffirm their goals and their motivation for accomplishing them. If you determine that an FC's goals were too big, help him to bring the goals closer to reality so he can experience success. We'll review key motivations in Section IV.

Remember to be sure that you haven't made great strides in one area by sacrificing growth toward your other goals. Lack of balance in one's goals is one of the greatest causes of failure further down the line and is a major source of stress and eventual burnout. Are your FCs' goals balanced? Are they leaving enough time for their family? Remember, if an FC's personal needs aren't being met, they will eventually interfere with the quality of his work.

Another source of stress is failure to budget the time necessary to meet any goal. Be sure that you leave both enough days and enough time in each day to accomplish any task/goal that you set for yourself or an employee. Even three projects that take a day each can overwhelm anyone if we expect them to be accomplished within one day.

Other Employees

Because your FCs pay themselves through the amount of production that they create, they have only to set their income goals and start to work to achieve them. However, never forget that without the help of their sales assistants and secretaries, often the lowest paid people in the firm, your FCs would accomplish little. You may find it very helpful for you, or one of your sales managers, to meet with them and discuss their career and financial goals. Meet with them selectively to discuss things that are going right and things that could be improved. By doing this, they can help quickly identify trends in problems and can often make excellent suggestions to increase overall office efficiency and the bottom line. Many an FC has been helped beyond measure by a registered sales assistant who was able to handle business in his absence. Also, your secretaries and sales assistants are usually the first contact that someone calling the branch has with your company. That can help, or hurt, business a lot.

Help them to establish and attain goals of their own, and reward them for good work. Their pay may be set by the company, but as a branch manager you have many ways of recognizing their work and showing appreciation.

Summary

If you don't have a goal to drive toward, movement in any direction can seem like progress. However, the individual with well-formed, written goals will always excel as he strives to attain them. Remember:

> People don't plan to fail. They fail to plan!

CHAPTER 4

Managing the 28-Hour Day

Today's branch managers seem to have a hundred things to keep in the air at the same time. Juggling that many responsibilities isn't easy. In fact, many branch and sales managers tell us that their firms place so many requirements on their time that they are left with virtually no time to manage their branches and the FCs that work for them. Despite this, have you ever felt that you could easily get everything done, if only the day had four more hours? We all feel that way at times. Yet, on other days, we not only complete every task that we face, we end the day looking around for more to do.

   One of the greatest sources of both stress and failure, for branch and sales managers, is loss of control over the events and information for which we are responsible. In fact, studies have shown that most of us waste between 40–50% of each working day through conscious or unconscious inefficiency. No wonder we feel stressed. However, if you are feeling overwhelmed, there's a good chance that you can begin to accomplish twice as much, with half the effort, by learning to manage your time.

Your first step must be to establish motivating goals for yourself (see Chapter 3). Next, establish a daily plan that includes all of the activities required to attain your goals. It has been said that, "If you fail to plan, you plan to fail." We agree! Every successful person makes a plan and works from it to achieve his goals.

It has been said that if you find a man on the top of a mountain, you can bet that he didn't just fall there. While he didn't fall there, you can also be certain that he didn't just wish himself there. When Sir Edmond Hilary climbed Mount Everest for the first time, he had a detailed plan of the routes that he would take, the equipment he would need, and even how far he should travel each day so that he wouldn't exhaust himself. Your goals are your Mount Everest, and you can achieve them if you establish and follow an effective plan.

As long as we are using the analogy of Sir Edmond Hilary, let's carry it one step further; he didn't just look at a map of the world one day, decide that it would be fun to climb Mount Everest, and quickly develop a plan to do so. He already had experience as a climber. In addition, he spoke to other climbers who had attempted the climb before him in order to gather information regarding the various routes, techniques that were effective or ineffective, and additional skills that he would need to develop so that he would be able to reach the summit. Then he developed his plan and practiced the skills he would need to prepare for his ascent.

> Plan your work and work your plan!

A few rules of thumb that can help to save you a great deal of time are:

- Handle each piece of paper that crosses your desk only once. You face a mound of paper each day. Constantly reshuffling them is a great time stealer.
- Avoid people who want to socialize in the office. Be polite, but firm. Each time someone comes to interrupt what you are doing, they are stealing not only your time, but your momentum. Tell them that you'd love to talk to them over lunch.

- Have your secretary or sales assistant screen your calls and arrange for you to return them during a "return call period" that you have scheduled in your day.

- If an FC or customer comes in without an appointment because he has an immediate problem, deal with his needs. However, if he just wants to socialize, or to discuss a problem that needs time and can wait, encourage him to make an appointment so you can give him more time and attention. Remember that you are a professional. Do you just drop in on your doctor or your boss and expect him to stop what he's doing to see you? As you act like a professional, your FCs and customers will treat you like one.

- Develop good working habits. Put a sign on your desk as a reminder to ask, "Is what I am doing NOW moving me toward one of my goals?" Most habits require about 21 straight days to establish. But, once they are there, they can be your most powerful ally in your battle for success. Remember what an anonymous author said:

> I am your constant companion.
> I am your greatest helper or heaviest burden.
> I will push you onward or drag you down to failure.
> I am completely at your command.
> Half the things you do you might just as well turn over to me
>   and I will do them—quickly and correctly.
> I am easily managed—you must merely be firm with me.
> Show me exactly how you want something done and, after a
>   few lessons, I will do it automatically.
> I am the servant of all great people; and, alas, of all failures as
>   well.
> Those who are great, I have made great. Those who are
>   failures, I have made failures.
> I am not a machine, though I work with all the precision of a
>   machine, plus the intelligence of a person.
> You may run me for profit or run me for ruin—it makes no
>   difference to me.
> Take me, train me, be firm with me, and I will place the world
>   at your feet.
> Be easy with me and I will destroy you.
> Who am I? I AM HABIT!

Make a habit of winning by making winning habits!

In Chapters 23 and 24 we will introduce a procedure that will help you to create the habits you want using a very effective mental programming technique. Having completed whatever training program your firm offers, you already have certain skills and knowledge that will be critical for your success as a branch manager. And, by reading this book, you are taking another step, seeking additional knowledge about skills that can help you to succeed. Seek out successful managers that have the kind of *character* and the type of business that you admire and find out how they did it. Now develop that plan. Then encourage your FCs to do the same. Encourage your experienced FCs and your new FCs to work together in a mentor-student relationship. Not only will this help the new FC to learn the art of the business more quickly, it can increase the sense of team work within the branch. *Note:* Ensure that the new FC arranges to receive the help he needs at times that will not detract from his mentor's production.

Setting Priorities

As a branch manager, you have so many tasks and so much information demanding your time and attention, that you must establish priorities or you will risk exhausting your resources on the unimportant while neglecting the critical. This is well-illustrated by the popular time management story of Ivy Lee and Charles Schwab, President of Bethlehem Steel Company.

Ivy Lee, a management consultant and "efficiency expert," had approached Charles Schwab to outline his firm's services. When he finished, Lee told Schwab that by using his services, he would know how *to manage better.*

Schwab was outraged, and replied that he didn't have time to manage as well as he knew how, now. What he wanted in his company, was more "doing," *not* "knowing." Schwab told Lee that if he could show him a way to activate his employees to do the things that they already knew they should be doing, he would not only listen, but would pay any reasonable price.

Lee accepted the challenge and said, "I can give you something in 20 minutes that will step up your action and doing by at least 50%." Schwab accepted the challenge and gave him just 20 minutes.

Lee pulled out a blank 3" x 5" index card and handed it to Schwab with the following directions: Write on the card the six most important tasks that you have to do tomorrow. When that is done, number them in order of importance. Carry this card with you and, the first thing tomorrow morning, review item one and begin working on it. Look at item one on the card every 15 minutes until it is completed. Then move on to item two and handle it the same way. Then three, four, and so forth, until you've completed all of your tasks, or until quitting time. Don't worry if you don't finish every item on your list. You'll be working on the most important ones. The others can wait. If you can't finish them all by this method, you wouldn't have by using any other method either. In addition, without some system, you might not have even initially decided which tasks were the most important.

Use the last 5 minutes of each day to plan the next by making out a "must do" list for tomorrow's tasks. After you've convinced yourself of the value of this system, have your managers try it. When you've given it a thorough trial, send me a check for what *you* think it's worth.

The entire interview lasted only 25 minutes. Two weeks later, Schwab sent Lee a check for $25,000—that works out to $1,000 a minute. In today's dollars, he would have been paid over $250,000. In five years, this method turned Bethlehem Steel into the biggest independent steel producer in the world and made Schwab a fortune of $100 million.

Today, a similar and popular technique is used to set priorities. Write down your tasks, and label them as A, B, or C.

Priorities labeled **A** *must be done*. They are absolutely critical for success in attaining your goal (if not for survival itself). **B** priorities are important and *should be done*, but are not an immediate threat if they are not accomplished today. **C** priorities would be nice to accomplish, but don't really need today as their deadline.

Unfortunately, too many of us tend to focus on the **C**s, first. Because they are unimportant, they are rarely threatening. Also, they frequently take little time individually, so we look to get them out of the way so we can focus our full attention on the **A** priorities. This is a rationalization that has resulted in more failure than almost any other. No **B** priority should be touched until every **A** priority is accomplished (or cannot be worked on at this time), and no **C** priority should be touched as long as any **A** or **B** priority is unfinished. Since 80% of most priorities are **C**s, this can save you a great deal of time.

Once you have established your **A, B,** and **C** priorities, number them according to importance within each category. Now put them into a daily plan.

Daily Plans

Just as you establish goals for your life, you also need a plan to accomplish each day's tasks. End each day by writing down a plan for the next. Include everything that you need to get done the next day (e.g., appointments, calls, etc.), and prioritize them. Then, when you get to the office, you'll be ready to start right to work. For example:

A1: 8:00 sales meeting

A2: Phone regional director re: new sales campaign

A3: Interview applicants for FC position

A4: See sales manager re: new sales assistant

A5: 5:00 p.m. appointment with Mr. Jones, re: new acct

B1: Read prospectus on XYZ mutual fund for Thursday's sales meeting

B2: Read Lesson 6 on the economy for fin. plan. course

C1: Update files

Remember that the purpose of prioritizing is to focus attention and energy on accomplishing the most important things each day. If you don't complete every task, let the unimportant be the ones you miss.

Establish a Work Schedule

Set up a daily schedule and establish blocks of time for specific activities, such as sales meetings, follow-up calls, customer meetings, planning and preparation, appointments, paperwork, dealing with operations problems, and so on. Once you have developed your schedule, post it and commit yourself to following it. We have included an example of such a schedule in Exhibit 4-1.

EXHIBIT 4-1. *Daily Schedule.*

7:00–9:00 a.m.	Interview FCs: review last month's production figures.
9:00–9:30 a.m.	Listen to company morning strategy broadcast. Comment to staff.
9:30–10:00 a.m.	Review any new financial information (e.g., *Wall Street Journal*, in-house news service, etc.).
10:00–12:00 a.m.	Meet with national sales manager.
12:00–1:00 p.m.	Lunch.
1:00–2:00 p.m.	Return morning phone calls. Contact operations re: follow-up on account problems.
2:00–4:00 p.m.	Tour new operations center.
4:00–5:00 p.m.	R&R (rest and racketball).
5:00–5:30 p.m.	Catch up on paperwork/records.
5:30–6:30 p.m.	Appointments.
6:30–7:30 p.m.	Dinner.
7:30–8:50 p.m.	Join FCs to make cold-calls.
8:50–9:10 p.m.	Planning and preparation.

This exhibit is just an example. Have your FCs do the same thing. *Note:* This schedule includes a period for rest and relaxation. As discussed in Chapter 17, burnout can easily result from neglect of your physical well-being.

Summary

Remember, by planning and prioritizing the events that take up your time, you can accomplish twice as much.

- List your goals and set your priorities.
- Make a daily "To Do" list.
- Start with As, not with Cs.
- Ask yourself, "What is the best use of my time, *right now?*"
- Handle each piece of paper just once! You don't have time to sort information several times.
- Spend a few minutes at the end of each day reviewing the day's activities and planning those for tomorrow.
- Have your FCs do the same thing!
- DO IT NOW!

CHAPTER 5

Running Effective Meetings/ Sales Meetings

At one time or another, each of us has had to endure meetings that were poorly run. Meetings with no agendas or with agendas that weren't followed; meetings that went way over the allotted time; or meetings where the presenters rambled. We all know what was wrong with those meetings; we probably discussed it at length with our colleagues, afterward, and everyone resented the whole thing. As a result, we also probably obtained a minimum of value from them. The purpose of this chapter is to provide you with a few simple rules of thumb for organizing and presenting effective meetings that will accomplish your purposes.

One way to look at organizing a successful meeting is as a problem of goal setting and time management (see Chapters 3 and 4). Hence, before you call a meeting, you must determine exactly what you wish to accomplish and how much time you have in which to accomplish it. In other words, what is the purpose of the meeting and will you be able to accomplish that purpose within the required time frame?

Make a Plan

Why plan? For one thing, you've already attended unplanned or poorly planned meetings. What did you think of the meeting and the individual responsible for it? Enough said. More important, any meeting you run will require the attendance of individuals who produce valuable revenue for your branch. While they are attending your meeting they will *not* be producing that revenue, so that meeting is going to cost you a great deal of money. In fact, the more people who attend, the more money it's going to cost you. So, you'd better make sure that what you present will result in the creation of more revenue than it costs. If your FCs leave the meeting confused or irritated about its purpose, that will certainly not be profitable in the long run.

To plan an effective meeting, following these simple steps:

- Determine what you wish to accomplish and state it in terms of a *specific* goal, following the five rules of goal setting (i.e., state it in positives). For example:
    - "At the completion of this sales meeting, each FC should be able to write an effective prospecting script for XYZ's new whole life insurance."
    - "At the completion of this meeting, each employee should have a clear understanding of the new employee benefits plan."
    - "At the completion of this meeting, each FC should have a clear understanding of the branch's goals for new account and assets under management for the new year, as well as what is expected of each FC individually."
- Evaluate your goals for the meeting in terms of the people involved in accomplishing them; include customers as well as employees. How will achieving these goals affect these people? Remember, in goal setting, achievement of a goal must maintain the positive aspects of the current situation. For example, let's say that your goal for a meeting is to convince your FCs to work late four to five nights per week during a sales campaign. You will have to find a way to

Creating a Successful Branch

convince the FCs (as well as their families, through the FCs) that the time they spend apart will be both well-compensated and replaced. If you don't, you may find both attendance and productivity lagging, with resentment as an additional by-product.

- Be sure that your plan of presentation is both well-organized and systematic.

Always Use an Agenda

Always use an agenda. You can't expect a meeting to succeed unless you have first defined its objective and scope to those involved. Several rules of thumb for planning an agenda are:

- Be sensitive to the time element. Many experts believe that the greatest mistake that many of us make is to try to present too much. Trying to cover too much during a meeting will result in either too long a meeting or inadequate coverage of the topics presented. Either will result in an ineffective meeting.

  - Remember the old saying, "The mind can absorb what the derriere can endure." Meetings that are too long lose the attention of the attendants. Numerous studies have demonstrated that 45 minutes plus or minus 10 minutes is the maximum amount of time that anyone can pay attention. A mental break is a necessity. The Japanese are said to avoid this by holding all of their meetings standing up. If you are planning a 1-hour meeting to handle general branch business, you will generally be able to handle only two to four major business items.

  - Stick to a single goal for any meeting, and avoid trying to develop more than two to four points from any idea. For example, in a training meeting, you might have a goal of discussing how an FC can increase his number of new accounts through effective prospecting. You might wish to break that presentation goal down into three parts, as follows:

    At the completion of this meeting, each FC should be able to increase his account base through:

    a. *Cold-calling* prospecting lists provided by the branch;

b. Actively seeking referrals from existing clients; and

c. Presenting seminars to small business owners on ways to save money on taxes.

You could elaborate on each of these three points through discussion, stories, and charts. Making use of a written plan also enables you to re-evaluate your goal in order to determine how successful you were.

- Provide a copy of the meeting's agenda to all involved at least one day in advance of the meeting. *Note:* If an individual is expected to make a report or presentation during the meeting, be sure to give him several days' notice. Providing a copy of the agenda to participants in advance will give them the time needed to give consideration to the items to be presented before they come to the meeting. This will increase both their interest and the value of their feedback during the meeting.

- Give those who will be attending the meeting the opportunity to submit items for the agenda. At the same time, make it clear that, with the exception of emergencies, items not on the agenda will not be considered during the meeting. This can be particularly important for weekly sales meetings. By allowing FCs the opportunity to submit items for the agenda, it is often possible to discover and deal with problems before they get out of hand. It is also an effective way to communicate interest in the FCs' concerns and to communicate a willingness to listen. If an item is submitted, check to make sure that it is of concern to more than one or two individuals. If it isn't, deal with it individually and you can achieve the same improved communications without spending precious meeting time on that issue.

- If a person brings up a point that is not part of the original agenda, use the *Relevancy Challenge*. Ask how the question, concern, or comment is relevant to the point at hand. This will provide you with greater control and will ensure that the meeting avoids going off on tangents. Using the relevancy challenge also trains people for future meetings. After the first few meetings, people become very aware of the rules of the game. They also become more willing to pay close attention because you have demonstrated that you consider their time valuable.

- Each agenda and meeting should teach the purpose and function of your organization to your FCs by the outlined presentation of business.

Preparing An Agenda

To effectively prepare an agenda, it is important to remember its purpose. Actually, the word *agenda* means *things to be done.* As such, it should give purpose and direction to the meeting, not merely provide a miscellaneous list of problems and topics to be covered at the meeting. Several rules of thumb for preparing a successful agenda are:

- While there are many ways to prepare an agenda, we prefer the outline method.
- First, list any opening remarks.
- Next, have the minutes of the previous meeting read. These should be read and approved for correctness. If the meeting is one of an ongoing series, providing a brief summary of the minutes will help to provide continuity. This can be particularly useful when you are providing training during sales meetings.
- List any announcements that have to be made. These are generally items that require no discussion and can be disposed of quickly.
- Then, list the goal for the meeting; outline the two to four points that you have broken the goal into.
- Having broken your goal into two to four major points that you wish to discuss, briefly outline the major ideas within each point. Doing so will accomplish two things:
  - It will enable each individual to adequately prepare for the meeting; and
  - It will act as a summary sheet following the meeting that will easily jog the memory of those who attended.
- Be sure that your outline is specific, and sufficiently detailed so that the participants can tell the purpose of the meeting and what topics will be covered. At the same time, avoid being so detailed that the agenda takes on the appearance of a training handout.
- Provide a listing for summarization and questions. This will enable you to gauge the effectiveness of the presentation in terms of the questions asked.

- Since a major purpose of any meeting is to convey information (even decision-making meetings are useless if no one remembers what was discussed or decided), it is important to ensure that participants remember what the meeting was all about when it is over. One way to accomplish this is by using the *Tell Them Three Times* technique.

    - As the meeting begins, provide a brief summary of what will be discussed/decided. This sets the mental framework for the meeting.

    - During the meeting, have the discussion. After all, this is what the meeting was held for.

    - When the meeting is over, provide a brief summary of what points were covered and what, if any, decisions were made. This will remind everyone of what occurred and pull everything discussed into a meaningful whole.

- In Exhibit 5-1 we have provided an example of an effective agenda for a sales meeting in which the importance of obtaining referrals is the topic of discussion.

EXHIBIT 5-1. *Weekly Sales Meeting Agenda.*

Monday, April 16, 1990
   I. Greeting.
  II. Minutes from previous meeting.
 III. Announcements and introduction of topic.
 IV. Building your business with referrals.
     A. Only three ways to build your business:
       1. Prospect/*cold call.*
       2. Obtain more business from existing accounts.
       3. *Seek new business from referrals.*
     B. Why FCs don't ask for referrals:
       1. Forget.
       2. Afraid of rejection.
       3. Don't want to impose.
     C. When to ask for referrals:
       1. At the end of an unsuccessful prospecting call.
       2. After you have provided a service.
       3. During a follow-up profiling meeting/call.
     D. How to ask for referrals:
       1. Tie in benefit to customer/doing him a favor.
       2. Use *his* memory sorting patterns.
       3. Report success or failure to referral source.
   V. Summary, questions, and group commitment.

44

Marketing Meetings

We've all sat through meetings with *marketing specialists* in which they tried to tell us how to sell a product to the wrong customer in ways that just don't work in the real world. While these are, ideally, already a rare experience for you, here are several tips that can make them almost nonexistent.

- First, be sure that the marketing specialist knows both the product *and* the target audience (i.e., both the FCs and their customers within your demographic area). As obvious as this may seem, the number of complaints we've had from managers and FCs about product marketing specialists who come to make a presentation to FCs and do not really understand how the FC works or the demographics of the population he serves are almost unnerving. *You* know the economic and cultural demographics of the area that you serve. For example:
  - You also know that people over 50 do not make purchasing decisions the same way that people under 35 do. Does your area predominate in one of these age groups?
  - In addition, California Hispanics and New York Italians do not use the same buying criteria. Neither is better or worse than the other, but knowing which you serve and how to appeal to their interests and needs can vastly improve the interest and effectiveness of a meeting.

- Another complaint we frequently hear is that while product marketing specialists often tell FCs how to sell a given product, they rarely give specifics regarding who should *not* be targeted as a customer. The result is too often a legal confrontation between an irate customer who bought a product that was inappropriate for his needs and the branch manager and his FC. To solve this, you may need to develop some form of *product marketing guide* for the branch, if one does not already exist.

  Most FCs resent the *hard sell* which says that this single product is the ultimate answer to all of life's problems. One would hope that your sales personnel are more sophisticated than that. The product specialist has to understand that he is one of many people who has a vested interest in having his product sold. Should product specialists sell to FCs? Absolutely! But, **selling equals persuasion. It does not equal force.** Ensure that the specialist does the same planning and affords the same considerations (e.g., time) that you do.

- Try to make sure that the product market specialist addresses not only the question of which type of customer is appropriate for a product, but also the kinds of problems which the product is designed to solve (e.g., retirement, college tuition, taxes, etc.). This can make it a lot easier for FCs to develop prospecting and sales scripts around the product. At the same time, avoid the opposite trap. Be sure that the specialist provides only pertinent details rather than every single trivial fact about a product or service.

- Finally, the marketing specialist should be available for a question and answer period following any presentation.

Preparation for a Meeting

The U.S. Army has an interesting memory jogger regarding the importance of good preparation. It's called *The Six Ps of Preparation*, which says *Proper Preparation Prevents (Pretty) Poor Performance*. Remember, if the meeting is worth having, it's worth a little effort at preparation. The following are a few simple steps to successful preparation.

- *Rehearse.* Be sure that whoever is making the presentation has rehearsed it for smoothness, timing, and its ability to hold the interest of (much less convince) the participants. Whether you are making a presentation to the CEO of your firm or your own FCs, if the meeting is worth holding, it's worth rehearsing. (*Note:* This becomes especially true if two or more people are involved in a presentation.) Just how much and what kind of rehearsal will depend on your experience as a presenter and the complexity of the material.

- Prepare any special *visual aids or materials* in advance. Visual aids can make any presentation more interesting and can be particularly important to individuals who think primarily in terms of visual concepts. Be sure to leave yourself sufficient time to prepare these aids. *Note:* if you don't have the time to put together visual aids, utilize the talents of people within the branch who do.

    - *Printed handouts* summarizing the topics you wish to discuss or teach are particularly helpful in some meetings. Not only do they help the participants to follow the presenter more closely, they also enable the participants to pay better attention because they preclude the need to take lengthy notes (*Note:* Obviously, they can also be used to take notes on some area being discussed).

- Always ***illustrate each major point*** or idea with an example to which the participants can relate. Of course, when illustrating a point, it is always preferable to use positive rather than negative examples. If possible, invite FCs (especially senior FCs) to share testimonials supporting the product. You may even wish to have FCs briefly *brainstorm* on ways that *they* intend to use the product. Finally, be sure to stop and periodically invite questions. All of this can set a better tone and be very motivating.

- Put together a simple ***checklist*** of everything that needs to be accomplished in preparation for the meeting. As simple as it is, it will help you to keep track of your preparations.

- Make certain that you have made adequate preparation for the ***physical comfort*** of those who will be attending. If the meeting is going to be long enough, arrange for refreshments and take periodic stretch breaks to keep the participants alert.

- ***Contact*** those who will be involved in time for them to make whatever plans are necessary for their attendance. If you wait until the last minute, you risk FCs being absent because they have prior commitments (e.g., with a customer). You also risk making them resentful because they had to cancel personal plans at the last minute.

- Be sure that everything is set up and that you are present and ready to begin at least 5 minutes before the meeting is to start.

- Always ***start on time*** and finish on time.

- Your greetings and opening announcements should be appropriate, short, and to the point.

Summary

Running an effective meeting can be easy. Despite this, we've all sat through too many that were poorly organized, unmotivating, and often confusing. By properly planning your meetings to achieve specific desired goals and establishing clear agendas, you can easily run effective meetings that will communicate, educate, and motivate your FCs to success. Finally, by ensuring that your outside speakers are adequately prepared and have something useful to say, you will be assured that your meetings will be well received.

SECTION *II*

Managers, Employees, and Customers: A Psychological Model

Managers and FCs have one thing in common; their success depends on their ability to convince someone else to do what they want. The FC must convince his customer of his professionalism and his ability to solve the customer's financial problems. You must convince your FCs to do their best, and prove your willingness to support them in their efforts.

The art of winning your employees' loyalty and cooperation will depend to a large extent on your ability to communicate both your desires and your understanding and concern for their needs. The ability to utilize effective communications tools, rapport building skills, and the ability to quickly determine an individual's psychological make-up can be powerful tools in both management and selling. They can enable you to step inside an FC's or a customer's world and demonstrate how accepting your idea or program will help him to meet his needs.

49

In this book, communication includes all of the behaviors, feelings, and expectations within a relationship between two people. In management, as in marriage, it is impossible not to communicate. Unfortunately, the extent of the information exchanged in any relationship, as well as the expectations that each individual brings to the relationship, can make effective communications very difficult. For example: If your FCs believe that your *only* interest in them is to make you look good with their production figures, this would probably increase their level of resistance toward ideas and programs in which they see no immediate benefit for themselves.

In this section you will learn techniques which will enable you to examine your own psychological profile and style of management, as well as how to psychologically profile an FC or a customer within the first few minutes of speaking to him. In addition, you will learn how to work with them in ways that will meet their emotional needs.

CHAPTER 6

Who Are We? General Personality Traits

Over the years, psychologists have developed a variety of systems to help understand people's actions. As a result, there are many systems available for profiling someone's behavior, even to the extent of psychiatric evaluation. For this book, we will provide a simplified system of categorizing the behavior you see in others in order to help you communicate more effectively. This system will also assist you in selecting which management techniques best fit your own personal style. This book will work with FCs' primary behavioral attributes, which are listed below, and then consolidate them into a psychological profiling system.

However, before we present the basis of the psychological profiling system, take a moment to think of the people that you know, or know of, who fit some of the elements of the following descriptions:

- Bill is always *hanging out with the crowd.* He bases his sense of self-worth on other people's reactions and perceptions of him.

Hence, he is eager to please, and may even appear to be a *social butterfly*. He is very garrulous, and tends to be very conscious of the latest fashions and trends.

- Jane always *goes by the book* because she believes rules were made for good reasons. She rarely takes chances and does not wish to stand out from the crowd. She does not wish to be the leader, but resents whoever does take the lead. She will frequently gossip about people, but will rarely confront them to their face. If a new idea is suggested, she usually has some reason why it won't work and shouldn't even be attempted.

- Jack is a person who is *very dogmatic and always has to be right*. When he is wrong, he tries to bully his way through, often at the top of his lungs. He always wants to be in control, and is often contemptuous of others. His three most frequently used words are *I, me,* and *myself*.

- Samantha is *an independent thinker who is respectful of other's feelings and opinions*, then makes up her own mind. A natural leader in any group, she is social, polite and friendly, but not insincerely so. When necessary, she is able to set limits on herself and others.

The chances are that you are already thinking of FCs, customers, and even other managers who fit quite well into some of these categories. In fact, most of us demonstrate at least some of the traits of each of these characters at one time or another, but tend to predominate in one. Think of some television or historical figures that might fit into each group.

The purpose of the above exercise is to demonstrate how true-to-life psychological profiling can be. Each of the following pages will provide you with additional insights into people that you already know as well as those you have yet to meet.

Primary Personality Traits

For the purpose of our profile, we have selected two basic personality types, the **Leader** and the **Follower**, and two modifying characteristics, **Hostile** and **Friendly**. These terms—Leader/Follower and Hostile/Friendly—have many more meanings (i.e., connotations) than their dictionary definitions suggest. They imply general orientations regarding how one deals with others, and will be explained in detail on the following pages.

Leader

The leader has a drive to take control in personal encounters and a desire to be paramount. This may manifest itself through a cluster of traits such as initiative, decisiveness, forcefulness, and independence, He is goal-oriented and self-motivating.

Follower

A follower has a disposition that lets others take the lead and make decisions in personal encounters. This may manifest itself in traits like dependence, indecisiveness, lack of assertiveness, and passivity. The follower demonstrates a willingness to be controlled, to avoid personal confrontations, and to comply with other people's wishes. Both his goals and his motivation must often be imposed from the outside.

Hostility

This trait is seen in a lack of regard for others and a concentration on self. Hostility demonstrates the attitude that other people matter less than oneself, and therefore deserve less care. It implies indifference to others, insensitivity to their needs and ideas, resistance to collaboration, and, in some cases, outright animosity. Hostile people are often cold, emotionally insensitive, and generally manipulative. Hostile people have a *self-oriented*, win-lose, or an *I'm OK, you're NOT OK* orientation.

Friendliness

This trait, on the other hand, is basically one's concern for others. It involves recognition of the value and dignity of other people and a sensitivity to their needs. Friendliness might be defined as the extent to which we are involved with people and are sensitive to their needs. It implies that we realize that we can only achieve our goals by helping others (e.g., our employees and peers) to achieve theirs. It has a win-win or an *I'm OK, you're OK* orientation.

The personality that we show others is a combination of the traits that we've just discussed, and can be demonstrated on a grid. Which traits predominate in any given situation are usually determined by the context of that situation. To enable you to understand the *grid system* that we will be using, we have divided the traits along two axes. See Exhibits 6-1 and 6-2.

EXHIBIT 6-1. *The Vertical Axis.*

This axis deals with the LEADER- and FOLLOWER-oriented traits.

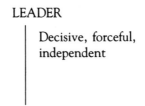

LEADER

Decisive, forceful,
independent

FOLLOWER
Indecisive, passive,
dependent

EXHIBIT 6-2. *The Horizontal Axis.*

This axis deals with the traits of HOSTILITY and FRIENDLINESS.

HOSTILE ————————— FRIENDLY

Self-oriented,   Other-oriented,
insensitive,   sensitive,
uncooperative   cooperative

Now let's merge these traits and see how they provide an easy-to-use psychological profiling system.

In Exhibit 6-3, we have combined the trait lines to show the interrelationship of the primary traits. As we discuss each personality type, we will show only that portion of the grid which applies to that type and show how the combination of traits leads to the personality

EXHIBIT 6-3. *Horizontal and Vertical Axes Interrelationship.*

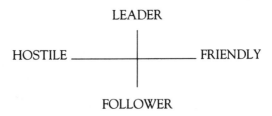

LEADER

HOSTILE ——————— FRIENDLY

FOLLOWER

types which we have labelled for easy identification. In Chapter 8, we will include the rest of the traits, further building the personality types.

The four extremes of leader, follower and hostile, friendly, presented above, form a grid. When the various combinations are considered, we find that these four categories produce a system which will enable us to easily recognize common personality types. In the next few pages, we will briefly outline each of the categories, then more precisely define the FC/Client/Manager characteristics associated with each primary type.

EXHIBIT 6-4. *Hostile + Leader = Dictator.*

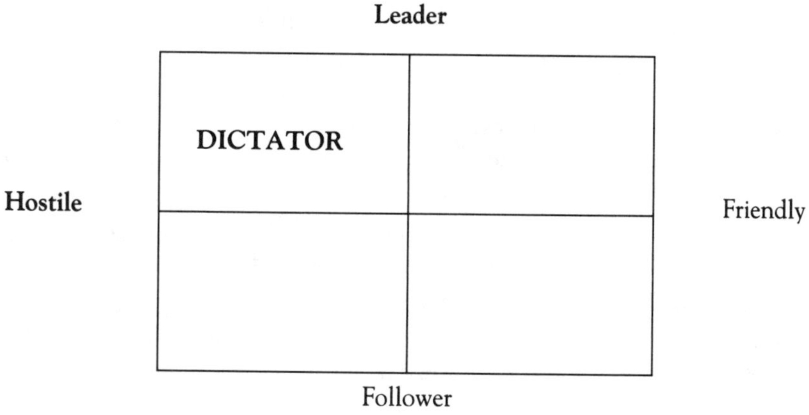

Leader

Hostile   Friendly

Follower

A **Dictator** (Exhibit 6-4) is a person who is very dogmatic and always has to be right. When he is wrong, he tries to bully his way through, often as loudly as possible. A Dictator insists on being in control and often is contemptuous of others. His most frequently used words are *I, me, mine,* and *myself.* His hostile and unresponsive nature often causes the Dictator to be labelled as aggressive (often with negative connotations). The Dictator feels that *I'm OK. You're NOT OK.*

In a sense, the Dictator really represents something of an extreme, since we all demonstrate the tendencies of this type (as well as the others) at some times. Actually, if we were to look at a scatter diagram of behaviors, we would notice that for the Dictator, the weighting occurs predominantly in one area. See Exhibit 6-5.

EXHIBIT 6-5. *Dictator Scatter Diagram*

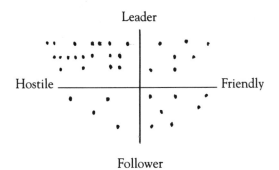

A **Bureaucrat** (Exhibit 6-6) is a person who usually *goes by the book* because "rules were made for good reasons." He rarely takes chances and does not wish to stand out from the crowd. He does not wish to be the leader, but resents whoever is. He will frequently gossip about people, but will rarely confront them. If a new idea is suggested, he usually has some reason why it won't work and shouldn't even be attempted. Of course, like the Socialite, the Bureaucrat is an extreme representation. He has an *I'm NOT OK, You're NOT OK* orientation.

A **Socialite** (Exhibit 6-7) is a *friendly follower:* someone who is often *hanging out with the crowd.* He bases his sense of self-worth on other people's reactions and perceptions of him. Hence, he is eager to please, and may even appear to be a *social butterfly* or a *good time Charlie.*

EXHIBIT 6-6. *Hostile + Follower = Bureaucrat.*

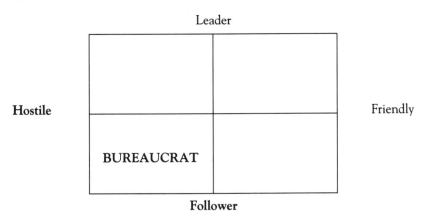

EXHIBIT 6-7. *Friendly + Follower = Socialite.*

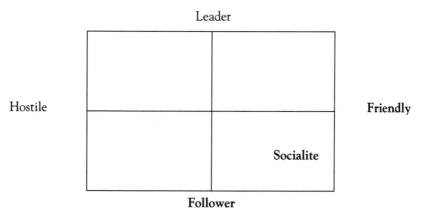

EXHIBIT 6-7. *Friendly + Follower = Socialite.*

He is very talkative and tends to be very conscious of the latest fashions and trends. Because he tends to subordinate his goals to the desires of the group, he rarely takes the initiative. He sees the world from a *You're OK, I'm NOT OK* orientation.

An **Executive** (Exhibit 6-8) is a person who is an independent thinker and is respectful of other's feelings and opinions, but makes up his own mind. A natural leader in any group, he is social, polite, and friendly, but not insincerely so. When necessary, he is able to set limits on himself and others. The warmth of the Executive's dominant behavior often causes him to be seen as assertive by others. Hence, he thinks, *I'm OK, You're OK.*

EXHIBIT 6-8. *Friendly + Leader = Executive.*

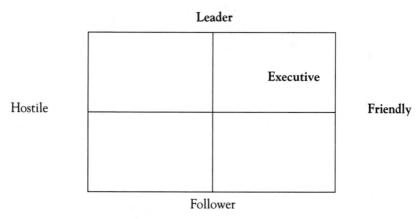

Summary

In this chapter, we have presented a broad summary of the four personality types that each of us demonstrates. Each of these types reflects a specific set of emotional needs. By recognizing which type of individual we are dealing with at any one time, it is possible to motivate them more effectively by recognizing and responding to those emotional needs.

In the chapters that follow, we will use the same grid system to explore how you can expect your FCs and clients to react to your presentations, based upon their psychological profile. Later, in Section III, we will deal with how to motivate and quickly build an effective relationship with any of these four types.

CHAPTER 7

Manager Types and Styles

What type of manager are you? How do your employees see you? Your ability to be an effective leader may well depend upon the answer to this and other questions. We've already mentioned that each of us demonstrates all four personality types at one time or another, but that we predominant in one.

As a branch or regional manager, you may have several other managers (sales, operations, administrative, etc.) under you, and you certainly have managers over you. Being able to recognize their *type* can be a great asset in working with them. Remember, while each of the types can be appropriate in some contexts, we've found that the **Executive** type manager is usually the most effective in working with others.

Beginning with the **Dictator**, let's look at each type and its strengths and weaknesses in dealing with other employees/managers and customers.

The Dictator as Manager

Historically, the **Dictator** (Exhibit 7-1) has been the most common type of manager in the financial services industry (primarily in securities and insurance, and less so in banking). This is hardly surprising when you realize that, traditionally, most FCs were hired because of their aggressive attitude toward cold-calling and selling. It took a tough hide to cold-call 100 people a day and be rejected 90 times. It was generally assumed that only someone who was naturally aggressive could survive. Since most sales managers and branch managers are selected from the ranks of successful FCs, most managers have been Dictators.

A significant problem that has arisen from the predominance of Dictators in the ranks of managers is the continued tendency to hire other Dictators as FCs. The architypical Dictator has a tendency to try to push his way through situations and to demand loyalty and total acceptance of his dictates because he is the manager and therefore probably not only has more market experience but is also better, smarter, etc. than anyone working for him. Unfortunately, his *I'm OK, you're NOT OK*, hard-nosed attitude does little to engender the loyalty and dedication that he both needs and seeks. A small change in behaviors would cause him to be perceived much differently, resulting in his more consistently attaining his personal and business objectives.

The Dictator tends to assume that the two main ways to motivate employees are with a carrot or a stick. The stick varies from public sarcasm and humiliation to threats of firing. The carrot is usually limited to financial rewards or public recognition, such as having one's name placed higher on a list of producers (note the implied threat of having one's name lower on the list than someone else's).

Because of his need to be better than everyone else, the Dictator manager is often ambivalent about his FCs. He is proud of the performance of his top producers, but may be threatened by the fact that they are doing better than he did when he was an FC and that they are currently making more money than he is. At the same time, while new FCs provide no threat to his ego in terms of being better than he, their potential failure and its reflection on his managing and hiring abilities can be a threat to his position. Because his top producers are often fellow Dictators who do not respond well to criticism (and he can hardly afford to antagonize them), this kind of manager tends to focus his attention and criticism on his new FCs, often driving them out of the

EXHIBIT 7-1. *Dictator Manager.*

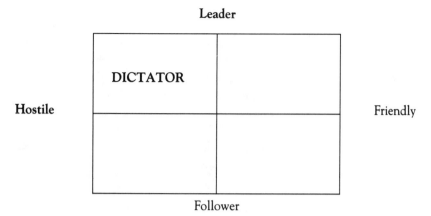

business from stress before they really get started. Ironically, his aggressiveness and hostility are often also very stressful to himself and frequently result in family problems and health difficulties. We'll deal in detail with specific recommendations for handling that stress in the section on stress management.

This manager needs to take some serious steps if he is to not only succeed, but also to enjoy doing so.

- First, he needs to evaluate his behavior and his attitudes about himself and his employees.
- Second, he must establish goals that target the behaviors and attitudes that will enable him to be most effective as a manager. To do this, he should use the techniques outlined in Chapters 2 and 3 on building character and goal setting.
- Third, he must produce a plan to achieve those goals, and follow it.

The one thing this manager must avoid is the tendency to assume that he cannot change. Remember Benjamin Franklin, a 20-year-old printer's apprentice with no character and no prospects.

The Bureaucrat as Manager

Outside of the banking industry, which rewards risk-avoidance behavior and those who follow traditional, accepted methods of doing things, there are very few **Bureaucrats** acting as branch managers (Exhibit 7-2). The reason is that few Bureaucrats have the flexibility and courage needed to do what must be done in order to be successful enough as an FC to be accepted into management. However, under enough pressure, any of us may tend to act like a Bureaucrat and to re-treat into a *by-the-book attitude*. This is both natural (such as when we are being pressured by upper management or a customer's lawyer) and occasionally appropriate. For example:

- When dealing with matters of compliance;
- When preparing for licensing exams; or
- When teaching the new employees how to prudently approach the market, by learning techniques that have already been proven to be safe and effective.

Unfortunately, this character trait in a manager can also be discouraging to employees and generally counter-productive.

An ultra Bureaucratic manager tends to be a rigid person who always follows the rules because they were made for good reasons. He rarely takes chances and does not wish to stand out from the crowd. In fact, he will most often be seen in the area of operations, where his attitudes and skills are both appropriate and helpful. He does not wish to be the leader, but resents whoever is. The extreme aspects of this personality would resent others in the office who are successful. He will

EXHIBIT 7-2. *Bureaucrat Manager.*

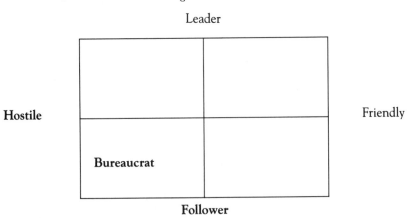

Managers, Employees, and Customers: A Psychological Model

frequently gossip about people, but will rarely confront them. If a new product, sales program, or idea is suggested, he usually has some reason why it won't work and shouldn't even be attempted. Hence, employees hesitate to bring him ways to improve the business. Our chapter on *Effective Questioning Techniques* will provide some insight into how to handle this issue/response when someone uses it.

Being hostile but weak, he will generally back down from individuals that he perceives as being more powerful than himself. He is generally sure that he is right, resents any form of criticism, and will harbor a grudge against those who disagree with him. At the same time, he will play the Dictator to people that he considers less powerful. Hence, you will usually see him take the side of FCs with large production against new FCs regardless of who is right. Because of this, he is hard to motivate and is not effective in motivating others.

He often has poor social skills and does not communicate his expectations and needs effectively. As a result, he may appear subservient to higher management and his peers, and hard to please to his employees. Of course, like the *Dictator*, the Bureaucrat is an extreme representation. He has an *I'm NOT OK, You're NOT OK* orientation.

This manager also needs to evaluate himself, his attitudes, and his goals and follow the same steps suggested for the Dictator. He can particularly benefit from the rapport building and other skills that will be presented in Section III on motivation. These skills will enable him to be perceived as more responsive and to obtain greater conformity from his FCs with significantly less resentment.

The Socialite as Manager

This individual is warm and friendly and appears easy to work for. Unfortunately, because the Socialite manager has difficulty in making decisions and setting policy, he can be very frustrating as well. See Exhibit 7-3.

A **Socialite** is essentially a *friendly follower*; meaning, by definition, someone who is generally not a leader, not management material. As a result, this person is also rarely seen in the ranks of branch management. As someone who is very conscious of other people's reactions and perceptions of what's popular, he is seen primarily in marketing and public relations positions. Because he tends to subordinate his goals to the desires of the group, especially those who he

EXHIBIT 7-3. *Socialite Manager.*

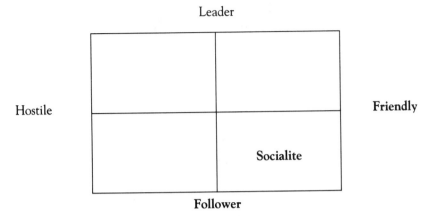

considers leaders and opinion formers, he rarely takes the initiative. He wants to be liked so much that he is unable to maintain the discipline necessary for a successful branch. His one chance of survival is to be assigned to a branch full of successful, self-starters that enjoy the pleasant atmosphere that he creates. He sees the world from a *You're OK, I'm NOT OK* orientation.

This individual needs an Executive sales manager who can maintain the control and discipline necessary to balance his warm friendliness. Any Dictator or Bureaucrat sales manager would undermine his position and take over. Barring that, he too must establish personal goals to overcome the inherent weakness of his position.

The Executive as Manager

In so many ways, the **Executive** (Exhibit 7-4) represents the ideal branch or sales manager. His leadership and warmth make him easy to follow.

An Executive manager finds it easy to support his company's various sales campaigns, while also adapting them to the circumstances of his FCs and customer base. An independent thinker himself, he is not threatened by FCs who have new or different ideas. He is respectful of others' feelings and opinions, but makes up his own mind and can be firm in maintaining his requirements where necessary. A natural leader in any group, he has good social skills, is polite and friendly, but not insincerely so. While his office door is always open, he is able to set limits on himself and others. One of his most important strengths as a

Managers, Employees, and Customers: A Psychological Model

EXHIBIT 7-4. *Executive Manager.*

Leader

Hostile

Executive

Friendly

Follower

leader is his ability to communicate his genuine interest in and concern for each of his employees, even in the midst of a disagreement. Hence, his assertiveness rarely results in defensive responses on the part of others. He communicates an *I'm OK. You're OK* attitude.

Another important strength is his flexibility. His self-confidence is based upon a sound self-image that allows him to deal effectively with employees and customers who are represented by the other three types. With Socialites, he can be friendly and meet their social needs while firmly encouraging them to work consistently toward required goals. With Bureaucrats, he can give solid direction regarding his expectations which they can follow by the book. At the same time, he does not accept their tendency to reject new products and ideas.

On the other hand, he works extremely well with Executive FCs because they have so much in common in their work and relationship styles. Finally, with the Dictator (often a prima donna FC), he maintains a firm, friendly relationship that lets the FC know that while he will provide consistent support, he runs the branch. No other type has the flexibility to effectively handle all four personality types.

Summary

We have presented the four personality types as managers to give you a chance to think about managers that you have known as well as about your own management style. How effective your style is in motivating the four types of FCs will be discussed in the next four chapters.

CHAPTER 8

FC and Customer Personality Types

As with managers, FCs and customers can be divided into having each of the four primary personality types. By understanding which personality you are dealing with, you can more effectively provide motivation by meeting the FC's/customer's emotional needs.

The Dictator as FC and Customer

The Dictator as FC

According to many clients, the Dictator is the most common type of FC (Exhibit 8-1). This individual thinks of selling as a win-lose situation. As a result, he perceives the client as prepared to resist any sale and feels that he must overwhelm that resistance. He relates in

EXHIBIT 8-1. *Dictator Personality Type Chart.*

Leader

DICTATOR	

Hostile   Friendly

Follower

an adversarial way and tends to use force and manipulation to obtain the sale, believing that *the end justifies the means.*

In the long run, his relationship style is, at best, self-defeating. While he may appear to temporarily excel in production quotas, he loses customers for the firm. He is also rarely trusted by his clients because his style does not establish rapport.

When this FC is successful, he is often difficult to work with in the branch. He naturally assumes that he is more important than other FCs and that his needs should always be placed first, even over the needs of the group. If he is not given what he wants, he may make veiled threats to leave the branch and take his production and clients where he will be more appreciated. At worst, if he perceives weakness in a branch or sales manager, he may be openly disrespectful.

General guidelines: There is little difficulty in dealing with *new* Dictator FCs. Because they tend to be authority-oriented themselves, most Dictators will respect and bend to any authority that they perceive as being greater than their own. A firm, friendly, no-nonsense stance will usually result in conformity to your standards and wishes. When a problem occurs, simply use the communications and rapport skills discussed in Section III and the counseling skills in Section V.

The problem in dealing with the *successful* Dictator stems from the hesitation some managers feel about risking the loss of any big producer. In reality, there are several things that can be done to make life with such an individual less stressful. These will be repeated in greater detail in Chapters 14–16.

- When this individual is upset, establish rapport and use *fogging*

Managers, Employees, and Customers: A Psychological Model

techniques (found in Section IV) to calm him down and determine the nature of the problem.

- Remember that the Dictator is motivated by a series of emotional needs. Look for ways to meet those needs that will not threaten the smooth functioning of the branch. In addition, utilize the motivational techniques found in Section III.
- Remain firm and friendly. Dealing with a Dictator who is an FC isn't really that different from dealing with one as a client.
- Use the counseling techniques found in Chapters 20–22.

The Dictator as Customer

This kind of prospect/client is very difficult to deal with because he tends to believe that all FCs are corrupt and are only interested in making money, even at the client's expense. The Dictator as customer (Exhibit 8-1) will tend to make flat assertions, be sarcastic, argue, and interrupt. He has strong security and esteem needs. He maintains both by attempting to remain in control, and by trying to rise above everyone else (*I'm OK. You're not OK*). He is most easily handled through the use of assertive warmth and the communications skills covered later. The rapport building skills in Section III can also be very powerful in working with him.

One good thing about these clients is that they can and will make decisions. Because of his need to appear better than others, this client is often willing to take risks that other clients will not. However, he can also become very hostile and quick to blame the FC if the risk does not pay off. He likes products that appeal to his ego needs. For example: Securities that are expected to turn a quick profit, high-performance mutual funds, insurance products that provide a large return on investment, sophisticated products.

General guidelines: Whenever he resists or becomes hostile, communicate your desire to understand, and your willingness to listen and to meet his needs. As you successfully communicate your sincere interest in him, his behavior will frequently change from being hostile and aggressive to assertive and less defensive, if not actually warm. Remember that this individual has a strong *need* to trust, but fears that he will get burned. How long it takes to win his trust will vary with the client (and some will never trust an FC). However, once their trust is won, these clients will frequently become the most loyal and the easiest to work with.

Stress the aspects of your product or service that will enhance their self-esteem and independence. Remember, they need to feel that they are different from, and therefore superior to, others. For example:

- "Mr. Jones, we are only showing this investment opportunity to a *few* of our clients whom we feel *have the experience* to really benefit from what it will provide."
- "Mr. Smith, this mutual fund will allow you to *achieve the independence* you want, to be able to *do your own thing*. Because of the particular features of this fund, you can basically divorce yourself from the market and concentrate on what you want. You'll be *one of the very few* to recognize this opportunity—which means that you *stand apart from the crowd.*"

When he is upset, let him get it out. Listen to him and then try to paraphrase his concerns back to him. Once you are sure that you understand his concerns, work with him to solve them. Always be sure that you have dealt with his opinions and concerns before bringing your own up, or he will not hear you. Don't let him upset you. Stick to your guns and don't let him overwhelm you. Frequently this individual really wants someone that he can depend on to be in charge. If you buckle in on him, he won't believe in your ability to help protect him from his own bad decisions. Make use of open probes, reflective statements, and summary statements. More information on how to deal with this individual can be found in Section III (*Rapport Building*) and Section V (*Counseling*).

In summary, Dictators have always been the individuals that most of us have liked the least. Overbearing and occasionally obnoxious, we tend to deal with them by avoiding them or giving into their desires. It is now possible to work with them and to turn them into the most loyal and hard-working employees and customers, simply by meeting their needs.

The Bureaucrat as FC and Customer

The Bureaucrat as FC

This kind of FC is relatively rare. He does not relate well to others and resents authority, yet he will rarely buck authority openly. The Bureaucrat FC (Exhibit 8-2) is passive-aggressive in the way that he

Managers, Employees, and Customers: A Psychological Model

relates to people and his resentment is frequently transparent within a short time; for example, when a new product or sales campaign is inaugurated, he has all the reasons why it won't work.

He feels that clients don't trust sales people and that customers will buy only when they are ready; and, hence, that there is little that he can do to influence the customer to buy. He is slow to make decisions, but will follow orders to the letter to avoid criticism. Often, the closest that he comes to success is in following specific directions to make a specific number of calls per day and to read a specific script. He demonstrates little creativity or leadership; in the end, he is little more than an order taker. His behavior parallels that of the classic bureau-taker. His behavior parallels that of the classic bureaucrat.

General guidelines: While few managers are motivated to hire someone who demonstrates the characteristics of our Bureaucrat, it should be remembered that none of us has a personality that is always one way. During an interview, the Bureaucrat may have been enthusiastic and even appeared to be something of a dictator with an aggressive, gung-ho attitude. However, under pressure, many dictators revert to bureaucratic behavior—and vice versa. Hence, the office Bureaucrat can become something of a bully to new brokers or support personnel that are unsure of themselves.

Let this FC know, early on, that a negative attitude is neither helpful nor acceptable in the branch. While he is not expected to support every new idea developed by marketing, he is to keep his negatives to himself unless specifically requested. Because this person

EXHIBIT 8-2. *Bureaucrat Personality Type Chart.*

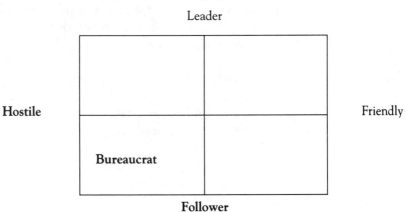

does tend to look for the negative in situations, make use of this trait. During brain-storming sessions, have him remain silent during the generation of ideas because his negative attitude may discourage the generation of ideas. However, when the generation period is completed, have him speak last and bring up all of the potential problems in each idea that has been discussed. Then, once a decision has been made, let him know that he will be expected to support it wholeheartedly. In this way, you can use his conservative attitude positively.

Be sure to give him firm goals and specific plans to attain those goals in each area of his business. Then follow up on a regular schedule. The regularity of the schedule will be important because it will provide a sense of security for him and enable him to plan for each deadline. Then be sure that you let him know how well he is progressing. If he is not making progress, use the tips given in the chapter on counseling to give very specific feedback regarding ways that he can improve. Make sure that he accepts responsibility for the changes he needs to make, as well as for his current failings.

The Bureaucrat as Customer

This client/prospect tends to believe that FCs are only out to sell him something that he doesn't want or need. However, unlike his more aggressive counterparts, he deals with this through avoidance behavior such as silence and noncommittal responses. The Bureaucrat as customer (Exhibit 8-2) also does not make decisions well. Unlike the Socialite, he speaks very little.

This individual has a poor self-image and a deep lack of trust that leads him to expect others to try to take advantage of him (*I'm not OK. You're not OK.*). Hence, he needs constant reassurance and support. As a result, he may appear to go along with a presentation but fail to make a decision; he may ask for more time, and then be impossible to reach for a follow-up conversation. Where the aggressive-hostile person will reject outright, this more passive-aggressive individual will avoid confrontation, but still fail to cooperate. For products, he prefers safety and things with a proven track record (e.g., certificates of deposit, investment-grade bonds, insurance, and, occasionally, investment-grade stocks and mutual funds).

General guidelines: Remember his security needs and stress benefits that will meet them. Don't push. Go slowly and be patient. Take the time to communicate your genuine interest and establish the trust he seeks. It is important to guide him firmly but gently. Draw out his feelings with open probes, pauses, and brief assertions of interest on your part. Emphasize that what you are recommending is the traditional, accepted, prudent thing to do. For example:

- "Mr. Jones, a municipal bond is one of the *most conservative* investments available to meet your need for tax free income, and has *traditionally* been the *method of choice* selected to solve this kind of problem."
- "Mr. Smith, a mutual fund is the most *traditional* and *judicious* method of accumulating wealth. It will *allow you* to *prudently* invest your money while achieving the added safety offered by diversification."

In summary, the Bureaucrat has traditionally been one of the most difficult individuals to work with. Unlike the Dictator, who speaks his mind, the more passive Bureaucrat may appear to be cooperating or agreeing with us, while internally shaking his head. By dealing with his emotional needs for order and security, it is now easier to motivate him to cooperate with you in obtaining your goals.

The Socialite as FC and Customer

EXHIBIT 8-3. *Socialite Personality Type Chart.*

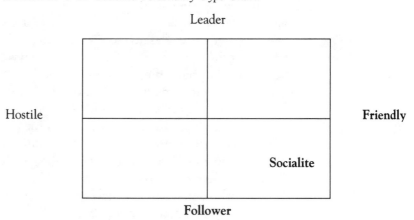

The Socialite as FC

As an FC, the Socialite (Exhibit 8-3) is easy to hire. He is enthusiastic, warmly agreeable, friendly and has great social skills. In fact, during the hiring interview you may find that he is extremely enthusiastic about your branch and the programs that you offer. He speaks easily and is very likable, generally making a good impression upon everyone he meets.

When he first begins to work, he usually does so with gusto, anticipating success because he feels that prospects and customers are nice guys who will buy from their friends. Hence, he attempts to make friends with all of his prospects. He is warm, friendly, and well-liked around the office. His Socialite tendencies make him popular with the clients he gets because he appears to put their interests before his own. However, because he dislikes unpleasantness, he has a tendency to avoid making decisions or confronting a client. This becomes apparent in his failure to close a sale or convey bad news about an investment. At the same time, he has the most success in obtaining client referrals.

He is also particularly vulnerable to rejection. As a result, he doesn't like to cold-call. While he establishes rapport well, he is insufficiently assertive to maintain production. As a result, he may waste a great deal of time socializing in the office or on the phone.

General guidelines: Establish specific daily and weekly performance goals in terms of calls made, new accounts opened, and assets gathered. Remember that his self-image is strongly dependent upon the opinions of others. Praise him when he meets the goals you've established together and encourage him to continue. Avoid publicly humiliating him if he fails to make the goals. When making goals with him, remind him that you are asking no more of him than of *everyone else*. Do not take his enthusiasm at face value. When you have completed a discussion with him, have him summarize what has been said, or ask him questions to determine whether or not he really understood you and accepted the goals. If not, probe to determine the nature of his doubts and deal with them. Keep him focused on the point being discussed as he may jump ahead of you as he becomes enthused with the topic being discussed. In motivational sessions dealing with rejection, he often needs to be reminded that a negative cold call is merely the result of someone who didn't appreciate what your company could do for them. The motivational techniques of Section IV will help here.

Managers, Employees, and Customers: A Psychological Model

The Socialite as Customer

This kind of prospect or client initially appears to be ideal: He assumes that the financial consultant has his interests at heart and appears to be easily maneuvered. The Socialite as customer (Exhibit 8-3) is warm, friendly, easy to convince and becomes easily enthused about anything presented. He is very *talkative*.

However, he also tends to have difficulty making decisions, and while he *appears* enthusiastic about a presentation, he will frequently end the conversation by saying that he needs more time (e.g., to talk it over with someone). He tends to meander and socialize during the presentation and frequently has to be brought back to the subject at hand. When he does listen, he glosses over the material. He has strong dependency needs (*You're OK. I'm not OK.*), and looks for security. This is manifested through his desire to take the most popular path and keep primarily to safe investments. He doesn't wish to risk losing his money or others good opinion of him.

General guidelines: When working with this individual, suggest to your FCs that they remember his need for acceptance and emphasize benefits that deal with acceptance, esteem, and security needs. They should concentrate on products that are both safe and popular (e.g., certificates of deposit, popular, high-quality mutual funds, insurance, and investment grade, well-known securities—be sure that investing in the market is popular before suggesting securities).

Remember that he needs to socialize. Meet this need, but do not allow it to override the purpose of the call. Firmly guide him through the presentation and be specific in your recommendations. Don't take his enthusiasm and easy acceptance at face value. Probe for underlying doubts. Finally, rely primarily on closed probes (they will not encourage the meandering that an open probe may), and frequently use summary and reflective statements. This individual can be sold by accentuating how your product or service will meet his needs for safety and for approval from friends and others. For example:

- "Mr. Jones, insured certificates of deposit are one of our most *popular* investments *among people* like yourself who are interested in achieving a good rate of return with excellent *safety*. They're very pleased with them."

- "Mr. Smith, a mutual fund is the most *popular* method for accumulating wealth. Most *smart people* allow responsive, professional managers to do their work for them. I wouldn't be surprised to find that *many of your friends* own some of the same funds as you. As various people talk about their investments, you can easily *participate* in the conversation because you'll be owning basically the same thing.

In summary, although warm and friendly and a pleasure to be around, the Socialite shares, with the Bureaucrat, the frustrating inability to quickly make and act on a decision. By appealing to their emotional needs for security and group approval, it is now easier to gain their cooperation.

The Executive as FC and Customer

The Executive as FC

This is the ideal FC and will be explored at length later. Essentially, he believes that clients will buy if they understand how the product or service that he presents will meet their needs. The Executive as FC (Exhibit 8-4) probes and profiles his clients to determine and understand their needs, and he links the appropriate features of the product/service to those needs to demonstrate the benefit to the client. We think he demonstrates the traits of the ideal executive.

General Guidelines: These individuals expect you to understand them, to meet their needs, and to effectively communicate to them

EXHIBIT 8-4. *Executive Personality Type Chart.*

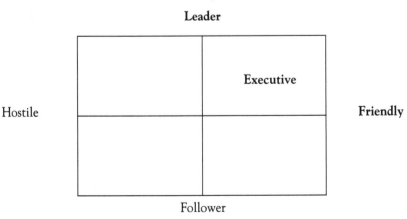

Managers, Employees, and Customers: A Psychological Model

specifically what you expect and what support you will provide them in their efforts to meet your and their goals. In terms of receptivity, they are willing to listen and are open to new ideas, products, and sales campaigns, but will tend to be impatient with hype. Do everything possible to involve them in the decision-making process while using open probes to determine their interests and concerns.

Be assertive and walk them through new products and campaigns, answering their questions and explaining how the product will meet the specific needs of clients. Tell them which clients a product is appropriate for and which it is not appropriate for, but do not attempt to oversell or manipulate. These FCs will respond to respect and will return it, with loyalty. They are also goal-oriented and can make decisions. They are emotionally secure and have a positive self image that allows them to be open to others (I'm OK. You're OK.). As a result, they are less afraid to cold-call or contact their clients in a bad market.

The Executive as Customer

As with Executive FCs, these individuals expect you to understand them, to meet their needs, and to effectively communicate to them just how you will meet those needs. In terms of receptivity, Executives as customers (Exhibit 8-4) are also willing to listen and are open to new ideas, but will also tend to be impatient with hype. It has often been suggested to FCs to *sell the sizzle, not the steak.* With these clients, present the steak first. If there isn't enough meat, all the sizzle in the world won't sell.

Do everything possible to involve them in the decision-making process while using open probes to determine their needs. Be assertive and guide them through the presentation but do not attempt to oversell or manipulate. These customers respond to respect and will return it, with loyalty. They are goal-oriented and can make buying decisions. In addition, they are emotionally secure and have a positive self-image that allows them to be open to the FC (again, *I'm OK. You're OK.*). In a sales situation, since they will respond to the steak rather than to the sizzle, you can show them any product or service as long as you tie its features into their needs.

General guidelines: Again, always emphasize the end benefits of their decisions by showing how your product or service will help them to achieve their goals. Demonstrate how the features of the solution that you have selected correspond to the parameters of their problem.

Involve them to the point that the decision that they make is always an informed decision. For example:

- "Mr. Jones, this XYZ stock is both investment grade (*meeting your requirements for high quality*), and is expected to grow at a rate of 12% per year over the next five years (*which exceeds your requirement of 8% growth*). What do you think?"
- "Mr. Smith, this mutual fund offers you the greatest probability of *meeting your goals* of _____, _____, with _____. Specifically, diversification and professional management will also allow you to *achieve the following benefits:* _____, _____, and _____."

In summary, whether FC or customer, the Executive is, clearly, the easiest individual to work with. Once he is convinced of the benefits of a course of action, he is well-motivated, organized, and able to make and act on decisions.

Summary

Whether you are dealing with a Dictator, Bureaucrat, Socialite, or Executive, knowing the personality types of your employees and customers can make life a lot easier for you as branch manager. By meeting their emotional needs, you will find that it requires less effort to motivate them to cooperate with your goals and it will be much simpler to keep them happy. Now explore the mastery exercises below.

Mastery Exercise 1: Personality Traits

Read each of the following statements and decide which psychological profile the individual speaking would fit into: Executive, Socialite, Bureaucrat, or Dictator. The answers can be found in Appendix 1.

"We all know just how important it is to perform exactly what is expected of you—no more and no less. A company ought to get what it pays for, and it doesn't pay us to make up new company policies." _____

"A department is run efficiently if all of the people are working in accord with one another. This virtually insures that the company is getting optimal performance."

_____

"The company requires that you pay attention to both the needs of the individual and the objectives of the department. Neither is always right."

_____

"There can be one captain of a ship and one captain only."

_____

"When I want your opinion I'll ask for it. Till then, just do what I told you. After all, I've been through these types of situations before."

_____

This person's office has pictures of various teams that he has participated in, family pictures, and mementoes of every office party ever attended. The placement of the seat is designed for easy, casual conversation.

_____

This person's office is rather stark and bare. The seat probably has a high back and is arranged opposite you and slightly above the visitor's.

_____

This person's office is somewhat stark but has company-oriented mementoes and plaques and awards placed throughout. It seems to be utilitarian.

_____

This person's office is stuffed to the gills with papers which are so scattered and messy as to be unbelievable. The person's organizational system is to remember approximately which side of the office something is located.

_____

"I wonder where all of the competent "Where did all the competent people go?," he asks. "The only way to get something done right is to do it yourself."

_____

"I know that management and the union are seemingly on opposite sides of the fence. Let's get everybody together to see how we can resolve the situation for our mutual benefit."

_____

Managers, Employees, and Customers: A Psychological Model

CHAPTER 9

Relationship Styles

We've already pointed out that no one is always a Dictator, a Bureaucrat, a Socialite, or even an Executive. After all, an individual who is a Dictator at the office will often be a Socialite when playing with his infant child at home. This is important, because each of us demonstrates each of the personality types at different times, depending upon the context. For example:

- At work, the warm, decisive leadership of the Executive type is consistently the most appropriate for a branch manager;
- for a soldier in combat, the hostile aggressiveness of the Dictator is most effective;
- when learning a new skill or job, the conservative, by-the-book mode of the Bureaucrat works best; and,

- when we just want to relax and have fun with our family and friends, the carefree warmth of the Socialite is often most rewarding.

The key to relating to others is flexibility. When we relate to someone the same way each time we encounter them, regardless of the context, we become locked into a rigid system that becomes self-defeating. In management, we frequently run into employees or customers who relate to us in a rigid style, always coming from the same personality type. If we are not flexible in our response to them, we can end up locking ourselves into a self-defeating pattern that may eventually force us or the employee to end the relationship. For example:

- Have you ever had an FC that always wanted you to make the decisions, but always found some reason for not going along with your idea?
- How about the opposite, an FC that always insisted on doing things his way, even when you know he's wrong, and then blames you when his idea doesn't work?
- Customers can be that way, too. We've all had at least one that always knows exactly what he wants, and then blames the bank when things don't work exactly as he thought they would.

Frustrating, isn't it? How do you respond to these employees and customers? When the first individual left all of the decisions to you, did you make the decisions or try to involve him? When the second individual tried to dominate you, did you give in and let him, or did you fight back? When we get locked into a relationship where we are always dominant when the client is submissive (or just the opposite), we have developed a *Relationship Style* with that client that will be frustrating and self-defeating at best.

Relationship style is basically a way of describing the way two people commonly communicate within a given relationship. The way that an individual relates usually varies with the context and the person to whom he is relating. However, it can become common to all contexts with a given person or even to all their relationships. When this happens, problems almost always occur.

We will describe three basic styles of relating: complementary, symmetrical, and parallel.

The Complementary Style

The complementary relationship is one of opposites (i.e., dominant-submissive, introvert-extrovert, hostile-warm, healthy-sick," and so forth).

The most common form is seen in the dominant-submissive mode. This is a rigid mode in which one person is *always* in control while the other is *never* in control. Conflicts are generally resolved by either the submissive person withdrawing in defeat or by the dominant person handing down an edict. You will see this whenever a Dictator relates to a Bureaucrat or a Socialite. For example:

- The aggressive FC and the pliant, eager-to-please customer; or the dominating manager and the pliant, eager-to-please FC (FCs certainly need to be teachable and to accept direction and instruction, but they must also be able to think for themselves).

- The dominating FC and the resistant prospect who is finally won over, but who never sends back the necessary paperwork to open the account; or the dominant manager and the apparently cooperative FC who speaks badly about the manager behind his back.

- The hostile customer and the over-accommodating FC (who can't seem to make a sale); or the hostile big-producing FC and the manager who can't get him to cooperate.

You should recognize that your submissive FCs and customers receive a great deal of *payoff* for maintaining their submissive role and will therefore try to maintain that role in your relationship. Don't let them. Move into the Executive mode and lead them into making their own decisions, and then support their decisions (even if they are not the ones you wanted). As you do so, they will begin to see you as a source of support instead of a threat and will begin to take more responsibility for their decisions.

In addition, submissive FCs or customers carry an all-powerful veto—they need only to appear to surrender, seeming to go along with what you wish, and then fail to follow through with whatever was agreed upon. This could place you in the position of having apparently *won* without obtaining your goals. Remember, dominating your employees and customers can become self-defeating.

The Symmetrical Style

This style may be found in situations and relationships in which both individuals respond identically, such as both dominant or both submissive. When power or control is sought, neither gives in and the struggle escalates until serious difficulties arise. Neither feels sufficiently secure in himself, the other person, or the relationship to relinquish control voluntarily. As a result, power becomes the primary source of validation in the relationship: "If I were really okay, I'd win."

When you run into aggressive employees or customers, do you find yourself confronting them and trying to overpower them? Or, when you work with passive employees or customers, do you have difficulty gaining their cooperation because you can't make yourself close for a commitment? In both situations you and the other individual are responding identically to each other, and nothing is getting accomplished. Frustrating, isn't it? Ultimately, in both cases, the other individual holds the ultimate veto. All he needs to do to win is *nothing*. He can even just hang up.

Whenever you meet a Dictator, Bureaucrat, or Socialite FC or client in this mode, you risk a symmetrical interaction. Move into the Executive mode and show the Dictator that you are not threatened/defensive, but that you also do not need to threaten. Show your interest and confidence and he will change his mode. When working with the Bureaucrat or Socialite, use your Executive skills to support them and help them to make decisions. If neither of you takes the lead, nothing can be accomplished.

The Parallel Style

The parallel style of relating is the healthiest and most effective of the three because it is the most flexible. It's a style in which neither you nor your employee is anxious about dealing with the other, and you both feel able to express yourselves without a struggle developing. In addition, you both decide the issues of power and control by the needs of the situation rather than by arbitrary or conflicting expectations. Remember, you may be the branch manager and have the power to hire and fire; but each FC is also the head of his own business and is used to making decisions about that business each day.

In practice, as the Executive in the relationship, you are able to maintain the necessary flexibility by supporting your FC's needs for self-esteem while providing the leadership to help solve his problem. It is a relationship in which neither of you wins all of the time, and it consists of honesty, openness, trust, and cooperation.

In the sales relationship, the parallel style occurs when you and your customer work together to solve his financial needs/problems. In most cases, a parallel relationship will result in your taking the lead in seeking and proposing solutions to the FC or customer, but in every case, it allows either to accept responsibility for the end decision.

> Flexibility is an important key to communicating.

There are four common elements which occur in all three relationship styles. These elements consist of the processes of control, communication patterns, change, and decision making. It is the variations among and within these four areas that determine the style of interaction or relationship.

- *Control* consists of the way each person in the relationship attempts to manipulate or coerce the other in an effort to maintain control of a situation and/or the relationship itself. This can be seen whenever either you or your employee or customer attempt to manipulate the other to obtain your own ends. (*Note:* Attempts to manipulate are almost always construed as negative by the person being manipulated.)

- *Communication* consists of each person's willingness to participate in two-way communication between peers rather than attempting to control the flow of information between them. How open is the flow of communication between you? Are you perceived as someone who communicates freely with your employees, or who only speaks to them when you have a new program to sell or are unhappy with their work? Do you perceive your employees as clearly sharing data about their needs, goals, and concerns, or as people who only come to you when they have a problem?

- *Change* consists of each person's willingness to risk altering their own behavior as well as the relationship itself without being threatened. This can be seen when you feel the need to suggest a change in strategy from one product line to another. How well do your FCs handle the change?

- *Decision making* consists of each individual's ability and willingness to place the needs of the relationship above his own desires relative to the decision at hand. You are the manager. In theory, it may seem that this means that you get to make all of the decisions and your FCs should cheerfully support them. For example, at times, you may feel that a particular product or service is exactly what your FCs need to sell to increase production and/or to relieve pressure on you from your management. However, your FCs should know their customer's needs best. If some of them are unwilling to emphasize a given product line, are you prepared to follow their inclination rather than risk damaging the relationship by insisting on your own point of view? Are your FCs willing to trust your judgment?

The elements of control, communication, change, and decision making will vary from relationship to relationship. As a leader, rather than a driver, you will find that by relating in a parallel style, with each of you taking your turn at the appropriate time, you will achieve a great deal more of *your* goals. The dominance, or overuse, of any characteristic is usually less effective than a more or less equal mix of these four factors.

Summary

The concept of relationship styles will help you to be sensitive to the need for flexibility in your communications with your employees and the branch's customers. Examine some of your current relationships and ask yourself if you are getting into a rut with any of them. If you are, note situations that always seem to start and end in a predictable manner and think about new responses that you can try. You'll be amazed at the results.

Section *III*

Rapport and the Elements of Leadership

Perhaps one of the most important, yet least understood and taught aspects of management is the concept of leadership. Today's graduate business schools teach their students how to manage finances and materials and tend to handle personnel as just another kind of material. Yet, any company's employees are its greatest single asset. This is especially true of the branch in the financial services industry, where a single employee can either significantly increase the branch's revenues or cause a lawsuit that closes the branch and ends the manager's career.

While most branch managers are chosen from the ranks of successful FCs, being a successful sales person does not necessarily translate into being a good leader. To be a good leader requires an ability to communicate with your employees in a way that they will desire to follow you and your/your company's policies. This is particularly important where you want to avoid using the carrot and the stick approach to encourage both obedience and loyalty.

As a manager, you are, by definition, an authority figure for the vast majority of people with whom you come into contact on a professional level. You may make them feel intimidated or nervous. Those responses, or even the common situation in which people are "Minding their Ps and Qs" in your presence, indicate that they are feeling at least mildly defensive and are NOT being totally open with you. Wouldn't it be useful to have the skills that can allow others to feel very comfortable in your presence?

The secret is to communicate both a genuine interest in and concern for your employees as well as the ability to understand how they feel about things and what motivates them. Simply put, if you want someone to follow your lead, you must first establish a meaningful rapport with them. Let's explore that idea for a moment.

> "Who is the most fascinating person in the world? I am! At least to me. And the second most fascinating person is someone who is just like me. The more that they are like me, the more comfortable I am with them. Now, I don't mean someone who mimics me; that can be insulting if taken too far. But someone who thinks like me, who *speaks my language*, who sees things the way I do (even if he doesn't agree with me). That's someone I'm comfortable with, someone I'll listen too."
>
> (Quote attributed to anyone's unconscious mind.)

Have you ever met someone that you seemed to agree with entirely, but with whom you couldn't get comfortable? On the other hand, have you ever met someone with whom you seemed to have nothing in common, but with whom you were very comfortable? We all have. The difference is that we had something called *rapport* with one and not with the other. That may have something to do with your selection of new FCs. We are far more likely to hire someone with whom we identify than someone with whom we don't.

What is rapport? Rapport might be defined as the ability to step into someone else's skin and to experience things the way that they do, from their point of view. As such, it is very much like empathy and helps us to communicate our understanding and acceptance of the other person. Yet, the ability to develop rapport with another person goes far beyond the words that we use when we speak. In fact, some psychologists estimate that as much as 90% of communication occurs on an unconscious level and has little or nothing to do with what is being discussed. That is why it is possible to develop deep levels of rapport with someone with whom you disagree.

Have you noticed that some of us seem to establish rapport naturally, while other have great difficulty? Frustrating, isn't it? Why is one manager very popular, successful, and listed to very carefully, while another, who may be much more intelligent, is ignored and has difficulty developing employee relationships? One reason may be their level of interest in people, their *warmth* (see *Psychological Profiling* in Chapter 6).

If the second most fascinating person in the world is someone who is just like us, surely tied for second is someone who communicates a genuine interest in us. Whenever we really focus our attention on someone and try to understand what they are saying, we almost automatically begin to build rapport. How to develop, enhance, and maintain rapport on the unconscious level is the subject of the next few chapters.

We like people who like us and who are like us.

Pacing

Key to the development of unconscious rapport is a process called *pacing*. We pace another person to the extent that we are in physical, mental, and emotional alignment with him. Essentially, it is a way of becoming similar to another person.

Since we respond to people on three primary levels (i.e., physical, mental, and emotional), people to whom we can related on multiple levels often become our friends, or at least our employees. Those with whom we don't relate never get close to us and rarely get hired. One way to increase the chances of making someone a friend, is to become as much like that person as possible. The same is true in terms of getting them to follow your leadership.

We have already pointed out that you unconsciously use many techniques in building rapport whenever you genuinely pay attention to someone in whom you are interested. A conscious understanding of what you already know how to do will enable you to become more consistent in your ability to establish and deepen rapport whenever you wish.

You should recognize that pacing is made up of a number of different aspects, no one of which is sufficient to accomplish your task by itself. *It is the combined effect of all of the methods of pacing that will virtually guarantee your ability to establish rapport with anyone you wish.* Rapport has a number of aspects and, while each aspect is important, it is the cumulative effect that makes each aspect powerful. What we are saying is that no single pacing method will automatically enable you to establish rapport with another person. However, *the cumulative effect of these basic techniques will assist you in creating "chemistry" with virtually anyone that you wish.*

Rapport and the Elements of Leadership

Chapter 10

Rapport Through Unconscious Physical Awareness

Have you ever been in a restaurant and, without even hearing what's being said, been able to tell who the friends and lovers were... or those who were angry at one another? How did you know? Unconsciously, we can tell who is in rapport and who is not. In this chapter we being to explore the *rapport-building process*.

As we said before, whenever we are very interested in someone (or even just in what they have to say), we tend to, psychologically, open ourselves to their influence. In doing so, we also tend to follow their lead and unconsciously seek deeper levels of rapport. Matching of body postures is just one of the ways that we do this.

Matching Body Posture—Mirroring

We like those who are most like ourselves—literally and figuratively. Matching body posture is one of the easiest and most effective ways of unconsciously influencing someone.

Matching is just what it sounds like. When you wish to establish rapport with someone, you match, almost as a mirror image, their posture, breathing, and gestures. This doesn't mean that you have to be exact, and it certainly doesn't mean mimicking them by moving as they move (that would be noticeable and insulting). What it does mean is that if someone were watching you and the other person, they would notice many similarities in your postures and gestures.

When you first meet someone, observe how he sits, then sit the same way. If you allow him to sit first, it becomes easy to sit the same way. If you are already seated, simply readjust your posture after he sits. For example: Have you ever gone to a party and looked at three people sitting together on a couch? Interesting isn't it? They almost always sit the same way. And, if one of them changes, they all change. That's matching on an unconscious basis.

When someone with whom you are speaking adjusts, or changes, his posture, wait a few moments and then *casually* adjust your own posture to match his. As long as you wait a moment first, your shift will rarely be noticeable. Remember, we are social beings and it is natural for us to establish rapport. As you sit, stand, or gesture like your employee you communicate a shared means of expression to him on an unconscious basis. This is true because the way we sit, stand, and gesture are all means of communicating, and anyone who does these things like we do is communicating like us in some way. Thus, they are already *speaking our language* on one level.

This may feel awkward at first. Sometimes it may even feel as though there are too many things to pay attention to at once. That's natural. What is ironic is that you already do this very well, at least part of the time, without even thinking about it at all. With a little practice, you'll be able to do it whenever you wish without having to think about it.

Test it for yourself. During a conversation with a friend or family member, begin by matching them. Notice how the conversation progresses. Then, after a few minutes, change your posture and mismatch them as completely as possible, and notice what happens to the conversation. Again, after just a few minutes, match them again and notice again what happens to the conversation. What differences did you notice? In yourself? In them? Fascinating, isn't it?

Initially, some people feel awkward following this procedure. However, after doing it a few times, it becomes automatic. You will soon find that your interactions with people are even more comfortable and easygoing as you employ these techniques.

You may notice that the other person will sometimes shift his body posture so that you are no longer matched. Merely wait a few moments, and then *casually* change your position until you are again somewhat matched. The key is to do it casually and to be as subtle as possible.

Sometimes simple matching isn't enough. Occasionally, you will run into someone who is so restless, or fidgety, that it seems that he just can't sit still. Trying to continuously match him would not only be difficult, but would also make you uncomfortable. A technique for dealing with this is called *cross matching*.

Cross Matching

When you are with someone who often shifts his body position, matching him move for move could make him aware that you are mimicking him. This could damage the rapport that you are trying to establish. To avoid this and continue to match, we utilize a technique known as *cross matching*. In this technique, you match some part of your body to a *different part* of your client's body. For example:

- If the person with whom you are speaking is sitting with his legs crossed, cross your arms but keep your feet flat on the floor.
- If his arms are crossed, cross your wrists, your legs, or your ankles.
- An individual who leans back in his chair might be cross matched by just leaning to the side and slightly back.
- If he puts his hand on his chin you can cross match him by putting your hand near your head. As long as you hand is in a *similar* position, you're fine.
- If you are interviewing someone who is sitting with his legs spread apart, cross match him by having your arms open (This is especially useful for women to know.)

The real key to matching is to adjust your body so that you *resemble* the posture of the person with whom you are speaking. Now, what about that restless, or fidgety client?

- If he likes to slowly bounce or move his legs to some internal rhythm, tap your fingers at the same rate that he moves his legs. There is very little chance that he will become conscious of what you are doing. Yet, unconsciously, you are maintaining your rapport.

An alternative to tapping your fingers could be a slight, almost unnoticeable, movement of your head (like nodding your head slightly to their rhythm). Again, there is very little possibility that he will ever notice this minute movement. Yet, *his unconscious is aware* and this awareness will correlate the rhythm of the two individual movements and will maintain or deepen your rapport.

Something this subtle might be difficult for a third person to observe. However, as long as you do this, you will increase the rapport that you need in order to develop really effective communication and leadership.

Matching body posture to obtain rapport is nice, but how do you know that you've achieved your purpose? The next subsection will give you a procedure in which you can *test for rapport.*

Leading: A Test for Rapport

How do you test to determine if you really have established rapport? One way to do this is through a process called *leading.*

Once you have matched a person's body posture for several minutes, change your posture slightly and wait a few moments (typically between 2 to 40 seconds) and notice if he readjusts his body posture to match yours. That is, once you change, does he follow your lead by repositioning himself? If he does, then you have established rapport on the unconscious level. If not, go back to matching him for a while, and then test again.

(**Note:** it is important to realize that often a half a minute will pass before he will follow your lead by changing his posture. Don't expect him to follow your lead immediately. You should also realize that it often takes several minutes of matching before you can successfully lead.)

While verifying rapport is very useful, leading has another important application. When you lead an employee or customer to move from one posture to another, the physiological change will often bring about a corresponding psychological change.

You can test this by being aware of your own internal, emotional changes as you conduct the following experiments.

1. Notice exactly how you are currently sitting or standing and the internal feelings that you associate with that body position.

2. Now change your posture to one that is either more relaxed or less relaxed, and again notice any changes in your internal feelings.

3. Now, sit absolutely straight, and then allow yourself to sink into the chair. Again, notice your internal feelings.

In which position could you most easily carry on a casual conversation? In which would it be the most difficult?

Do you associate specific emotional states with certain bodily postures? If you associate certain emotional or psychological states with corresponding physical states, then consider the ramifications of this thought: You can influence your mental and/or emotional state just by changing your posture!

> You can change how you think and how you feel just by changing your body's posture!

Try it out. Take a moment and stand as you usually do when you are proud of something you've accomplished. Be sure that if someone were watching you that they would be able to tell how proud you are. Stand tall, throw your shoulders back and your chest out, and smile.

Notice how easy it becomes to suddenly remember the many times when you have felt proud of something you've done. Notice how those feelings return and how proud you actually begin to feel. Take a moment and fully relive one of those accomplishments. Experience it as if it were happening again. Fantastic, isn't it? How might this help you when making a presentation?

Now, change your posture and let your shoulders slump. Slouch and let your chest sink. Lower your head and your gaze. What happened? Note how the intensity of the feeling changes. Now, return to your original "Proud" position again.

Psychologists call these positions, or postures, *anchors*. Anchors allow you to modify your internal state merely by changing your body posture.

Leadership and Rapport

You have just demonstrated to yourself that you can change the way that you think and feel simply by changing the way you sit, stand, or even breathe. Wouldn't it be useful to be able to move your employees the same way? Now you can!

When you are speaking to an employee who is in a *negative state* (e.g., discouraged or angry, or any other state that would keep them from listening openly and positively to what you are saying), you can *lead* them into a more positive state by following these simple steps:

- Establish rapport by matching your body to theirs; and
- gradually shift your body into a posture which will lead them into a different mental state as their own anchors take effect.

Remember that their anchors may be different from your own. So, if the first state that you lead them to is not an improvement, continue to lead them through different postures until you obtain the response that you desire. Here are some examples:

- You may wish to lead an anxious FC into a relaxed posture/state from a stiff or rigid posture/state. This will make it easier for him to prospect more effectively.
- Try leading an FC who is too relaxed into a posture/state that is normally associated with being excited and enthusiastic (e.g., sitting up straight, smiling, leaning slightly forward, and maintaining good eye contact).
- Lead an irritable FC or customer into a relaxed posture/state.
- Lead an indecisive FC into a dynamic, decisive posture/state (e.g., the proud pose you experienced earlier).

As you combine leading his posture with leading his breathing and rate of speech, you will be able to achieve even deeper levels of rapport and greater influence over your staff.

> You can modify your employee's feelings and thinking by leading him into a more positive state!

Matching Breathing

Matching your rate of breathing to that of someone with whom you are speaking is one of the most powerful techniques for enhancing rapport. This is a simple technique whose impact occurs below the level of conscious awareness and, if combined with the previous techniques, can significantly increase your level of rapport. To match breathing, simply breath at the same rate as your employee.

- If you are conversing, time your breathing to match the inhalations and exhalations of your employee's speech rate. In addition, time your sentences to match his breathing. This can be especially effective when speaking on the telephone, since it is one of the few things you can match over the phone.
- Watch the rise and fall of your employee's chest or shoulders since this correlates with his breathing. (*Note:* When dealing with female employees and customers, focus only on the shoulders or you may communicate the wrong message.)
- Remember that there will be times that you do *not* wish to match a client's breathing (e.g., if they suffer from asthma or emphysema). When this occurs, use a cross matching technique such as moving your head, finger, or foot at the same pace as their breathing.

Summary

You can see that *matching* and *leading* add an entirely new dimension to the concept of leadership. When you think about it, isn't that what charisma consists of. If matching someone's breathing along with their posture can significantly enhance the depth of your rapport, just imagine what you can accomplish if you really do "speak their language."

Chapter 11

Speed and the Communication Process

The *fast-talking salesman* and the *slow-minded customer* have become cliches. Yet, have you ever spoken with a person who talked so quickly that *you* felt rushed? How about a person who spoke so slowly that you wanted to try to speed them up? How did you feel as you conversed with them, comfortable or uncomfortable? How did you feel if that person were a superior? An employee? At some level, most of us feel discomfort when this happens. Even when we can't put our finger on just what, it's obvious to us that something is wrong.

Think about it. If you feel uncomfortable when your boss or employee is too fast or too slow for you, he probably feels the same way. In the same way, if he's too slow for you, you're probably too fast for him. Now both of you are experiencing that slightly uncomfortable feeling. Even though you may not be consciously aware of it, such differences contribute to what we call *bad vibes.*

99

> People generally prefer to listen
> at the same rate as they speak.

Think about the traditional door-to-door salesman. He is almost always portrayed as speaking too quickly. It could be that he's just so excited about what he's selling that he gets carried away. Or, he may be afraid that if he doesn't get his message out fast, his customer will slam the door before he gets to his point. Or, maybe he's just nervous. In any case, his rapid speech pattern can be self-defeating unless his customer speaks just as quickly.

Think about the last time you attended a meeting and the presenter spoke so rapidly that you became uncomfortable. While he was giving you fast-paced information, you may have needed time to think. However, to give you that time to think, he had to slow down. Did he? After all, it's not easy to listen to him *and* process what he's saying at the same time. If he didn't slow down, one of three things probably happened:

- You processed the information that you caught but didn't hear everything that he said;
- you listened to him but didn't get a chance to think about it; or,
- you tried to do both and ended up confused.

When you think about it, frustration was an almost inevitable result of any of the possibilities. After all, asking someone to just absorb information and make a decision without thinking about it doesn't show much respect for your listener and frequently makes him feel pushed. At the same time, speaking too slowly can leave him bored, and just as frustrated. Hence:

> Matching someone's speech can help you build rapport!

Think about what effect this might have on your FCs during a sales meeting when you are trying a new campaign or a new product. If the person from marketing speaks too quickly or too slowly for your FCs, he may lose most of them. Result: Less interest and enthusiasm for the product or program. Remember, whenever you think, you need time to do it. If you get the time you need, you can make a decision and act upon it. If you don't, you are likely to feel pressured and frustrated or confused. Show your employees the same thoughtful respect that you would like to have.

Of course, some people are very fast thinkers, even if they don't speak quickly. How can you tell when your FCs are following you? Note their expressions, the relevance of their questions, and changes in their voice quality, speed, tone, or affect which might be indicators for them. Remember, if you speak slower than your listener, speed up. If you speak faster than he does, slow down.

Leading

In the last chapter we showed how you could test for rapport through *leading*. Once you have established rapport, simply modify your posture slightly and see if they follow your lead. If they do, you have established rapport.

You can also test for rapport through modifying your speech. Once you have matched someone's rate of speech you can incrementally change your rate, making it either faster or slower, and see if they follow your lead. If they do, you have established rapport. They usually will, without even consciously becoming aware that they are doing so. Think of some of the ways leading someone into a more effective state might help you:

- Increase the effectiveness of any sales presentation.
- Build rapport during an employment interview.
- Make a proposal to your boss; or
- try to calm down a customer (initially, match their rate of speech and then lead them into a calmer state by gradually slowing your own rate of speech).

Summary

Whether you match posture or speech, your behavior sends an important message to your listener. If you want to lead him around to your way of thinking, you'll become more effective the more levels on which you match.

Chapter **12**

Speaking Your Employees' Private Language

We've mentioned the concept of "speaking someone's language" several times. So far, we've shown how everything that we do (how we sit, stand and breath, and even how fast we speak) affects our ability to be like others. Now let's look at language itself and the ways that even the words that we use tell us something about the way people think.

Have you ever heard someone say, "It *looks* good to me" or "It *sounds* good to me" or "It *feels* good to me"? These phrases, and others like them, provide important information about how people think or process information. By learning to recognize and use the clues that people give you about how they think, you can literally communicate in a way that will make them feel that you are just like them. Considering what we've already discussed about people's natural "resistance" to others perceived as "outsiders," you can see how powerful a tool this can be.

Some of us think by **seeing** images in our mind, others by **discussing** a concept with ourselves so as to **hear** how it sounds, while still others of us need to determine how something **feels**. Regardless of how we process information, we tend to verbalize our thoughts using words and phrases that most closely match how we think.

This occurs for several reasons. One of the most important deals with our five senses and our experiences as we mature. Although we are born with five senses, as we mature we begin to rely upon one or two more than the others. One result of this is a tendency to remember that aspect of an experience more completely than any others. Hence, if we tend to rely upon our sight, we are more likely to remember the visual aspects of an experience. As a result, when we relate it to someone, we will tend to use visual terms to describe it. The same would be true of the other senses. For example:

- "I think that my favorite memory of spring is of the *beautiful colors* that *appear* as the trees and flowers come into bloom. You can *see* it everywhere, even as you *watch* the birds return for the summer, their *colors* enhanced as they prepare to mate." **(Visual)**

- "I think that my favorite memory of spring is of the *sound* of children playing in the parks after a silent winter. You can *hear* spring everywhere, even as you *listen* for the first *song* of the robin building its nest, and the *buzz* of the bumble bee moving from flower to flower. **(Auditory)**

- "I think that may favorite memory of spring is of the first *sensation* of *warmth* returning in the spring sun after a *cold* winter. You can *smell* the flowers and the trees and *feel* the rebirth of the world around you. **(Kinesthetic feelings)**.

Of course, some experiences will dominate a specific sense regardless of which one we tend to rely upon. For example, a cold shower would dominate the kinesthetic sense, while a symphony would compel the auditory and a rainbow, the visual. Because of this, even a person who relies primarily upon his sight will sometimes use auditory and kinesthetic terms.

Once we begin to rely upon one sense over the others, the data received through that sense would tend to dominate our thought processes. As a result, we may even begin to *specialize* in that sensory mode in the way that we think. This means that if you tend to think by

104

making pictures, you are probably someone who also tends to rely upon your sight and to be most aware of the visual aspects of your experiences. Of course, this doesn't mean that you can't remember the sounds and feelings associated with an experience. They probably just aren't remembered as being as obvious as what you saw. This can result in our using some of the other senses so infrequently that we can actually become confused when we receive too much information through them. Psychologists refer to this as *sensory overload.*

Since we understand the familiar more quickly than the unfamiliar, we understand words and phrases that most closely correspond to those that we use in our thinking process. In short, something as simple as our choice of words can make the difference between whether or not we are understood by others. For example: If your listener uses words and phrases that are primarily visual (sight-oriented), and you use phrases that are primarily auditory (sound-oriented), you may actually confuse them. We call these sensory-oriented words *predicates.*

In the same way, if you want to communicate clearly with someone who uses a particular sensory orientation in their thinking, you will be most successful if you use predicates that match the way that they process the information. Try it! You'll be amazed at the improvement in understanding that occurs when you match predicates compared to the difficulty created when they are mismatched.

Read the following scripts, and after you finish them, determine which FC you think has the best chance of continuing the conversation with this client.

Reading I

FC #1: I just came across a report on a stock, the XYZ Company, that looks interesting, and if you have a moment, I'd like to show it to you.

Client: Sounds interesting. I'd like to hear some more.

FC #1: Well, I just saw something that shows the company's earnings have really improved in the last few months.

Client: What do you mean? I've heard that XYZ is in really bad shape.

FC #1: Yet, this financial report clearly shows that it has really improved, which is why you...

Client: (Interrupting) My gut reaction is that it hasn't changed at all.

FC #1: What have you seen to make you think that way. I perceive the change as very positive.

Client: Well, I've been hearing just the opposite.

FC #1: Look, I want to show you a few things that should give you a better picture.

What was your gut feeling as you read this dialogue? Were you comfortable, or did you feel that, somehow, the FC and the client just weren't on the same wavelength? Go back and read it again, then go on to Reading II.

Reading II

FC #2: I just came across a report on a stock, the XYZ Company, that looks interesting, and if you have a moment, I'd like to show it to you.

Client: Sounds interesting. I'd like to hear some more.

FC #2: Well, I just heard something that states the company's earnings have really improved in the last few months.

Client: What do you mean? I've heard that its in really bad shape.

FC #2: Yet, this financial report clearly states that it has really improved, which is why you...

Client: (Interrupting) My gut reaction is that it hasn't changed at all.

FC #2: What have you heard to make you think that way. I feel the change is very positive.

Client: Well, I've been hearing just the opposite.

FC #2: Listen, I want to tell you a few things that should give you a better picture.

Which financial consultant do you think has the better chance to continue the conversation? Most people think that FC #2 has the better chance. They usually comment that FC #1 was more confrontational, and aggressive, etc. FC #2 is usually labeled as being more supportive, understanding, and responsive.

Let's compare them word for word.

FC #1: I just came across a report on a stock, the
FC #2: I just came across a report on a stock, the

 #1: XYZ Company, that looks interesting, and if
 #2: XYZ Company, that looks interesting, and if

 #1: you have a moment, I'd like to show it to you.
 #2: you have a moment, I'd like to show it to you.

Client: *Sounds* interesting. I'd like to hear some more.

FC #1: Well, I just *saw* something that *shows*
FC #2: Well, I just *heard* something that *states*

 #1: the company's earnings have really improved in the last
 #2: the company's earnings have really improved in the last

 #1: few months.
 #2: few months.

Client: What do you mean? I've *heard* that it's in really bad shape.

FC #1: Yet, this financial report clearly *shows* that
FC #2: Yet, this financial report clearly *states* that

 #1: it has really improved, which is why you...
 #2: it has really improved, which is why you....

Client: (Interrupting) My *gut reaction* is that it hasn't changed at all.

FC #1: What have you *seen* to make you think that
 #2: What have you *heard* to make you think that

 #1: way? I *perceive* the change as very positive.
 #2: way? I *feel* the change is very positive.

Client: Well, I've been *hearing* just the opposite.

FC #1: *Look,* I want to *show* you a few things that
FC #2: *Listen,* I want to *tell* you a few things that

 #1: should give you a better *picture.*
 #2: should give you a better *feeling.*

If you're like most people, after a second reading you're amazed that the mere change of predicates (mismatched by FC #1 and matched by FC #2) makes all the difference. The change in response occurs outside of conscious awareness. You can see for yourself the difference that matching someone's predicates can make in a sales situation.

> Matching someone's predicates
> creates more effective communication.

For example: Someone from regional sales approaches you to discuss a new mutual fund, and says, "I've been *looking over* this new mutual fund and I'm sure that you'll agree that it *shows* excellent potential. Let's take a minute and I'll put you in the *picture.*" You might respond in any one of several ways:

1. "It certainly *looks* good to me. Have you *shown* it to the other people in the office yet?"

2. "It certainly *sounds* good to me. Have you *told* the other people in the office about it yet?"

3. "It certainly *feels* good to me. Have you *shared* your *grasp* of it with the other people in the office yet?"

All three responses *mean* essentially the same thing, don't they? But note the difference. Which response most closely matches the way that the sales campaign was presented? The first response. The other two responses mismatch the speaker and may actually result in a misunderstanding or in confusing him. You might say that the last two responses might convince the speaker that you just can't *see* what he's getting at.

If you've ever tried to learn a foreign language, you can probably recall how you had to mentally translate the new language into your native tongue. Frustrating, wasn't it? Whenever someone speaks to us using a sensory style that is different from our own (e.g., if we're speaking in visual terms and they say something in auditory or kinesthetic terms), we have to unconsciously translate what they are saying into our terms. This takes a moment and can confuse us. They're not "speaking our language." At this point, we can either attempt to shift gears and speak in their terms, or allow ourselves to become frustrated and annoyed. The method we choose will depend upon how important it is to make that person comfortable.

Rapport and the Elements of Leadership

For example: Have you ever explained something very *clearly* to an employee only to have him respond with confusion? Did his understanding improve the second or third time that you *explained*? If not, it may not be a case of his being stupid. Rather, it is possible that the two of you were *speaking* different languages and that he just wasn't *grasping* what you were *saying*. If you were using one set of predicates (perhaps visual), while he was using another set (such as auditory), your visual concepts may have caused his confusion.

Leadership consists of selling your ideas to your employees. Matching predicates allows even more effective communication and is really worth utilizing to improve your leadership with your employees. Literally and figuratively, matching predicates allows you to speak the same language. Hence, if you want to lead someone, speaking their language will greatly increase your effectiveness. Listen for the predicate system an individual uses before giving directions or answering a question. Then match it. You'll probably get a much more satisfying response.

Since mismatching someone's predicates can lead to confusion and misunderstanding, how do you open a conversation before you know their sensory preference? Just as there are predicates that match a particular sensory orientation, there are others that are neutral and can be used with any orientation. We call these words *unspecified*. They can be very useful when opening a conversation with someone new.

For example: "Mr. Jones, our company *anticipates* significant growth over the next year which we think will be very exciting. As you *contemplate* this, I hope you'll *consider* joining us."

For your convenience, we have provided a brief listing of predicate words and phrases in Tables 12-1 and 12-2.

Being able to speak their language by matching predicates is valuable in virtually every situation where it is important for us to relate to another person. Do you have an employee that has previously, been difficult to communicate with? Do you know someone who doesn't *see* what you're *showing* him, *hear* what you're *saying*, or *grasp* your *meaning*? Try matching their predicates and see what a difference it makes, not only in your communication, but also in your relationship. Remember:

> We like those who are most like ourselves.

TABLE 12-1. *Sensory-Oriented Words (Predicates).*

Visual	Auditory	Kinesthetic	Unspecified
See	Sound	Feel	Think
Picture	Hear	Grasp	Decide
Appear	Mention	Firm	Motivate
Outlook	Inquire	Pressure	Understand
Imagine	Scream	Grip	Plan
Focus	Tune	Moves	Know
Perception	Shrill	Flow	Consider
Foresee	Oral	Stress	Advise
Vista	Earful	Callous	Deliberate
Looks	Listen	Moves	Develop
Clear	Ring	Warm	Create
Observe	Resonate	Numb	Manage
Horizon	Loud	Dull	Repeat
Scope	Vocal	Hold	Anticipate
Notice	Remark	Affected	Indicate
Show	Discuss	Emotional	Admonish
Scene	Articulate	Solid	Activate
Watch	Say	Soft	Prepare
Aim	Announce	Active	Allow
Angle	Audible	Bearable	Permit
Aspect	Boisterous	Charge	Direct
Clarity	Communicate	Concrete	Discover
Cognizant	Converse	Foundation	Ponder
Conspicuous	Dissonant	Hanging	Determine
Examine	Divulge	Hassle	Resolve
Glance	Earshot	Heated	Meditate
Hindsight	Enunciate	Hunch	Believe
Illusion	Interview	Hustle	Cogitate
Illustrate	Noise	Intuition	Judge
Image	Proclaim	Lukewarm	Evaluate
Inspect	Pronounce	Motion	Reckon
Obscure	Report	Muddled	Imagine
Obvious	Roar	Panicky	Contemplate
Perspective	Rumor	Rush	Assume
Pinpoint	Screech	Sensitive	Conceptualize
Scrutinize	Silence	Set	Conceive
Sight	Speak	Shallow	Influence
Sketchy	Speechless	Shift	Accept
Survey	Squeal	Softly	Prove
Vague	State	Stir	Depend
View	Tell	Structured	Communicate
Vision	Tone	Support	Comprehend

TABLE 12-2. *Sensory-Oriented/Predicate Phrases.*

Visual	Auditory	Kinesthetic
An eyeful	Blabber mouth	All washed up
Appears to be	Clear as a bell	Boils down to
Bird's eye view	Clearly expressed	Chip off the old block
Catch a glimpse of	Call on	Come to grips with
Clear-cut	Describe in detail	Cool/Calm/Collected
Dim view	Earful	Firm foundation
Eye to eye	Express yourself	Floating on thin air
Flashed on	Give an account of	Get a handle on
Get a perspective on	Give me your ear	Get a load of this
Get a scope on	Hear voices	Get the drift of
Hazy idea	Hidden message	Get your goat
In light of	Hold your tongue	Hand-in-hand
In person	Idle talk	Hang in there
In view of	Idle tongue	Heated argument
Looks like	Inquire into	Hold it
Make a scene	Keynote speaker	Hold on
Mental image/picture	Loud and clear	Hot-head
Mind's eye	Outspoken	Keep your shirt on
Naked eye	Power of speech	Lay cards on the table
Paint a picture	Purrs like a kitten	Light-headed
Photographic memory	Rap session	Moment of panic
Plainly see	Rings a bell	Not following you
Pretty as a picture	State your purpose	Pull some strings
See to it	Tattletale	Sharp as a tack
Short-sighted	To tell the truth	Slipped my mind
Showing off	Tongue-tied	Smooth operator
Sight for sore eyes	Tuned in/out	So-so
Staring off into space	Unheard of	Start from scratch
Take a peek	Utterly	Stiff upper lip
Tunnel vision	Voiced an opinion	Stuffed shirt
Up front	Within hearing range	Topsy-turvy
Well-defined	Word for word	Underhanded

Summary

If charisma consists of the level of rapport that someone feels with you, your ability to speak their language is critical to that rapport. In addition, it can radically increase the chances of their understanding and accepting something that you are trying to tell them.

Mastery Exercise 2: Sensory Modes

Read each of the following, and decide which sensory mode is being used. Underline the key words. The answers can be found in Appendix 1.

"Let's take a look at all sides of the proposal and decide which avenue is most attractive."

"What we have here is a failure to communicate. Everyone's always just talking about what they want, but they never seem to get it down on paper. Talk is cheap, but let me have some time to study the figures. Then I'll know whether or not I'm interested."

"Did you ever get the sense that they don't know exactly what's coming down? They move their mouths, but seem to be missing the entire idea."

"I think that we should consider the proposal very carefully. There are numerous points that need to be pondered."

Mastery Exercise 3: Accurate Responses to Sensory Modes

Choose the best response for the following statement (the answer is in Appendix 1).

"After I look over the literature, I want to speak with a few people who already own the product. Based upon how satisfied they are, I'll know whether the literature is telling the truth."

1. Let me show you some information which you should find interesting. Then I'll relate some comments from satisfied customers which should help.

2. I'm sure that you'll get a good feeling once you read over the literature. There are a lot of excellent things that people are saying.

3. After you get a sense of what is going on, I'll show you a few things that will make you feel even better.

4. I can see that once you read some of the literature, you'll be able to make a decision based on a positive gut reaction.

Mastery Exercise 4: Predicates and Criteria for Personality Types

Read each of the following and underline the predicates and the key criteria for determining the individual's personality type. Check your answers in Appendix 1.

"I want to get a sense of the proposal to ensure that it doesn't diverge too significantly from standard operating procedure. I know that this has been important to you, but I don't want too much decentralization. You know what happened to our arch rival. He let things get out of control and subsequently lost significant market share to me, I mean us. It made me laugh for weeks. But, there's no way that'll happen here. I'll personally attend to that if I have to make them toe the line myself."

"Most of us have decided that it would be a good idea to attend the lecture on stress management. You know how it's important to the company that we learn as much as we can about it. Anyway, it will be a good chance to get together."

"Numerous factors have led to the creation of this new administration. The people have decided that they want to have the control necessary to positively affect their destinies."

"I chose this company because of its reputation for reliability. I've heard many good things about it over the years and it seems that it warrants those comments. Over time, I've become more familiar with it and find that the assistance I've received conforms to the level of service that should be provided."

"My friends know that this is the right place to go. This is where it's at and you can just tell from the vibes. It's like where everyone else hangs out and, you know, I have to maintain my image."

Chapter *13*

Think and Speak Positively

How many times has someone told you, "Don't worry?" What did you do? You worried! After all, "What is it that I'm not supposed to worry about?" The problem is that in order for us not to do something, we have to think about doing it first, and then add *Don't*. Doesn't help much, does it? Try this: *Don't think about the Statue of Liberty!* How did it work? If you're like most of us, you thought about the Statue of Liberty, even if only for a microsecond, before moving on to something else.

Interesting, isn't it? When you are on a diet, what is it you're not supposed to think about? Food, right? But what fills almost every waking thought? **Food!** The harder we try to push the thought out of our heads, the more attention we must focus on it (food) to avoid it. No wonder so many of us have difficulty losing weight. The point is that in order to *not* think of something, you *have to* think about it first. That's because our language mediates the way we think. Remember, we also communicate with ourselves, and communication is the purpose of language.

Here's another thought; what do you do when you lose something? You look for it until you find it. For many of us, the same thing happens when we lose weight. We seem to search until we have not only found every pound that we've lost, but also a few more that we weren't even looking for.

> Don't think or speak negatively!
> Or, in better words: **Think and speak positively!**

Considering the previous comments, have you thought about the effect of negative statements on your employees?

"Don't worry about the commission."

The FC has to think about potential commission problems so that, in the end, he doesn't have to worry about them. The probability is then increased that the FC will become concerned about problems with his commission credits. After all, why did you bring them up unless you thought that they might cause a potential problem. Makes sense, doesn't it? How about a few others like:

- "Don't be late!"
- "Don't forget about tomorrow's sales meeting."
- "Don't make a decision until you've heard what our research department has to say about the stock."
- "Don't buy certificates of deposit at a bank."

This may explain a lot of the misunderstandings and surprises that occur with FCs and customers who forget something important, or bring up concerns about future commission credits. All that they are doing is exactly what we directed them to do unconsciously. We literally set ourselves up to obtain the very results that we wished to avoid.

Think about what might happen differently if we speak in positive terms. We might say:

- "Be on time."
- "Remember tomorrow's sales meeting."

- "You can depend upon the dividend."
- "Look at your alternatives carefully. We're confident you'll purchase your CD from us."
- "Look over what our analysts have to say before you make a decision on the stock."

Our words are very powerful because they can direct the thoughts and memories of our listeners (especially when we're the listener). These thoughts and memories then influence their attitudes, behaviors, and beliefs. If we accept that:

- Our unconscious mind cannot deal in negatives (try to think of nothing); and
- our minds have to briefly focus upon the unwanted concept in order to make sense of a negative statement, then we get the following communications formula: **The Original Statement (OS) minus the Negation (N) equals the Unconscious Message Received (UMR).**

$$OS - N = UMR$$

This means that a negative statement becomes unconsciously transformed into literally the opposite of what we intended, whether we are thinking to ourselves or talking to someone else. For example:

- "Do not feel bad." $-$ *not* $=$ "Do feel bad."
- "Do not forget." $-$ *not* $=$ "Do forget."
- "I do not want to be late." $-$ *not* $=$ "I do want to be late."
- "Do not worry about the next delivery." $-$ *not* $=$ "Do worry about the next delivery."

Summary

It's obvious how easily we can program ourselves to fail in obtaining our objectives. Speaking in positives is much more effective.

Speak positively!

Leadership and Motivation

Effective communication and rapport are important aspects of establishing the charisma we call *leadership*. The ability to motivate people to follow is just as important in establishing leadership. Each and every person has a series of emotional needs, decision-making criteria, and other elements that determine his motivation. The chapters in this section will discuss the nature of those elements and how to both elicit and use them to motivate yourself and your employees.

Positive Motivation

How wonderful it would be if we knew what made an employee or a customer tick. How much easier it would be to meet their needs. In fact, one of the most important puzzles that any manager is called upon to solve is how to motivate his personnel, especially his FCs.

119

While money and recognition have traditionally been the most popular motivators among managers, they are rarely the most effective with employees. In addition, if you are the manager of a bank branch, or if you are dealing with salaried employees, money may not really be available to you as an option. Fortunately, each of us is motivated by a combination of key themes that drive our behavior and are very easily ascertained once you know where to look. Some of these are fully explained in Section IV, "Leadership and Motivation." In addition, the sales applications of these themes are explained in detail in our sales book, *Consultative Selling Techniques for Financial Professionals* in the chapter called "Discovering The Client's Buying Motivations."

Once you understand the motivational themes that control our lives, people will become much easier to both understand and manage. Then, when motivational problems occur, you will be able to more effectively deal with the problem at hand. This is the mark of a true leader.

In addition to the communications and motivational aspects of leadership, this section will also provide useful information that will enable you to successfully select and recruit winning personnel. Finally, the last chapter in the section will deal with creating and maintaining a *State of Excellence*. Overall, the applications are enormous and the techniques that you are about to learn work with virtually everyone.

Chapter 14

Motivations Ruling Our Behaviors

Psychologists have found that each of us has various unconscious motivations, or criteria, that we use to make decisions. These criteria, such as *quality, image,* and *convenience,* become motivational themes which often form the basis of our decisions. To a large extent they determine what we like or dislike, what we are attracted to or repelled by. These themes are consistent for most of us, most of the time.

Identifying these constant themes is one of the concepts behind *benefit selling* as presented in our book *Consultative Selling Techniques for Financial Professionals.* With this information an FC can make presentations to the *individual* customer instead of the *generic* customer. The information becomes personally meaningful because the FC makes the presentation using the customer's unconscious motivational themes. This substantially deepens the rapport already established and further allows the customer to feel comfortable with the FC's level of competency.

We will shortly apply these same concepts to what motivates an individual to strive for success. This information will be combined with the tools presented in Chapters 15 and 16. For a few people, the motivation to succeed is the "stick" of fear, the fear of failure, or the fear of being fired. For others, it is the "carrot" of success, a higher standard of living, wealth, the admiration of peers, or security. However, each of us is different, and motivational techniques that are limited to fear, financial rewards, or fame miss a large number of employees who could become stars in their own right if only the correct button were pushed.

It has been said that people work for one of three reasons: Fear, duty, or love. Of the three, the individual that works out of love is obviously the best employee. It is he who looks forward to coming to work because it's exciting and fulfilling, rather than going to work because it's the right thing to do or because there are bills to meet. As managers, it is our job to help each employee develop a love for his work that will help ensure his *success* as well as create a more self-motivated employee.

Why are some people natural self-starters and easily motivated? Usually, these people have a clear understanding that performing certain actions will lead them, step-by-step, towards definite, clearly defined goals. They have a type of mental image of where they want to be and also a way of measuring the incremental steps needed in order to achieve that goal. Finally, they get some type of personal satisfaction from the steps being made. Rather than eventually becoming *successful,* these highly motivated individuals are always in the process of *succeeding.* Success is a daily activity rather than something which will eventually be attained.

Here is a brief exercise which should demonstrate something significant to you—or anyone else who takes it. For each of the six questions that follow, circle the words that are applicable to the situation for you as an individual.

What do you want in a car that you might purchase?

1. Reputation	6. Bargain
2. Available options	7. Dealer integrity
3. Style/Looks	8. Dependability
4. Location of dealer	9. Warranty
5. Service from dealer	10. Performance

What would you like about a company that you either work for or would consider working for?

1. Reputation	6. Money
2. Career alternatives	7. Company integrity
3. Appearance	8. Reliability
4. Location of office	9. Contract offered
5. Service orientation	10. Company track record

What would you consider important qualities in a business associate?

1. Reputation	6. Worth the effort
2. Diverse interests	7. Honesty
3. Cleanliness/Looks	8. Reliability
4. Accessibility	9. Fulfillment of promises
5. Helpfulness	10. Consistent performance

Why do you frequent certain restaurants?

1. Reputation	6. Reasonable prices
2. Good selection	7. Integrity
3. Atmosphere/Ambiance	8. Consistent quality
4. Location	9. Satisfaction assured
5. Good service	10. Improves with each visit

What do you pride yourself on as a manager; or what would you choose as the attributes of a person to emulate?

1. Good reputation	6. Paid for work rendered
2. Seeks new challenges	7. Trustworthy
3. Provides good image	8. Reliable
4. Accessibility	9. Fulfills verbal word
5. Offers assistance	10. Constantly improving self

What are some of the qualities you would want in a friend or spouse?

1. Reputation	6. They're worth the effort
2. Wide range of interests	7. Trustworthy
3. Attractive	8. Dependable
4. Is there when needed	9. Keeps promises
5. Helpful	10. Self-improvement conscious

The numbers listed below will allow you to indicate how often you chose a particular response. For example, if you chose the answers associated with number 1 on five of the six questions, you would write the number 5 at the appropriate place. Please do this for each of the 10 numbers.

1. _____   6. _____
2. _____   7. _____
3. _____   8. _____
4. _____   9. _____
5. _____   10. _____

Most people have a few numbers that received rather high usage. The words associated with each number were synonyms—all the number 3s, for instance, mean basically the same thing. Any words or equivalents used on three or more occasions can be considered a personal *key criteria* or motivation for you or for whoever took the test.

We've presented variations of this exercise to over 6,000 people and found that the vast majority of people have at least two or three major criteria that affect multiple decisions. The point we're making is that if you learn someone's basic themes you can package your presentation much more powerfully.

Think of how this can make your FCs' sales presentations more effective. Instead of presenting a variety of features, benefits, and advantages and merely hoping that your customers can figure out what it means to them, the FC can now do something substantially better. He or she can elicit customers' *unconscious* buying motivations and then feed them back to them in a way that completely matches their thinking pattern. This allows the FC to tailor-make a presentation that is both directed and highly meaningful to the customer.

When combined with knowing a person's psychological profile (Dictator, Bureaucrate, Socialite, or Executive) and their mode of thinking (Visual, Auditory, or Kinesthetic) and with their meta-programs (power, affiliation, achievement, etc., see Chapter 15), the FC has the ability to become extraordinarily persuasive. It's as if the customer would have written the presentation himself.

As a manager you have the same opportunity for extraordinary persuasiveness as you motivate, coach, teach, and lead your office personnel—whether it be the sales or operations staff.

Remember, this information is all discovered beforehand, during prior elicitations or discussions. You would have taken notes to remind yourself which frames of reference would be most useful with a particular person. Therefore, your effectiveness will be substantially enhanced.

"What do I listen for?" you may ask. We're glad you asked that question. Table 14-1 provides a brief listing of personal motivations and their synonyms. If you hear some of these words used in a variety of contexts, you can bet that they will be highly persuasive when you use them to further empower your people.

TABLE 14-1. *Key Personal Motivations and Synonyms.*

Advertising:	Reputation	Familiarity	Awareness
Alternatives:	Variety	Selection	Product line
Appearance:	Looks	Atmosphere	Ambiance
Courtesy:	Consideration	Service	Respect
Credit:	Cash Flow	Bargain	Discount
Dependability	Reliability	Reputation	Confidence
Habit:	Tradition	Familiar	Sentimental
Image:	Style	Status	Prestige
Integrity:	Honesty	Trustworthy	Honor/Trust
Professional:	Competent	Expert	Authority
Quality:	Value	Craftsmanship	Reliable
Relationship:	Loyalty	Friendliness	Affiliation
Safety:	Security	Guarantee	Warranty

Although people tend to use consistent themes to make decisions, they rarely describe these themes using the same words all the time. For example, someone may go to a particular gas station because of the *large product line*; a particular clothing store because of its *good selection*; a restaurant because of the *variety of dishes* on the menu; and may select *diversity of interests* in friends. In each case, the theme of *available alternatives* was dominant.

To motivate such a person, you could emphasize in your discussion the concept of *multiplicity of choices* by using synonyms that indicate choice. Perhaps you would offer the person 10 different approaches to take when prospecting. You allow them to make the decision on which three approaches they will try and some flexibility in terms of when this week they will initiate one of the ideas. (You, of course, made note that they *had* to choose three items and they *would* do it this week. You feel good *and,* most importantly, they feel good.)

It's generally easy to discover key motivations if you merely ask a few astute questions over a period of time. Simply ask your employee questions that might normally come up in a social or business situation or meeting, such as what do you like about a given product or restaurant, and note the criteria that are consistently raised. For example, read the conversation below and look for potential decision-making criteria from the FC. The important probes from the manager are set in italics.

Mgr.: Bill, I notice that you own a Jaguar. I'm thinking about buying one myself, but I haven't quite made up my mind. *What do you like about yours?*

FC: Well, I think that it's a well-made car, and it's lots of fun to drive.

Mgr.: *Anything else?*

FC: Sure. It's a sharp-looking car. Not like some of the boxes they're selling today. And my friends like it.

Mgr.: They certainly look great. Where do you get it serviced? I mean, I'd guess you must want a factory-trained mechanic to work on it.

FC: That's for sure. I don't take any chances with it. I take it to the dealer where I bought it, in Smithtown.

Mgr.: That's a little out of your way, isn't it? *What made you choose that dealer?*

FC: Frankly, I didn't like the quality of the service that I was getting at the dealer here in town. The dealer in Smithtown always has the car when he says he will and does a quality job. For that, I don't mind the inconvenience of paying a little more and having the extra drive. Besides, he always gives me a loaner while the car's in the shop.

Did you notice the information that the FC revealed? We'll provide it again, this time we've set the possible criteria off in italics.

Mgr.: Bill, I notice that you own a Jaguar. I'm thinking about buying one myself, but I haven't quite made up my mind. What do you like about yours?

FC: Well, I think that it's a *well-made* car, and it's lots of *fun* to drive.

Mgr.: Anything else?

FC: Sure. It's a *sharp-looking* car. Not like some of the boxes they're selling today. And my *friends like it.*

Mgr.: They certainly look great. Where do you get it serviced? I mean, I'd guess you must want a factory-trained mechanic to work on it.

FC: That's for sure. I don't take any chances with it. I take it to the dealer where I bought it, in Smithtown.

Mgr.: That's a little out of your way, isn't it? What made you choose that dealer?

FC: Frankly, I didn't like the *quality* of the service that I was getting at the dealer here in town. The dealer in Smithtown always has the *car ready when he says* he will and does a *quality* job. For that, I don't mind the inconvenience of paying a little more and having the extra drive. Besides, he always *gives me a loaner* while the car's in the shop.

Let's examine the criteria that the FC mentioned and suggest possible correlations.

---

well-made = quality
fun
sharp-looking = appearance or status
friends like it = opinions of others
don't want to take any risks = security
quality (mentioned twice again)
gives me a loaner = services

Two or three other questions (e.g., about favorite restaurants, etc.) can easily confirm and/or provide additional criteria. You can also ask questions about products that the FC is knowledgeable about (yours or that of a competitor), or what the FC likes about the job or the firm. These can be particularly useful because they are more closely related to what you are trying to accomplish.

In addition, while the FC is answering these questions, you are also finding out about her psychological profile, her thinking preferences, and her primary programs. Your future discussions will be more productive and will be structured to meet the employee's multilevel needs.

This takes practice. One way to practice eliciting someone's criteria is to occasionally ask your friends or associates, "What do you like about _____?" It doesn't matter what you ask about. Just be curious. After asking this a few times about different things, you may notice that you are beginning to receive similar responses from people. Remember that you will probably be getting this information over several conversations.

Summary

Everyone has multiple decision making and motivational criteria. The ability to elicit these criteria will greatly enhance your ability to motivate virtually anyone. There are numerous ways and opportunities for you to elicit and utilize this information. One idea is to psychologically profile the best producers in your office and determine if there are similar themes in terms of motivation or work ethic. If there are, then look for new employees who have similar motivational themes. Your sales meetings will take on added power if you specifically meet the needs of the entire group.

Our next two chapters will further explore ways to elicit any individual's psychological needs and thinking patterns. Take a moment to go through the mastery exercises below.

Mastery Exercise 5: Key Motivations

Read the next three paragraphs and decide which themes have the greatest frequency. See Appendix 1 for the answers.

- "I chose this company to work for because it has an excellent reputation for quality. Everything they do indicates that. The fact that it offers me so many career paths is also important to someone like me who is upwardly mobile. It's also a very well-known company."

- "There's a great restaurant down the street which I'm sure you'll enjoy. It has a large menu which always gets rave reviews from those of us who know about it."

- "I like people who have a lot of different interests because it makes them interesting to talk to. But, more than anything, I must know that I can turn my back on them without fear."

Chapter *15*

Primary Motivational Programs

It's amazing how predictable people are once we know how they work. In the previous chapter, you found that a person's key motivational themes are easily elicited once you ask the right questions and know what to listen for. In a similar vein, key patterns which drive behavior are easily ascertained once you know what to look for. With an understanding of these motivational themes, people become more easily understood and manageable. Then, when motivational or behavioral problems occur, you can more effectively deal with the problem at hand.

This chapter deals with some of the key, unconscious mental programs that drive behavior. It is information that you will be able to immediately employ in a variety of situations. For example, you'll be able to use these techniques in coaching and counseling sessions and sales meetings. They can also be used for selecting and recruiting personnel. This will allow you to choose your employees with a greater degree of accuracy than was previously possible. In addition, these techniques will help you deal with creating and maintaining a *State of Excellence* (see Chapters 23 and 24) in yourself and in your employees. Overall, the applications are enormous and the techniques that you are about to learn work with virtually everyone.

Over the years many studies have been made to determine what motivates people. Unfortunately, various research conclusions have used words and labels that often contradict each other.

Rather than go into too many details, suffice it to say that each person has a variety of needs. We need food, clothing, and shelter in order to survive. Once these needs are met, other needs such as entertainment and luxuries can be addressed. Eventually, as a person goes up the economic ladder, the purchase of gadgets, gizmoes, and toys may dominate one's thoughts. At this point, all of the key needs have been easily met and it is *assumed* that they will continue to be met. Of course, a major disaster may seriously challenge this very common assumption.

Consider the feelings that people had immediately after the Stock Market Crash of 1987. People who had invested heavily in the market were frightened that day; their very foundations were shaken. The results were expressed in a prolonged period of caution-laden investor psychology following the *pullback* that had been expressed in *the flight to quality.*

Accumulated capital was destroyed overnight. Confidence in the future was affected similarly. People who were purchasing all of the toys of the *Yuppie* generation had substantial *erosion of capital* and went into a survival mode with the *flight to safety* being the theme of the day. Without belaboring the point, the investment game changed on that day. In one form or another, everyone reading this book was mentally affected. Your subsequent response was partially determined by what you saw, heard, and felt over the days that followed the crash. It was also determined by your background and the way you approach the world in your normal day-to-day affairs. The key point is that the dividing line between cool, calm, and collected versus frightened is often extremely thin. This is true of all of us. When someone's economic security is threatened, the reactions that you get may be substantially more than you anticipated.

Crisis situations not withstanding, most people habitually employ, and are motivated by, certain common patterns called *primary programs*. In the next few pages, we'll describe three of those programs, the Need for Power, the Need for Affiliation, and the Need for Achievement. In the following chapter you will be introduced to additional programs.

As you read this material, it will be easy to identify someone you know who employs each pattern. Remember, no single pattern is good or bad in and of itself. Rather than labeling people, think of it as useful information. Later you will combine some of these patterns to make a whole that is far greater than the sum of its parts.

The first major patterns to be discussed have enjoyed a degree of popularity over the years because their concept makes so much sense.

Power, Affiliation, and Achievement

The Need for Power

Do you know someone who always wants to take charge of the situation and likes to direct and control others (either directly or from behind the scenes)? Interestingly, there are many reasons that someone may want or need to take charge. The people who take charge because it makes them feel good and/or powerful and/or in control are the ones who demonstrate a Need for **Power**. If they say *jump*, they want someone else to ask *how high*.

You see them everywhere, in all walks of life. If the person is in sales she likes to make her clients do as they're told. These FCs are usually very forceful and react negatively to questions or any type of delay (this is often viewed as a personal affront). In a word, the typical *Dictator*. In a bureaucracy, this person is the clerk who takes great pleasure in enforcing each and every one of the rules. Our *Bureaucrat* may be this type of person if control of others is a primary motivation. (See Chapter 7 for a review of the *Dictator* and *Bureaucrat* personalities.)

They respond very favorably if you publicly ask their opinion about things—whether it be some strategy that the office should employ, or a financial recommendation. However, the extreme cases would then use the opportunity as a public forum for *dictating from on high*. If appropriate, delegate some responsibility to them, and let them and others, know that there may be more to come. This can create a good deal of personal loyalty to you from such individuals.

There are other things that you can do to effectively motivate and persuade a power-oriented person. These will become obvious as other primary motivational programs are explored in the next chapter. A summary of power-oriented motivations and ways to deal with them are presented below.

> People desiring power have a strong need to take control of others and various situations. They want to be the boss. "Do it my way," and, "Follow my directions," are key patterns.

- Power motivations:

    Position of real or implied authority.

    Position and status.

    Ability to influence, supervise, or control other people.

- Methods for dealing with a power-motivated person:

    Acknowledge their achievements, status, position, and authority.

    Provide symbols of authority such as preferred location.

    Obtain their opinion (preferably publicly).

    Publicly acknowledge their contributions.

    Delegate authority to them, but always be certain to effectively supervise the use of that authority.

    Show them how doing what you want will also get them what they desire.

- Words and phrases used by power-motivated people:

    Me, Myself, I.

    Control.

    Power.

    Authority.

    "Do it my way."

    "*I'm* the boss."

    "That's *my* decision to make."

- How to recognize a power-motivated person:

  They try to stand apart from the crowd.

  Their desk and office tend to be rather stark.

In essence, the way to deal with power-oriented people is to give them as much power as they demonstrate an ability to handle appropriately without disrupting the office or your authority. Let them know that they win when they support you. Everything will become much more powerful when you add other major motivational programs that will be discussed in this and other chapters.

The Need for Affiliation

The person whose primary motivation is **Affiliation** is substantially different from the power-oriented individual. For him, the goal is association with other people. The need to be part of a group and to be accepted by others is of paramount importance on the unconscious level. You can easily identify these people because they tend to have pictures of groups and group activities surrounding them. They like to be around others. They feel demotivated and perhaps even depressed when they have to work alone.

In fact, *alone* is not a word that they are comfortable with in virtually any environment. This is not to say that they cannot work alone or that they are never alone. However, if you were to offer this person a private office, you would not get the same favorable reception as you might from someone who is power- or achievement- oriented. If you were to remove them from the mainstream of the office and have them work on an independent project where they would need to spend the majority of their time alone, you might have a disgruntled employee who would spend significantly more time around the coffee machine, in the lounge, or visiting other people at their work area.

Think of the water cooler gang and its needs. Often, it is the contact and the support that comes from the group that is important. There are significant disadvantages to most of these groups; that is, they tend to be self-perpetuating, support maladaptive behaviors, and are often associated with reinforcement of negative attitudes. Of course, there are many exceptions to the traditional rule.

Essentially, the affiliation-oriented person has a need for personal contact. He knows he is good, based upon the consensus of opinion. The group is always right. The team is important. The members of the group are key in this person's determination of his self-worth. The group can be composed of members of the same profession, church, social organization, family, or some combination of similar items. Affiliation-oriented people use the pronouns we, us, let's, and variations of these themes. Working in association with others dominates their thinking. They are very similar to the *Socialite* introduced in Chapter 7.

- Affiliation motivations:
  - Being a member of the team.
  - Needs to be liked.
  - Needs acceptance and interpersonal relationships.
  - Wants/needs to work with people.
  - Minimizes conflicts.
- Actions to take with an affiliation-motivated person:
  - Reward contributions to the group (e.g., social function).
  - Thank them for helping others.
  - Smooth over potential conflicts.
  - Talk in terms of group effort and what others are doing.
- Words and phrases used by the affiliation-activated person:
  - We, Us, Let's, All, and Others.
  - "Let's get together."
  - "Let's do something for. . ."
  - Group participation.
- How to recognize an affiliation-oriented person:
  - Pictures of groups to which they belong on their desks.
  - Dress like their contemporaries.
  - Go to the popular restaurants, activities, etc.

In essence, the way to deal with someone who is highly affiliation-oriented is to present them with concepts in terms of the needs of the group. Present ideas by defining them in terms of other people. Get them involved with the process. Throw them a party. Be warm and friendly.

The Need for Achievement

Achievement-oriented people place a high premium on the accomplishment of the task. They are task-oriented as long as the task has measurable results and they can feel a sense of pride in accomplishment. They respond well to plaques, awards, and other types of certificates that can be prominently displayed on their walls and desks.

They can be left alone to do a job. While they usually work well with others, their primary motivation is to get the job done, not the social interaction derived from group activities. They will take control and occasionally take power, but to get the job done, not for personal aggrandizement.

Simply put, these people want and need a sense of accomplishment. They obtain this sense of accomplishment from challenging and/or competitive situations. Realistic and achievable goals are set within a framework of achieving personal excellence.

- Achievement motivations:

     Set long-range, accomplishable objectives.

     Plan for contingencies.

     Compete against a motivating standard.

     Satisfaction from the job/task being done.

     Satisfaction also from working on the task.

- Actions to take with an achievement-motivated person:

     Recognize their achievement through words and/or awards.

     Encourage initiative.

     Encourage independent thinking.

     Allow participation in goal-setting activities.

     Keep projects interesting and challenging.

- Words and phrases used by achievers:

     Innovative ideas.

     "Let's plan ahead."

     "Let's get the job done."

     Feeling of accomplishment.

- How to recognize an achievement-oriented person:

    Awards/Plaques/Certificates.

    Participation in group social activities only after the work has been done.

    Task orientation.

    Asks specific questions about objectives, deadline, and details.

    Remains focused on the task.

    Rarely involved in power struggles or in socialization.

In essence, you work with an *Achiever* by providing challenges which are meaningful to them. They respond well to recognition that a job was well done.

In Closing

The need for *power, affiliation,* and/or *achievement* are themes that drive behavior. They are quite pervasive, but not quite as black and white as presented. Most of us have all three needs to some extent, with one consistently predominating **within a given context**. For example, a person who is power-oriented at work may have a strong achievement orientation at home. A person who is predominantly affiliation-oriented may also have a strong affiliation orientation at home. A person who is predominantly affiliation-oriented may also have a strong desire to achieve a particular goal. For the duration of his work toward that goal, his behavior will appear to be more achievement-oriented.

Situations and people change. Yet, this information, when combined with key motivations and other primary programs, will enable the aware observer to more completely understand the individual involved.

Chapter **16**

Additional Motivational Programs

Extremes in Thinking

Individuals who think in terms of black/white, good/bad, right/wrong, etc., literally tend to think and respond in extremes. They appear to be very definitive and opinionated. They see the world through their own *rose-colored glasses* and, as far as they are concerned, everyone should think and believe exactly the same way as they do. These individuals have made up the ranks of the world's zealots since history began.

It is very difficult to argue with someone like this concerning one of their beliefs. They are right and they know it and are willing to tell anyone and everyone who will listen. Confronting them in front of a group is usually a disaster because they just dig in their heels and stay put. This can easily lead to an escalation of the argument where either you back down or are forced to take punitive action. Obviously, neither solution is desirable.

You must deal with them one-on-one. When you need to convince them that there is something beyond the level of their own experience, merely search for the exception that negates the extreme statement. Usually, if you find even one exception, they have to admit that, just possibly, they do not have all of the answers. For example, during one sales meeting we recall a salesman informing the manager that he had no intention of selling a particular mutual fund because the fund was worthless. The sales manager had finally had it with this salesman and employed the procedure that we had suggested. The manager made a statement something like the following: "You sound very certain. What specifically did you read in the prospectus to allow you to come to that conclusion?" The salesman got flustered and had to admit that he associated this particular mutual fund with another fund that had performed poorly in the past. The blustering salesman became significantly more cautious in future sales meetings.

It would have been better if the manager had confronted the FC on an individual basis. However, the FC had effectively challenged the manager in front of the entire office. The manager was careful with his tone so that his question sounded curious, rather than sarcastic or confrontational. More than one FC got the message.

Past, Present, and Future Orientations

One's orientation to time is an important key to how some people think, respond, and are motivated. We all know people who constantly refer to the *good old days*; while others constantly refer to *how things will be*. Whether a person is oriented to the past, the future, or is among those who are popularly called the *now generation* (present orientation), knowledge about people's time orientations can be very important to the process of managing and motivating them.

Past-Orientation

Past orientation is exemplified by the theme song from the television show "All in the Family," in which Archie and Edith Bunker sing about "the good old days." Many people seem to live their lives in the past and use the past as their primary basis of reference.

"They don't build cars like they used to," and a series of other past-oriented phrases would let the astute manager know that the key to dealing with such an FC would be to emphasize the *continuance of quality* and the *enhancements to the basic designs that have served us so well over the years.* The phrases used by the manager indicate a past reference which would then match the FC's past time orientation.

The way to demotivate such as FC is by emphasizing the modern, state-of-the-art, tradition-breaking aspects of the product or service. This focus would appeal to people with *present* or *future* time orientations.

A past orientation is fine as long as long as there is also a good grounding in the present.

Present-Orientation

People with a strong orientation to the present are involved in what is happening at the moment. They occasionally review past memories and plan for the future, but they live in the present. Now *is the time to get things done.*

Future-Orientation

People with a strong future orientation are more concerned with the way things will eventually be rather than working right now. They tend to live in a fantasy world in which things will always work themselves out. They are always talking about the things they are about to do. "Things will be better/different, tomorrow" is typical of the way they deal with problems. Unfortunately, many of them never get anything done.

Future-oriented people are often people who are always talking about their next big deal that will save them. Unfortunately, most of these great deals never happen, and the FC continues to live in a fantasy world where some magical happening is about to occur.

A future orientation is fine as long as there is also a good grounding in the present.

When dealing with such people, emphasize the benefits they *will* receive for a particular project. They will modify their behavior as long as they have a goal to look forward to.

People, Places, Things, and Activities

People-oriented individuals are usually talking about others. *Relationships are very important* to them. This pattern is synonymous with the *Socialite* presented in Chapter 7 and the *Affiliation-Motivated* individual presented in the previous chapter.

A person-oriented employee can be motivated by making references to group activities that everybody could benefit from or by telling them that everyone would appreciate what they are about to do. For example saying, "You'll be able to proudly tell all of your friends" would be another approach to persuading this person.

Place-oriented people are generally talking about all the places they have been. "Last year we went to Europe and spent some time in Paris. Oh, what a wonderful city. Have you ever been there?" Motivating this person with a sales trip or a dinner at an exclusive restaurant would work much better than a plaque or a round of applause from the group.

Thing-oriented people are exemplified by the yuppies who accumulate things for the sake of ownership. "He who dies with the most toys wins" was a popular saying. While making fun of the extreme, it is interesting to note how many people get motivated by being able to select from some type of catalogue of prizes for achievement. You know this person by the number of gadgets he owns.

Place-oriented individuals associate places with their self-worth and frequently wish to travel. However, before labelling someone as *place-oriented*, remember that the key question is "WHY." If they like to travel to visit the various places, then the person is *place-oriented*. However, if the person intends to ski the Alps, and hike in the Black Forest and do a series of other activities, you know that he is really *Activities-oriented*. This person goes to a resort because of the things that can be done.

Global versus Linear

Global thinkers often see the big picture and are generally not interested in the details of a situation. Present a concept and they grasp the meaning and are often mentally exploring other potentials and ramifications while their contemporaries are still trying to understand the basic ideas. While global thinking is great for some things, it can be disadvantageous for certain types of jobs which require a more step-by-step orientation.

140

Linear thinkers take things one step at a time. They tend to be great at procedures and relatively poor at *what if* scenarios. Yet, it is usually good to have at least one person who can do linear thinking on your team because they will make sure that the logical sequence is taken into consideration and few, it any, things are left to chance.

Chunking

Chunking refers to the detail required in presenting information or ideas. Information chunk size can often be correlated to global or linear thinking. However, the correlations are not precise. If an employee needs a tremendous amount of detail in order to understand what is necessary, provide it. Mentally make note of it and, the next time you give instructions, you'll be able to provide it in the most advantageous way for the individual.

Of course, you must take into account the person's relative familiarity with the task that he is about to undertake. Even a global thinker, who prefers the big picture, will need additional details if the task is new.

The trick is to be able to explain something using both extremes—details versus global. If you can do that, you can then explain to anyone in the middle.

Emotional versus Logical

Emotional people often have an intuitive method of coming to a conclusion. (i.e., "I *feel* that this is the right way" or "I just know that..."). They often react very quickly and with a great deal of emotionalism. The Dr. McCoy character on "Star Trek" would be a good representation of the emotionally driven person.

In contrast, the Mr. Spock character would be the epitome of the logically oriented person. Things need to be logical. Oftentimes they appear to be dealing exclusively with their head and not their heart. Hence, they are sometimes thought to be cold and aloof and certainly detached. They rarely get very excited, nor do they easily get depressed.

Emotional employees would be influenced by you *sharing your feelings* with them. They also respond more readily to the rah-rah of many motivational speakers. Of course, they could have the opposite response and be turned off by such speeches. Either way, they will have an emotional response.

The logical person responds to appeals to the intellect. Try to motivate him with an emotional appeal and you'll find he has a decided lack of interest and even the possibility of mild disgust that someone would do something so illogical.

I/We; Us/Them

"I think that the way to do it is my way. I remember when I told a client what I thought and, of course, I was right." You probably know someone who somewhat represents this extreme *I orientation*. These people are not going to be motivated by team spirit. "What's in it for me?" must be clearly, distinctly, and exquisitely stated. "This is what's in it for you," is the way that you would present any idea. A power or achievement orientation may increase the persuasiveness of your comments. Affiliation is a very remote possibility.

We-oriented individuals are similar to the *affiliation-oriented* person discussed in Chapter 14. "Let's get the gang together and all pull toward the common objective for our mutual benefit." However, the regular use of *we, us, let's* etc. is not a guarantee that affiliation is the approach. You'd want to consider other behaviors to verify your suppositions.

Internal versus External Motivation

How a person is motivated is a key to working with him. Some people are internally motivated and maintain their own pace. They know they are good by an internal check. A person who is externally motivated needs reinforcement from others. Sometimes a pat on the back. For some, it's an award, while for others, it's money.

An internally motivated person enjoys contests with himself by beating his own personal best. An externally motivated person would be more responsive to a sales contest.

A person's motivational needs are one of the key hiring characteristics to consider during the initial interviews. It's easy to observe FCs in their day-to-day activities and make note of who is an internal versus an external motivator. It is substantially more difficult to do this in the interview. Not too many people would respond "No" to the following question: "Are you a self-starter?" Unless the person has come from a different planet, he is going to indicate that he has always been and always will be a self-starter who requires little or no supervision.

Toward versus Away as a Goal-Setting Strategy

People tend to look either ahead or behind. Some people move through life seeking positive goals (*toward orientation*), while others take the same journey to avoid unpleasantness (*away orientation*). While their actions may be identical, their motivation patterns are not. What motivates one, leaves the other cold.

For example, an *away-oriented* individual might say, "I don't want a job with a lot of rules and regulations" or "I'm not interested in being constantly supervised." These two statements are indications that he is moving away from something, not toward it (i.e., away from rules, regulations, and supervision). He seemingly knows what he *doesn't* want, but does he necessarily know what he *does* want? Remember, just because he doesn't want a lot of rules and regulations doesn't mean that he is not a good job candidate. After all, his opposite number may speak of *wanting* the independence to make his own decisions, and a willingness to accept responsibility for the outcomes. Both of these individuals may represent the ideal candidate. The difference is in the way you appeal to them.

The *toward-oriented* individual is constantly striving to attain certain conditions that he perceives as positive, while the away-oriented individual focuses his efforts on avoiding conditions perceived as negative. Hence, when trying to motivate the *away-oriented* person, you might say something like, "I know you'll enjoy this new campaign. The prospectus is much simpler and there aren't nearly as many restrictions on sales as there have been with previous issues." However, to the *toward-oriented* person, you might sell the same campaign by saying something like, "I know that you'll enjoy the tremendous freedom offered by this new product line. It will give you the flexibility you've been seeking in terms of trying out some of your own sales ideas." The campaign is the same, and each FC will probably perform excellently, but neither will respond to the other's motivation pattern.

Similar to Good/Bad, All/None, and so forth, this pattern identifies almost everything in terms of *Did I win or lose?* Some people get into the habit of being a *loser,* while others allow losing attitudes to affect their lives to a significant degree. Consider what is called *The Murphy's Law Syndrome*—if anything can go wrong, it will go wrong. When something goes wrong they blithely say, "Murphy's Law" as if that excuses everything. Certainly this is fine and even healthy occasionally. Sometimes this attitude allows us not to sweat the small stuff and to rationalize a problem as something basically trivial. It's also good to plan for contingencies by taking into account all of the things that can go wrong. This is great for strategic and tactical planning, but has no real place in everyday affairs because these people who have losing attitudes are mentally giving up control of their actions by putting their success in the hands of fate.

In an FC, most of us would want someone who makes his own success, someone who doesn't wait for opportunities to occur, but makes his own opportunities. When a problem occurs we want this person to either fix it or deal with it, but then go forward from there without dwelling on what could have been.

There are many other characteristics of perfect FCs, but an additional one that comes to mind when considering this section is that they have the drive to want to win and want others to be winners as well. It would be ideal if they would also regularly assist others in winning, but if they merely allowed others to win without sabotaging, that would be good too. It's interesting to note that the *stars* in your office, and in any industry, will usually have this *win-win* trait. They have already made it. It is okay for other people to shine also.

Compare them to the members of the dreaded coffee klatch, who knock, berate, sabotage, bend, fold, and otherwise mutilate those who are not members of their little group. This is the type of affiliation that can be detrimental to your office and your career.

There are many different patterns that people commonly employ. Very few are intrinsically good or bad. Almost all of them can be either advantageous or disadvantageous depending upon the context. The trick is to pay attention to these patterns in your day-to-day dealings with people.

As you learn to first recognize and then respond to these patterns in ways that make sense to the other person, your overall effectiveness will be enhanced. It will demonstrate your acknowledgement that you have a series of individuals in your employ rather than a generic nonentity. It will also enable you to motivate people to achieve more of their potential which is a *win-win* situation. Finally it will allow you to recognize when problems with a particular person are occurring and provides the tools, along with other elements of this book, to more quickly and easily resolve those problems.

Summary

The patterns that have been presented thus far are but a few of the standard responses which allow you to predict behavior. We have presented the ones that are easily observable and which should give you the greatest personal leverage. It is important to combine this information with the characteristics presented in other chapters. Extending the concept a bit further, we can psychologically profile current *ideal employees* to determine which criteria contribute most significantly to their success.

As an experiment, think of an ideal FC and respond to the following questions so that you can get a feel for the potential ramifications of having this information. Is this person:

- Oriented to the past, present, or future?
- Self-motivated (i.e., able to maintain a good work pace without reliance on external sources)?
- Interested in power and/or affiliation and/or achievement?
- A global or linear thinker?
- Moving toward a goal or moving away from something?
- Pro-active or reactive?
- Interested in continuing the job in the same way as usual or does he always try to do things differently?

The answers to these questions are important because they literally determine how successful this person will become. By eliciting the motivational themes and programs of a few of your star performers, you can develop both a clearer picture of the mental and behavioral characteristics necessary for success, and better guidelines to use in determining who you hire.

A potential difficulty you face is that most people will consciously indicate that they are pro-active or global thinkers or whatever most closely matches their self-image or their ideal. You cannot just ask people what they are. However, you can determine it through multiple observations of behavior, in addition to asking certain astute questions to decide whether a new candidate will fit the same mold as the star producers.

Chapter 17

Stress and Motivation

In the last few chapters, we've discussed important ways that you can effectively motivate your employees to give their very best while enjoying what they do. In this chapter we will explore *stress overload,* one of the great *demotivators* which, if ignored, can cost you lost production, high personnel turnover, and an increase in costly errors.

How does stress affect our level of motivation? Is it possible to overstress our FCs in our efforts to motivate them? We've all seen FCs who lose their enthusiasm and seem to give up, or become frequently ill, or develop family problems or a drinking habit. We've also seen FCs who are so hard charging that when the burnout comes, we're hardly surprised. The fact is that stress and motivation (or lack of motivation) frequently go hand in hand. But, what is stress, and where does it come from?

"Everyday in every way... (things are getting more and more stressful)." At least, that's what most of us seem to think. Financial

147

consultants have very stressful jobs. In fact, stress-related burnout is probably the single greatest cause of failure among FCs—the average length of their careers is five years in many areas of the financial services industry. If that statistic is true for FCs, what about branch managers? You have all of the strain that you had as an FC, as well as the responsibility for everything that happens or fails to happen in your branch. But managers and FCs aren't the only ones who find their jobs stressful.

According to pollster Louis Harris' book, *Inside America*, 89% of all adult Americans (roughly 158 million people) report experiencing high levels of stress. Almost 60% say that they feel "great stress" at least once or twice a week and nearly one-third (over 30%) say they feel they are living with high stress every day.

Stress has been shown to be a major contributor to physical and mental illness (insurance companies and medical authorities indicate that over 75% of *all* time lost from work can be attributed to stress), family breakup, drug and alcohol abuse, and suicide. Many psychiatric authorities believe that stress is the major cause of mental illnesses. Among high-stress jobs (e.g., police, fire fighters, stock brokers, insurance salespeople, executives, and psychotherapists), stress may easily be the single greatest cause of physical and mental problems, especially divorce, suicide, and burnout.

Insurance studies have shown that the families of stock brokers tend to submit claims for mental health services significantly more frequently than the norm. In addition, informal research studies have shown that the divorce rate among brokers exceeds 85%, and some studies show brokers running third, behind dentists and psychotherapists, in suicide rates! One million-dollar broker told us that of the 16 men who had come to training with him 10 years ago, *all* had since been divorced at least once.

These are grim statistics and, considering the nature of the responsibilities of today's manager, it might be useful to explore the nature of stress and how to combat it. After all, stress may cost you not only the efficiency and effectiveness of your employees, it may also affect you! At the same time, anxiety over stress can be overdone. After all, it's possible to have too little stress, too!

What Is Stress?

Probably the simplest way to define stress is as the amount of challenge you experience. Physiologically, stress can be defined as

148

anything that moves your body out of a state of *homeostasis* (balance). This can include eating, playing tennis, or even being affectionate with your family (none of which are usually life threatening). Overall, most authorities agree that stress overload results from feelings of losing control over events that affect our physical and emotional well-being and our sense of self-worth. Once this is added to a gradual loss of hope that things will improve, we become stressed and begin to risk experiencing *burnout*. Let's look at Exhibit 17-1 which shows how our level of stress, or challenge, affects both our efficiency and our enjoyment of life.

As you can see, too little stress, or challenge, can lead to boredom and loss of energy and enthusiasm. We need challenges to keep up our enthusiasm. However, too much challenge can lead to stress overload, which can further lead to burnout, loss of production, family problems, and even a breakdown in our immune system with subsequent loss of health.

As a branch manager, you have far greater control over many of the factors that affect your well-being than most people. However, while you have more control than your peers in the home office, there are still many events that affect you which you cannot control. Examples might include such elements as the state of the economy, foreign competition, interest rates, etc. All of these factors influence the potential productivity of your branch, but you cannot control them. In addition, while you have only limited control over your FCs' productivity, you are held accountable for it.

To avoid, or to overcome this sense of being helpless and out of control, it is important to develop personal values in terms of what is

EXHIBIT 17-1. *Effect of Stress on Enjoyment/Efficiency.*

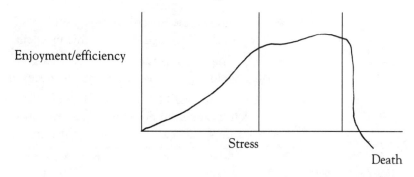

meaningful and important to you (see Chapter 3). Remember, too much stress suppresses your immune system, leaving you vulnerable to illness. In addition to potential physical ailments, you may also develop feelings of a loss of identity and self-esteem.

Do you have any FCs who have performed well in the past but who seem to be losing their sales ability now? Someone who may even appear to have given up? How about an FC who has become virtually obsessed with work and trying to get ahead? For many of us, stress overload can lead to feelings of anxiety, depression, even a sense of being driven and, in our attempts to regain our sense of control, many of us literally cross the line from productive to self-destructive behaviors. What is most ironic is that stress overload is a self-inflicted wound.

Today, we are constantly surrounded by reminders of what we have to own, look like, and accomplish in order to be considered successful. If we accept advertising's concept of success, it is easy for us to develop feelings of inadequacy over failure to obtain it. This can lead to a sense of being trapped and the development of feelings of hopelessness and helplessness in trying to get what you really want out of life. According to Dr. Robert Eliot, a noted heart specialist, a far more important question to ask is, *"Am I winning?"* Also, ask yourself whose standards you're using to determine your success level. Then look at those standards and decide whether anyone could meet them. Too many of us demand the impossible of ourselves and others. If you are impatient with anything short of perfection, you may be setting yourself up for failure, frustration, and strong feelings of hopelessness.

To help avoid this kind of trap, review the chapter on coaching and counseling where we suggested that you explore your (and your employee's) goals and plans for achieving them. If you are feeling stressed, look at what you're trying to accomplish and ask yourself three questions developed by Dr. Joseph Yeager in his book, *Thinking About Thinking With NLP.*

- "Do I know **how to** achieve this goal?" In other words, do I have the technical knowledge to solve this problem?

- "Do I have a **chance to** achieve this goal?" That is, is the goal reachable? Do I have the resources necessary to achieve it?

- "Do I really **want to** achieve this goal?" Is this really my goal or one which has been imposed upon me by someone else? If the goal has been imposed, can I really make it mine? If so, do it!

150

Once you've answered these questions satisfactorily, there are three others that need to be explored to clarify the source of stress:

- "Is this goal **real**?" Is it really achievable? (To a degree, this is an extension of *chance to*.)
- "Can I **win** the goal using my current strategy?" Often, we choose excellent goals but fail to achieve them because we have selected an ineffective strategy to achieve it. Evaluate your problem-solving strategies for effectiveness before committing significant resources.
- "Will achieving my goal be **worth** the cost and effort required?" There are many financially successful people who would gladly trade their success to regain the good health or the family they lost in attaining it.

Hot Reactors

With all of this talk about the effects of stress, you may be wondering, "How does all of this affect me?" Dr. Robert Eliot, the author (with Dennis L. Breo) of, *Is It Worth Dying For?* has made a series of discoveries regarding the way our responses to situations affect our physical and mental health.

One of his discoveries indicates that some people respond in the same way to simple challenges (e.g., completing a billing form or figuring a commission) in the same way that they would a life-threatening situation. He refers to these individuals as HOT REACTORS. In addition, his research has indicated that nearly one-fifth of all people who feel that they are under stress are hot reactors, and in some professions (e.g., top insurance salespeople), the number reaches as high as 40%. (During a recent study involving a major brokerage firm, Dr. Eliot found that as many as 80% of the top producers were hot reactors.)

If you are a hot reactor, you may experience the physical reactions of an *alarm response* and adrenaline production (see Appendix 4 for details of the **Alarm Response**) to simple challenges as often as 40 or more times a day without even being aware of it. In some cases, your blood pressure may even double. In any case, subjecting your body to this kind of reaction on a constant basis will eventually cause it to break down.

In addition, if you feel overly challenged, or threatened, over a period of time, your body goes into the *resistance mode*, adding the hormone cortisol to your system (see Appendix 4 for details of the **Resistance Mode**). This hormone raises your blood pressure and keeps it up. Then, when the alarm occurs again, your body's system begins its alert from higher levels of blood pressure, blood thickness, and stomach acidity. This addition of more adrenaline to a system already flush with cortisol can literally lead the heart muscles to tear themselves apart—one of the common findings in sudden cardiac death (87%).

The worst aspect of being a hot reactor is that this person is not easy to spot the way *Type A personality* is. Recent research by the American Medical Association indicates that there are just as many *Type B* hot reactors as Type As.

Each year, more than 1.2 million people suffer from heart attacks. Over half of those heart attacks are caused by too much stress and, in nearly one-third of the attacks, the first symptom is *death*! That means that **over 1200 people die from stress-related heart attacks every day!** How many FCs do you know who have died of a heart attack?

In addition, remember that stress overload attacks more than just the heart. Few people seem to realize that too much stress is probably the single greatest cause of impotence in men and frigidity in women. Failure to recognize this and to discuss it openly and with understanding has hurt many marriages when one or both partners began to fear that they were losing their sexuality. Needless to say, an FC who is worrying about divorce or family problems is not giving his full attention to his work.

The Million Dollar Round Table

In 1985, Dr. Robert Eliot conducted a study with the members of the Million Dollar Round Table (the insurance industry's highest producers). He found that 39% were hot reactors, and another 25% were undiagnosed hypertensives. That is, two out of three of the top producers in the insurance industry were in imminent cardiac danger. He also found that 80% felt that their lives were not fulfilling and, consequently, they were not happy. Interestingly, these kinds of numbers are not unique to the insurance industry. In fact, recent studies have indicated that things are even worse for stock brokers. How healthy are your top producers?

These are grim numbers for anyone who wants to be successful, especially in sales. However, there is a happy ending. Dr. Eliot and his group worked with the members of the study to help them learn how to deal with and reduce stress in their lives, and the results were phenomenal. **Six months later, all of the participants were healthy.** *None* were hot reactors and *none* were hypertensive. All reported that life had taken on new meaning and that life was good. In addition, the average work week for these individuals dropped from 70 hours per week to just 40-50 hours per week. Best of all, each had significantly increased their production during the same period.

The year 1986 was a fantastic one for the insurance industry. On the average, members of the Million Dollar Round Table increased their production by 11% over the previous year. When Dr. Eliot did a follow up of his test group in January 1987, he found that everyone was still healthy and happy. In addition, the smallest increase in production for a member of the group was *40%* (*note:* he was undergoing a divorce), while the average increase was in excess of *100%* over the previous year.

Summary

What all of this boils down to is that you can have it all. Success doesn't have to mean ulcers, heart attacks, and an early grave. In fact, it can mean just the opposite. **You can succeed and enjoy yourself while you do it!** All you have to do is learn how to handle stress in your life.

In the next chapter, we will provide you with a series of techniques for reducing both your own stress and that of your staff.

Chapter 18

How to Manage and Reduce Stress

Stress Isn't All Bad

As we mentioned before, stress, or challenge, isn't *all* bad. Effective time management (or event management) is an important tool in coping with stress (see Chapter 4). Review your life for a moment and try to determine whether you have too much stress, or not enough. If you have too many challenges (which seems to be the most common complaint among branch managers and their sales personnel), begin to learn to say, "no" to additional responsibilities. You may even need to cut back on some of your current work load or social obligations.

However, if you don't have enough challenge in your life, begin to say, "yes" to additional challenges and responsibilities. You may find yourself not only with more to do, but also more energy to do it with. Note: We realize that as a manager, you probably don't have this particular problem.

155

In any case, make a list of your current activities. When you have completed it, determine which activities you are involved in because you really have to do them, which you're involved in because you really want to do them, and which you're involved in for any other reason. Then make a notation next to each for *have to, want to,* and *neither.* When you are done, start eliminating the activities that you've marked as neither on your list.

Make a Plan

Hyrum Smith, the great time management expert, points out that no one can manage time. What we can do, is manage those events that impinge upon our time. To do this, write down those events and factors that have the most impact on you. Those which you can control (e.g., what time you leave the office each day), and those which you cannot control (e.g., the economy). Once you have determined which is which, develop and follow a plan to *take control of the things that you can control,* and to lessen the negative impact that those things that you cannot control have upon you.

> Take control of the events in your life.

Attainable Goals

The importance of establishing attainable goals for ourselves cannot be overemphasized. Without goals, our behavior becomes directionless and lacks meaning. If we set goals that are not attainable, they quickly become a source of frustration and stress. Below is a summary of the five conditions necessary to establish a well-formed goal (see Chapter 3 for more details):

1. State your goal in positive language: Write down what you want rather than what you don't want.

2. The goal must be within your control. If you are sixty-years-old, a goal of winning the decathlon in the Olympics is probably not within your control.

3. The goal should preserve your *ecology*. That is, will attaining the goal cost you more than it's worth? (Remember *real, win, worth.*) We know of many a millionaire who lost his family in gaining his success who would gladly trade his millions to have them back again.

4. Be very specific both in describing your goal, and in how you will know when you have achieved it. From your description, someone else should be able to recognize when you have reached your goal.

5. However you view your current state, there are probably many positive aspects about it. Your goal must maintain these positive aspects or you may find yourself unconsciously defeating your efforts to obtain it.

Once you have established your intermediate and long-term goals, break them down into daily increments. Each day set yourself a goal that you can attain and then reward yourself for attaining it. The nature of the reward is up to you (watching a ball game, reading a novel, a treat, etc.), but see that you earn and give yourself a little reward every day. You'll be surprised what it does for your attitude.

Point of View

One interesting result of studies in stress management is that far more important than the actual events in your life is the way you interpret those events and the meaning that you assign them. In his book, *Man's Search for Meaning*, Dr. Viktor Frankl speaks of his years in a Nazi extermination camp. While there, he would frequently try to determine which prisoners might survive and which would be unable to cope. At first he made his determinations based upon the youth and physical strength of the prisoners, but too frequently, young, healthy prisoners would come into the barracks and announce that they had given up. The next day they were found dead in their bunks. When they lost the will to live, they died!

Others, who were aged 40 to 60 and were not in top physical condition, survived. Despite all of the odds against them, they were still alive when the camp was liberated, four years later. Frankl determined that there was one factor that separated those who gave up and died from those who held on until they were liberated. That factor was the *meaning* that people assigned to their lives and to the events that occurred.

Dr. Frankl says that if life has meaning, then all suffering has meaning and can be borne, no matter how great. If life is meaningless, then all suffering is meaningless and is unbearable, no matter how small. Remember, **it is not the event that causes stress, it is the meaning that we assign to the event.**

When something doesn't go our way, do we interpret it as a failure, proof that we are unworthy? Or, do we look for what we can learn from the experience? As you explore the motivational criteria of your employees, you will also discover the way that they assign meaning to events, especially failure. One of the great blessings of failing is that it makes us more willing to try something different.

What's Your Point of View?

Ask yourself, "What is the meaning of my life?" If you are not sure, think about it. How would you like to be remembered after you are gone? Do you just want to be remembered for being a million-dollar producer, a successful branch manager, or are there other, more important things? What are your motivational criteria and belief systems?

Thoughts versus Feelings

Perhaps Solomon said it best over 4,000 years ago, **"As a man thinketh, so is he."** What you think about and how you think about it (the meaning that you assign to events), determines how you feel and the impact that the event will have on your health. Try this simple exercise:

Relax and get as comfortable as you can. Take a deep breath, hold it for a slow count of three and let it out. Now think back and remember the happiest moment of your life (perhaps the day you got married or proposed, your third birthday party, or possibly the first time the doctor handed you your new child to hold). Try to really get into the memory, and rather than seeing yourself doing something, feel yourself doing it. Reexperience everything as if you were actually there and reliving it all again. Do this for about one minute and then return.

How do you feel? Pretty good? Now do the same thing, but this time relive a moment of minor irritation such as a traffic delay, getting yelled at for something, or missing an important putt in a golf game. Again, relive the experience for about one minute and then return.

How do you feel now? Not as good? Finally, return to the happiest moment of your life. Again, relive it as it was then and make it real. Do this for one moment and then return. Notice how good you feel. What happened? Did you notice how what you thought about determined how you felt?

Now, take a 3″ × 5″ card and on one side of its write down 10 qualities that you possess that others might find admirable or attractive (e.g., your concern for others, your professionalism, etc.). On the other side, write down five of the happiest moments of your life and five successes in your life (times when you felt that you could do anything, overcome any obstacle, such as winning a race or solving a major problem in your branch).

Carry the card with you, and take it out to read the next time that you feel discouraged. Remind yourself that you are a good, competent person. Then turn it over, relax, and relive each of the 10 moments you've written there for one minute apiece. Before you complete number five, you will find that you have completely regained your confidence and positive outlook. By following these methods, you can *take control of how you feel!*

Take control of how you feel.

Humor

Developing a good sense of humor and the ability to laugh at ourselves and the situations in which we find ourselves is one of the easiest and most effective ways to regain control of the impact that circumstances have on our feelings. It also lets us see ourselves and our circumstances from a different point of view (humorous instead of ego- or life-threatening). In their book, *Frogs into Princes*, Richard Bandler and John Grinder point out that since we often say to ourselves, "Someday I'll probably look back on all this and laugh," *why wait?!* Laugh now instead of letting circumstances overwhelm you. Set the example in the office. If you can laugh at problems, it will be easier for your employees to do so, and you will easily reduce the level of stress within the branch. *Note:* Of course we are not suggesting that you develop a flippant attitude toward problems. We are suggesting putting them into proper perspective and not letting them cost more than they are worth.

```
Laugh now and avoid the stress.
```

Helping Your Family Help You

Your family can either be a lifesaving support or an additional source of threat. Today, nearly 26% of all sudden cardiac deaths occur on Monday mornings. An additional 25% occur on Saturday mornings. These are the times when we switch from one source of stress to another. There are several steps that you can easily take that will not only help you to cope with stress in your own life, but will also help you to avoid becoming a source of stress for your family and employees. You may wish to encourage your employees to take some of these steps and support them in their efforts to do so.

Keep Your Balance

Anyone can lift and carry two to three times more weight if it is well-balanced than if it is unbalanced. This is also true of psychic burdens such as stress.

To really cope with the complexities of today's world we must develop and maintain a sense of inner balance between our mental, physical, emotional, career, social, and spiritual selves. If any one of these areas is overemphasized at the expense of the others, it can leave us without the resources to fully cope when circumstances put us under pressure. We all want FCs, especially new FCs, to stay late and prospect several nights a week. However, it's important to take into account the cost to families and the potential backlash from that source if we overdo it.

Prepare for Change

In the competitive arena of sales, change is more than inevitable; it is constant. To deal with change we must learn to expect it and prepare for its impact upon our lives and the lives of our families.

160

If you are new to management, the odds are high that your family and loved ones are not prepared for the changes that will occur in their lives as a result of your change in career. After all, your level of responsibility increased significantly with your promotion. **Be certain that you discuss your job with them regularly and, especially, that you discuss not only your own goals for your career, but also *their* goals for your career.** After all, you are asking them for their support of your work. Encourage your FCs to do the same.

Just one of the changes that your family will have to deal with is your new work hours. To succeed in a new job, especially as a manager or an FC, you may need to work at least two to three nights per week for several years. If your family and loved ones are not already familiar with such a pattern, this can be a severe disruption. If you have already told them and they seemed understanding and supportive, don't be lulled into a false sense of security. Until they have experienced the change, they won't really know what kind of an impact it will have upon them.

Once a pattern has become established (e.g., your being home every night), it is natural to unconsciously expect that pattern to continue. They develop further patterns of meeting our needs around that pattern, and when one person changes, it affects everyone. Imagine the typical family of five as pictured in Exhibit 18-1.

EXHIBIT 18-1. *Family of Five Pattern.*

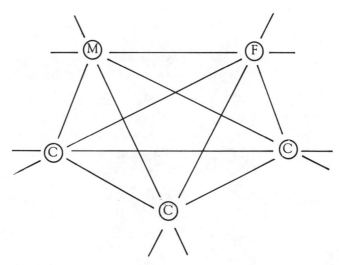

Each circle represents a family member, and the lines connecting the circles represent relationships among the members and between each member and their outside commitments (e.g., work, friends, church, etc.). Notice what happens in Exhibit 18-2 when one member changes his or her accepted role (e.g., begins a new job, becomes an adolescent, etc.). The relationships stretch, adding tension (and stress) to *all* of the relationships in the family.

EXHIBIT 18-2. *Change in Member's Status.*

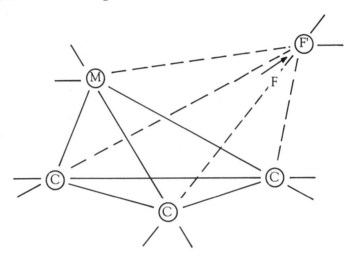

There are only three ways to reduce those tensions.

1. The best and hardest method is for the family to work together to adjust to the change (see Exhibit 18-3).

   Your family's ability to do this effectively can radically affect their ability to cope with stress in their lives. If this does not occur, you may find that the tension you bring home from work shows up in your child's poor grades or behavior in school.

2. The family can exert so much pressure upon the person who has changed, that he changes back (e.g., quits his job), as in Exhibit 18-4. A lot of new FCs leave the business because of this.

EXHIBIT 18-3. *Adjustment to Change.*

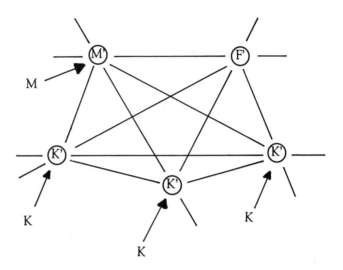

EXHIBIT 18-4. *Return to Origin.*

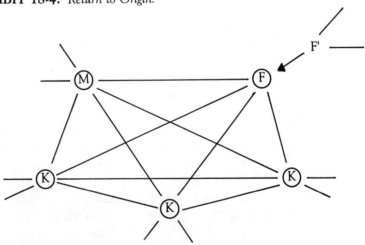

This occurs because, like your body, your family is a system and no system can tolerate tension for very long. As a result, it always moves to reduce that tension. This is one reason why so many alcoholics have difficulty staying sober: Once their families have adjusted to the individual as an alcoholic, they resist the further adjustment needed to cope with him sober. They often unconsciously subtly pressure him to drink again.

3. The most tragic way to adjust occurs when the family system cannot cope with the tension any longer (see Exhibit 18-5) and it cuts the relationships to the stress-producing individual.

EXHIBIT 18-5. *Relationship Is Severed.*

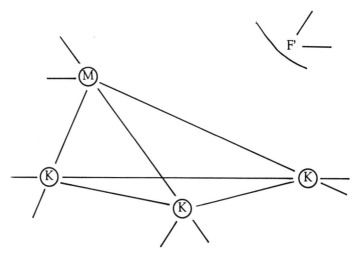

This can result in divorce, suicide, murder, runaway, alcohol and drug abuse, or mental illness.

Keep Courting

What can you do to avoid having your family see your job as a rival for your time and attention? Court your spouse *and* your children. For so many couples, the courtship ends as soon as they have said, "I do." Everyone needs to feel courted, needed, and loved. One way to do this is to make sure that the time that you do spend with your loved ones is *quality time*. That is, time in which your main objective is to meet your family's needs. This isn't easy since it requires periods of time when they have your total and undivided attention.

If you are going to work two to three nights per week, suggest that your spouse bring the children to work at six, and then go out to eat as a family (e.g., MacDonald's) instead of remaining in the office. Help the children to see your late nights as potentially fun instead of dreary. When dinner is over, take one of the children back to the office and let him use the desk next to yours to do his homework. Branch and sales managers who have encouraged their FCs to do this report very positive

164

results in the form of increased family loyalty to the firm and more work at night to increase sales.

If your children are teenagers, let them help you with chores such as stuffing envelopes, so that they can feel that they are actually a part of helping to attain the family's goals. If an FC's children are older teenagers, and if you approve, it may be possible for them to cold call potential customers for your FC. When the evening is over, stop for some ice cream together on the way home. By having the children take turns, you can have a special experience with a different child each week.

If possible, have your spouse join you alone for dinner once a week. After dinner, ask your spouse to join you and do whatever work he or she brought home from the office in the desk next to you. If there is no work, let your spouse help you in any of your tasks where he or she may be useful. At the very least, your spouse can keep you company by watching television in the meeting room while you work. On the way home, stop for a milk shake or something.

Call your spouse and go out on a real *date* together once a week. The nature of the date will be far less important than being able to look forward to it.

Family Council

Hold a family council each week to discuss each family member's progress toward *their* goals. Find out their needs and discuss their responsibilities, their goals, and any help they need from other members of the family.

Mail a note home to your spouse and each of the children each week (or slip it in their lunch or pocket) telling them that you are thinking of them. Bring home a surprise that you know they like to let them know they're special. It doesn't take a lot of money to say, "I love you," but it can be very important.

Loving Memories

Last of all, always try to make going home a reward to yourself. Don't let family problems overwhelm your family's beneficial effect on you. Have you ever experienced a time of great difficulty with a family member? Have you dreaded going home because you knew that there would be a fight? One way to alleviate this dread is to take a moment before leaving work to relax at your desk, close your eyes, and remember a loving moment shared with that family member. If the problem is with your spouse, remember and relive how you felt the day you got engaged. If the problem is with a child, remember and relive how you felt the first time the doctor handed him or her to you as an infant. You'll be surprised at how unimportant problems and misunderstandings become, and as *you* change so will *they*.

Family and friends can either increase your level of stress, or they can reduce it. You make that choice. Take the time to strengthen your support groups.

Positive Mental Attitude

In computer terminology, *GIGO* means, garbage in—garbage out. Your brain is the most sophisticated computer known, yet this rule applies to it as well. Each day, little discouragements, news items, business changes, FC, operations or customer relations problems fill your brain with negative information. All around you there are people and circumstances telling you that you can't win and there's no point in trying. Even if you don't listen to them with your conscious mind, your unconscious picks it up and after a while even the most optimistic person can become discouraged. When this occurs, pull out the index card we discussed earlier and bring your spirits back up. But to avoid letting self-doubt happen in the first place, program your mind to think positively.

PMA Books

Your local bookstore has hundreds of excellent books on maintaining a positive mental attitude. Most say the same thing in different ways (just as most bad news falls into several categories stated in slightly different ways), but all are good. Each carries the message that *you are a winner, and you can accomplish anything that you set your mind to!*

Read a chapter each morning before you go to work to program yourself for success, and encourage your FCs to do the same. If you have a rough morning, read another chapter during lunch. Finally, read a chapter before going to bed (reading this aloud with your spouse can be excellent for a marriage). Psychologists have found that the last thing you think about before sleep programs the unconscious for the remainder of the night. If you go to bed worried and upset you will spend the

166

night that way and awaken suffering from the *Wrong Side of the Bed Syndrome*. That's when you wake up grouchy and no matter how many things go well that day it was just luck (if you even notice at all). Why not program yourself to wake up with the *Right Side of the Bed Syndrome?* Then spend the rest of the day feeling good, despite any unimportant setbacks. Consider building a lending library of PMA books in the branch.

PMA Tapes

Another aid in maintaining a positive mental attitude consists of audio tapes with the same messages as the books. You can listen to them while commuting or getting dressed in the morning. The important thing is to take control over what gets programmed into your mind. Many branch managers we know have a substantial collection of such tapes in the branch which they loan out to FCs.

Work Environment

Many branch and sales managers encourage their FCs to eat at their desks during lunch. This may have unfortunate results in terms of health and overall production. The unconscious mind tends to label areas as work areas, play areas, eating areas, and so on. In addition, customers and operations centers are rarely impressed with materials that are sticky or have coffee rings.

Eating away from your desk becomes particularly important at lunch. Trying to eat while dealing with the stress of calls from customers or other managers is a very effective way to give yourself heartburn if not gastritis, an ulcer, or worse. When you eat, leave the office behind and go somewhere where you won't even think about work. Recharge your batteries. Read a novel or a positive mental attitude book. Go window shopping or take a brisk walk. Studies have shown that doing so can radically increase your effectiveness after lunch, while failing to do so can leave you ineffective and exhausted by the end of the day. Remember, always eat away from your desk.

Watch out for the office cranks. Almost every office seems to have one or more individuals who think that the world will end tomorrow. Be pleasant about it, but let them know that you're not interested in their talking about negative things.

Mickey Mouse

Do you have someone at the office or elsewhere who is upsetting to even think about? Take a moment to mentally see him now. While you think of him, imagine him with ears like Mickey Mouse and a beak and voice like Donald Duck. Does he still upset you? Change other things about this person until thinking about him doesn't bother you. With a little practice, every time you see this person you'll see Mickey Mouse and hear Donald Duck.

The important thing to remember is that you are in control of your life and your health.

Take control of your life.

Change Your Stress

When you have worked all day at a desk, it is often difficult to come home and just sit down and relax. If this occurs, first change the nature of your stress. If you've been working on mental problems, do something physical like playing tennis or taking a walk. Afterward you will find that you will be able to relax more easily, if for no other reason than the fact that you will have burned off some of the stress chemicals stored up in your body during the day. (*Note:* The physical stress should be something you *enjoy* doing.)

Eat Right

There are many excellent books out on diet and stress. Or, you may wish to consult about a diet with your physician. In any case, a safe rule of thumb is to always eat intelligently and avoid extremes. Avoid the use of tobacco and alcohol as both exacerbate stress (see Appendix 4 for details).

Be sure to get plenty of fiber, and concentrate on complex carbohydrates such as vegetables. Finally, eat because you are hungry, not because you are tired, working, or watching television.

Exercise

Exercise is also a matter of moderation and intelligence. Handled properly, it can not only burn off stress chemicals, it can also raise your metabolic set point and burn off excess weight.

Before beginning an exercise program, be sure to check with your doctor to determine what is appropriate for you. After that, find something that you enjoy doing and do it three to five times per week gradually working your way up to 30 minutes a session.

In school, the coaches used to tell us, "No pain, no gain." In reality, this is not true. When your body hurts, it is trying to tell you something important and you should listen to it. If you are exercising and it hurts, *stop!* Cool down gradually and call it a day. Continuing could lead to injury.

Summary

It is possible to have both too little and too much stress, or challenge, in our lives. Too little can leave us dull and bored while too much can leave us feeling hopeless and helpless, exhausted, and even ill. Both are demotivating. By actively taking charge of our lives and the meanings we assign to the events in our lives, we can control the level of challenge we face each day and use it to help us to maintain maximum efficiency and enthusiasm at all times.

Section V

Coaching and Counseling

One of the most important roles of the branch manager is that of supervision. Because you are responsible for everything that happens or fails to happen in your branch, it is sometimes necessary to counsel an employee regarding his performance. Unfortunately, this can make the employee very defensive and result in resentment instead of the change you desire.

In addition, managers sometimes meet with disgruntled employees, customers, or even superiors. When this happens, it is necessary to calm them and to elicit the specific cause of their unhappiness, as well as the specific parameters of any desired solution before you can even begin to act upon their complaint.

The chapters in this section will provide you with a series of techniques which can be used in your roles as coach and counselor to improve the efficiency and effectiveness of your employees, and to soothe the feelings of those who are upset. In addition, Chapters 23 and 24 will provide ways to achieve and maintain a state of personal excellence in all that you do.

171

Chapter **19**

Overcoming "Telephone-a-Phobia": The Unprofitable Fear of Using the Phone

You see it everywhere. People staring at the phone as if it were going to bite. Individuals unable to lift the receiver. FCs turning gray at the thought of calling another prospect. Anticipation anxiety can be masked under many guises: "I'm too busy doing something more important"; "My ear didn't get enough rest last night"; or, "I will as soon as I get organized." "Enough already!" you say, "I've heard it all before."

Telephone-a-phobia (the unreasonable fear of using the phone) has reduced many FCs to total ineffectiveness. However, FCs are not the only ones whose discomfort in communicating on the phone can virtually incapacitate them. For service reps, and many other types of employees, this fear of rejection becomes a palpable dread. Unfortunately, people fail out of the financial services business every day because of it. What do you do when this happens? What do you say? How do you get a person through this fear?

Perhaps the first step is to recognize the causes of telephone-a-phobia. When you think about it, there are only a few causes for avoiding the use of the phone:

- fear of rejection;
- fear of a customer's or prospect's anger (frequently seen in customer service reps or in FCs following a sharp downturn in the market);
- making 100 or 200 calls per day can quickly become extremely tedious; and,
- some people just aren't sure of what to say on the phone (you see this particularly among new FCs who don't really know the firm's products and services well enough yet and who fear looking foolish when asked a question that they can't answer).

The following sections are a few techniques that have worked successfully with numerous sales professionals from a variety of industries, including the financial services industry. The thing that they all had in common was a decided reluctance to meet new, potential clients on the phone or face-to-face. They evidenced what could typically be labeled as *avoidance behavior* and, in the extreme, *burnout*. If their situation had continued much longer, they would have been terminated. Of course, the techniques also work with virtually anyone.

Making Friends

Fear of rejection often results from the tendency to take personally the negative responses of total strangers during prospecting. The first part of this multilayered technique is to give the individual a more complete appreciation for the real meaning of *rejection*. All of the techniques will be presented as though you, the reader, were an individual suffering from telephone-a-phobia.

Look outside and imagine a large parking lot with 1,000 people there, or imagine an auditorium filled with 1,000 people. Your task is to meet each of those 1,000 people during the next five hours. At the end of five hours you have to know which people are worth developing as friends. Basically, you will need to meet 200 people per hour, or approximately one person every 15 to 20 seconds.

Think about this situation for a moment. Now, approximately

how many people of the 1,000 do you think that you would want to really develop a friendship with—remember that you can only develop one friend at a time and that it is impossible to develop a friendship with each and every person.

If you're like most people, your answer probably falls within the range of from 5 to 50, with the majority agreeing at around 10 people (approximately 1%) statistically being worth your individual attention.

How did you make that determination? Most people we talk to tell us that, essentially, they would shake hands briefly, mutter a few comments, and make a quick decision as to whether the person is "like me" or "not like me." If the decision is "not like me," then they walk to the next person. The *yes/no decision* has extremely little to do with the individuals involved. Do they dress poorly? Do they remind you of someone you don't like? Do they seem nervous? A *yes* to any of those questions could cause a negative determination and cause you to walk away in search of someone else.

The main point is that most people mentally accept or reject entire groups of people on purely subjective determinations. The yes/no decision probably had little, if anything, to do with the individual in question. Should the people you bypassed feel terrible about themselves because you walked on? Are they terrible people unworthy of love? *Of course not!* Now, ask yourself this key question: "Did you actually reject them on a personal level?" *Of course not!* The point is that it didn't have anything to do with them on a personal level.

(*Note:* We realize that this concept is nothing new. Most people in the business understand the concept of not taking rejection personally. Yet, **despite this intellectual knowledge, people regularly leave the business because they *do* take rejection personally.** The mere intellectualization of what is actually happening has nothing to do with the feelings that can occur because of the rejection. That is why we developed the multiple level approach you see here. We find that once an individual tries out our ideas, he can much more easily deal with all the "No" responses that he receives on a daily basis. At this point in our discussions with an FC, we often explain what was just stated. If you go too far with the visualization, many adults will become resentful that they are being treated as children. If you stop halfway, as we just did, then it becomes much more reasonable to continue playing the game.)

Now imagine someone else doing the same thing that you just did, and you are now a member of the crowd. As you meet the person you *both* make an immediate subjective determination. A "No" means absolutely nothing, whether you are evaluating him or he is evaluating you. If that person bypasses you, he does so using the same process you used. You were not bypassed or rejected because he knows anything about you. He don't know you well enough to reject you.

Automatic Defense Mechanisms

Now let's do the same thing in terms of cold calling. It is easy to determine that people whose automatic response to you is "No" are responding to an idea, a concept, or a business name, but certainly not to you as an individual. They don't know you well enough to reject you.

Almost everyone has a series of *automatic defense mechanisms* which they use to keep others at a distance. For example: The last time you walked into a store to buy something, what was your response when a sales person approached and said, "Can I help you?" For most of us, the almost automatic response is "No thanks, I'm just looking." *We say this automatically! We say it without thinking.* Our prospects do the very same thing!!! It has nothing to do with the salesperson. *Rejection* from a prospect is really just another automatic defense mechanism being triggered.

If nothing else, it is much easier to deal with 25 automatic defense mechanisms in a row than it is to deal with 25 incidents of being rejected. It's all in how you perceive something.

Friendly Faces

In counseling sessions with FCs we've found two additional problems in people who dislike cold calling. Both of these problems involve mental images of the prospect that can unconsciously get in the way. In one case, the individual has difficulty in communicating/dealing with a faceless voice over the phone. In the second case, the individual has had a prior negative experience and is still carrying the baggage of that experience with him. Often, this individual forms a mental picture of an unfriendly face answering the phone and prepares himself for rejection.

For those who are able to deal with people they have already met over the phone, but have difficulty with faceless people that they have not met, the answer is simple. Give your generic prospect a kind-looking face! Just think of someone that has a pleasant face and then pretend that you are talking to that person whenever you call a prospect. Or, an alternative is to look at a picture of a group of people and mentally associate a randomly selected face with the yet-to-be-met person on the other end of the phone. Try it. It's absolutely amazing! We usually see people change their entire attitude and phone style when they can actually visualize someone pleasant at the other end of the phone. After you've consciously done this a couple of dozen times, you'll automatically do it in the future. Any remaining awkwardness and fear of the phone will tend to disappear very quickly.

The second technique is for those who have had a bad experience and tend to mentally replay that bad experience each time they get on the phone. These people suffer from anticipation anxiety. They imagine the worst, and they get it. As they begin to dial, their tonal qualities change, their confidence level diminishes, and they become afraid.

In an extreme case, the person actually develops a phobic response to making prospecting and/or sales calls—hence the title for this chapter: "Telephone-a-Phobia." The resolution of an actual phobic response will not be provided in this book because it requires training that is not easily presented in text format. However, most people find the following idea so humorous that it tends to work for them with virtually anything short of a phobia or traumatic experience.

Try it on yourself as an experiment. Take a moment and think of someone from your past who was very upsetting. Someone who, whenever you think of that person, you say the equivalent of, "That bum!" (*Note:* For this experience it is important that it not be a family member or someone very close to you. Rather it should be an ex-client or someone that you *had* disliked.) Then let it go. Now, how do you feel? You probably have a slightly tight feeling associated with the memory of that particular individual.

From a mental picture of that person we can feel the twinge of emotion associated with the memory. Now, just for the fun of it, listen to circus music in your head and see that person with Mickey Mouse ears, a Donald Duck nose, the eyes of a clown and Goofy's voice. See that individual in this new light and make your new mental picture of him as vivid as possible. (See Chapter 18.)

Enjoy the crazy picture. What happened to that tight feeling? The vast majority of people we've worked with tell us that the feeling dissipated or was neutralized. How about for you? Think of the person again and discover what happens. Did the clown's face come up? How about the feeling that you used to have? Was it neutralized? For most people it is.

We invite you to try it, using the same parameters, with other people. It is important **NOT** to try it on people who are very close to you because the funny face may not be able to offset the intensity of the feeling. That requires more sophisticated techniques which are part of another book. (*Note:* Be careful of using it with those people whom you currently deal with at work. While everyone likes to be smiled at, few people will enjoy being laughed at every time you see them.)

Dialing for Dollars

For many FCs, the hardest thing about prospecting by phone is the tedium of dialing number after number, day after day, without immediate reward. To make things worse, in the financial services industry, the average FC may obtain only 10 good contacts and one new account from every 100 prospecting calls. Let's face it, cold calling can be boring.

However, let's look at another method. On average, this new account results in a first sale with an average commission of about $500.00. That means that every time you pick up the telephone and dial a prospect, you are earning $5.00, whether the prospect answers the phone and accepts you, rejects you, the line is busy, or the prospect doesn't even answer. Regardless of how the call ends, every dial you make is worth a five-dollar bill in your pocket.

With that motivating thought, how many numbers can you dial in an hour? In a day? As you improve, your level of success will increase and the value of each call will increase with it. (*Note:* The actual statistics will vary with the products that your company sells and with the experience of your sales force. The above figures have been true for the average FC across the securities and insurance industries.)

Know What You're Going to Say

Fear of sounding stupid is another thing that keeps many people away from the phone. Often this is caused by an inadequate level of knowledge of one's assigned area. In the case of the customer service rep, it may mean not knowing the ins and outs of operations. For the new FC, on the other hand, the problem is often the result of a case of information overload wherein he has been taught so many new products and services that it is difficult to sort them out.

A simple solution to both problems can be found in the preparation of easily accessed reference materials for their area of responsibility. For customer service reps, a simple three-ring binder with a summary of each area of the branch and the name and number of each individual with their area of expertise can be a big help. In addition, a one-page summary of each type of account or product along with the most common problems that have arisen and the solutions to those problems can be very useful. Be sure that they are encouraged to call the experts for additional information or help if they don't know the answer to a customer's problem. Then, be sure that you never berate them for calling the expert. If they become too afraid to contact you or someone else in the branch, they may become tempted to sweep problems under the rug or to solve them themselves even when they don't know how. Needless to say, this can be expensive.

Whenever you want your new FCs to prospect using any product, or your more experienced FCs to prospect using a new product, prepare or have the marketing rep prepare, a one-page summary of the features and benefits of the product, as well as answers to anticipated questions. Give them some time to study the sheets, then call them together and have them field questions about the product/service until you are comfortable that they know it thoroughly. In the end, you'll all feel more comfortable.

Be sure that new FCs have a good prospecting script. In our other book, *Consultative Selling Techniques for Financial Professionals*, we demonstrate precisely how to write prospecting scripts that will build confidence and get new clients.

Summary

Being hesitant to prospect or to return a customer's call is the most natural thing in the world. Unfortunately, in this business, it's also a sure way to fail. At this point you can use:

- The discussion regarding meeting people (the parking lot or auditorium metaphor);

- the discussion regarding automatic responses (the salesperson in the store analogy);
- the insertion of a positive picture or the neutralization of a negative memory (friendly faces);
- the discussion/analogy regarding getting money each time the FC picks up the phone (dialing for dollars); and
- the importance of basic preparation for handling questions (scripts and help sheets);

This should all make FCs and customer service reps more confident in cold calling and in dealing with people over the phone. If the FC still has difficulty, return to the *How to, Chance to, Want to Approach* that was discussed in the chapters on goal setting, coaching, and counseling.

Chapter 20

Effective Questioning Techniques

Have you ever felt that you and another person were speaking two different languages? Although the words were all in English, they no longer seem to mean what you thought they meant. Frustrating, isn't it? Yet, this happens to all of us at some time. Maybe that's why we all chuckle when we see this sign on someone's desk.

> I know you think you understand what you thought I said. But I'm not sure that you realize that what you heard is not what I meant.

The following is an example of such a conversation between a job applicant and an interviewer.

Interviewer: We're looking for a person who is absolutely honest and can be trusted around important data.

Applicant: That's me. I've always been known for my absolute honesty. You can ask any of my previous employers. There have been many times when confidential matters were discussed. I can assure you that I'm the soul of discretion.

Interviewer: You do look honest. However, the position that I'm trying to fill requires a person who can work alone and who is a self-starter. There are times when little or no direction can be offered, so the ideal candidate would also have to take the initiative to solve any unusual problems that may occur.

Applicant: I also appreciate those qualities in others because I've always prided myself on having them and, unfortunately, find that relatively few people have them. I've spent the majority of time in positions where working alone was normal. If it were not for a high degree of self-motivation and a personal desire for excellence, some of my tasks would not have been completed otherwise. I can assure you that I am a self-starter and highly motivated to succeed.

As for the ability to take the initiative, let me respond by letting you know that I once received a company commendation for handling an unexpected problem in an expeditious manner. I know how to follow the rules, and I also know when to make exceptions.

Interviewer: Well, enough for now. Please send us a completed resume. You are certainly a strong candidate for this position.

Applicant: Thank you very much. It will be in the mail tomorrow. I am definitely interested in being associated with your corporation.

Interviewer to Sales Director: I think I've found our candidate for night manager.

Applicant to Spouse: Honey, I think I got the job as night guard!

"I know that you think you understand what you thought I said. But I'm not sure that you realize that what you heard is not what I meant." If this interview weren't so common it would be funny. However, situations of this sort occur all of the time.

There are times when precise communication is imperative; when a miscommunication can be detrimental. At these times, it becomes important to insure that the message was transmitted clearly and concisely. To assure this, it is useful to have a set of specific tools to insure more precise communication. These techniques, associated with effective questioning, are very important to any individual, but they are particularly important to you, the branch manager.

The ability to effectively communicate presupposes that we have a relatively good understanding of what the other person is trying to say. Yet, many studies on communication have suggested that approximately 90% of all communication problems occur because we *assume* that the other person actually knows what we are talking about.

Some of the common assumptions in everyday language may come back to haunt us. That's the bad news. The good news is that this chapter will provide a number of very effective tools to deal with this very common problem. You'll be able to employ these techniques with your FCs, customers, friends, and family. The techniques are universal in their application and are derived from the cutting edge in psychology. These techniques are not something that you would normally use in day-to-day conversations. Their purpose is to both impart and receive specific and exact information when it is necessary to clarify what is being said. It is important to know both *how* and *what* to clarify.

There are certain language patterns that are so pervasive that we fail to hear them because they are so common. Becoming aware of them is the first step toward more effective communication. One of them is to make the assumption that the words we use mean the same thing to our listener as they do to us, and vice versa.

Service is one of the most overused words in business. "I want good service," says the customer. The salesperson, of course, replies, "I'll give you great service." The customer may expect the salesperson to return his calls within five minutes. The salesperson may think that one hour is exemplary. The customer service department may be happy, given their volume, with a one-day turnaround. Each person could literally do his absolute best and be thoroughly proud of how well he had done, while the other two parties in the transaction end up being totally dissatisfied. Unless the salesperson knows what the client wants, he can't win. Unless the salesperson knows what the customer service department can deliver, neither he nor the client can win. Little things like this can ruin a relationship.

Service is one of those vague words that has a different meaning for each person who utters it. Other words that are equally vague are: comfortable, satisfaction, safety, and risk.

The typical response to the comment, "I feel satisfied" is, "I know what you mean." That's impossible! The other person can only have a vague idea of what is meant because the word *satisfied* represents an internal state. It is interesting to realize that many people automatically assume that you have the same meaning, or connotation, for words that they do.

It's important to understand the difference between a word's denotations (dictionary definition) and its connotations (the emotional meaning we each assign to it). For example, the word *family* has the same denotation for everyone. The dictionary defines *family* as, "A social unit consisting of parents and the children that they rear" or "a group of people related by ancestry or marriage." However, the *meaning* of the word *family* may vary widely. It could encompass:

- A warm, nurturing environment in which one was raised;
- a place where an alcoholic father physically or sexually abused one member;
- a place that had no father (or no mother); or
- an idealized concept in the mind of one who was raised without a family.

Obviously, anyone using the word *family* in an effort to communicate something, might find himself obtaining a very unexpected response, depending upon the experience of the listener. Hence, skills that enable you to make sure that you correctly hear and understand what someone is saying can be very important. This chapter was started with an interviewer and an applicant both using the same words with entirely different meanings and interpretations. Although it was quite exaggerated, situations of this sort do occur.

The basic problem results from the fact that people naturally delete, distort, or even over-generalize information. While this is rather immaterial most of the time, there are numerous occasions when failure to get complete and accurate information can result in serious problems.

You'll undoubtedly find that you already employ many of the techniques listed here. Many of them are based upon natural language patterns that are only called into play in relatively rare instances. In many ways, the questioning techniques that you are about to learn are really a sophisticated way of saying "Huh?" These techniques will help you:

184

- Resolve organizational problems more quickly;
- deal with interpersonal conflict;
- understand and deal with your employees' personal problems;
- clear up confusion (muddied thinking);
- deal with distraught FCs or clients (when combined with other techniques not yet introduced);
- clarify legal issues; and
- conduct effective interviews.

As mentioned earlier, people often delete, distort, or overgeneralize information in their head. This is true of everyone and occurs on an unconscious level. Rather than go through lengthy psychological proofs, let's just say that it is a common problem that you will face on a regular basis. For instance, if a customer service representative told you: "They told me that I had better get it resolved to their satisfaction." Your response might be, "Huh?" After your initial reaction you would still have to determine:

- Who *they* are;
- what *it* is that needs to be resolved;
- what needs to happen for them to be *satisfied*; and
- the meaning behind the implied threat, "...better get it resolved...".

In this example the customer service representative deleted information that was needed for you to understand what was really going on. He needs to provide you with more explicit information on the meaning of some of the key words.

We know, intuitively, that *satisfaction* for one person is not necessarily *satisfaction* for another. One person may merely desire an apology, while another may need specific operational action(s) to be taken, while still others may require some combination of both, plus other things, to occur. Given the specific example, we also know that the specific criteria to satisfy this customer would be important. After all, what a customer wants may or may not be possible (or even reasonable). However, until the issue is addressed, we have an angry customer on our hands who has implied an undesirable next step. The nature of that next step has yet to be determined.

When taking the same concept and applying it to coaching, counseling, and performance issues, we find that similar situations arise when employees say that they have *motivation* or need more job *satisfaction*. Each person using the word means something different. As we explored motivational issues earlier in the book, we already discussed the need to refine our understanding of what motivates our employees.

One Cause of Burnout

Have you ever seen people burn themselves out? Work so hard that they can't see straight, or become inefficient and ineffective? Those people are *driven* by some internal motivation that is literally getting in their way. Wouldn't it be great if we were able to install some of that internal drive in other employees who just sit around doing nothing?

"I *have to* get this done by tomorrow." "If this doesn't get done, there will be trouble." "We need to do this." These are statements which represent a psychological imperative that is driving the behavior or thought. It has created a need that *must, ought to,* or *should* be fulfilled. The consequences of not performing the action are intimidating. But, are they really?

So, what? What's the problem?

Often, people give something a significantly higher priority than it actually deserves. They *have to* do something, even if it's to the detriment of something else. They *must*, for instance, work on a Mr. B's account, even though the phone is ringing and a dozen other clients are not being serviced. At these times, such an individual becomes very narrow-minded and very focused. Sometimes this is good, but sometimes it isn't.

The situation just described would drive most office managers crazy wondering what is wrong with this individual's priorities. We might ask her what she is doing and why. Then, depending upon the answer (there may be contingencies that we are unaware of), we might ask her the equivalent of, "What would happen if you didn't do that right now?" Usually, nothing. This can enable the employee to mentally discover that failure to work on Mr. B's account *at that moment* will have few, if any, consequences. Of course, afterward we may then wish to help her reprioritize her duties.

Consider some of your FCs who spend all of their time organizing and preparing for production. Other FCs spend a substantial amount of time on customer service problems (paying credit balances, checking on operational issues, etc.). While these things need to get done, it becomes obvious that some people use them to procrastinate. At those times, it may be necessary to confront them and bring their lack of prioritizing into the forefront. However, you will find that many of these people honestly believe they are doing what is required. They may not have the same understanding that you do. You could handle them by asking questions and leading them through the logical consequences of doing or not doing certain things. Of course, some managers prefer to just yell or tell. Fortunately, we already know that motivation through intimidation is counter-productive in the long run. It usually results in resentments and other behaviors that become equally defeating.

If an employee comes to you with a problem, or if you are involved in any sort of difficulty, you'll find that a good part of the problem is muddied thinking. "They can't see the forest because of the trees" is a common situation. The fact is, that it is hard for anyone to be objective when he is too close to a problem. However, this lack of objectivity is reflected in people's communication and often leads to misunderstandings and destructive feelings. Hence, people get into arguments and get off track.

When a person has a problem, we must assume that it is real, at least to them. Almost by definition, if people go for help, their problem is real to them. Have you ever gone to your friend, spouse, or boss and inquired, "What did you do that for?" Once they gave you the answer, you may not have agreed, but you were probably at least satisfied. However, before they gave you their answer, important information was missing; the rationale for their behavior. The missing or deleted information was necessary for you to feel comfortable and, if not provided, can remain in your mind like an unresolved question. That's true for others as well. They also have issues, conflicts, problems, confusions, and frustrations which result from missing information or muddied thinking.

Each questioning category that follows is presented so that you can easily recognize it and use it with others. You can also teach it to your employees to reduce or avoid the normal, day-to-day miscommunications and conflicts. The smooth functioning of your office is dependent upon people doing their jobs in active cooperation with each other. Office conflicts may be very common, but they are easy to avoid if you have the right tools available. The following sections discuss a few of those tools.

Vague/Fuzzy/Undefined, yet Seemingly Meaningful Words

An example of these kinds of words and the confusion that they can cause was introduced in the beginning of the chapter. As a rule of thumb, whenever you are expected to do something, that is, perform some action to satisfy another person, you need to clarify exactly what they expect. A customer who says, "I want you to give me good service," is an example of a statement that would need clarification for reasons that were previously provided.

If you told your employees, "Our job is to provide good service to the client, to answer the phone in a courteous way, and provide a timely response," the vast majority of your personnel would nod their heads in total agreement, without having any specific understanding of what you mean by the word *service, timely,* and possibly *courteous.* Language has certain conventions which are theoretically understood. Yet, one person may think that service means providing what is asked for, while another person may understand it to mean going the extra step and anticipating client needs. Timely can mean anything from five minutes to five weeks. What is the response time that you require, in what context, and with what exceptions? Any misunderstanding or different interpretation could cause a problem for someone. Finally, try to define courteous.

Words that are subject to individual interpretation will often be interpreted in as many ways as there are individuals doing the interpretations. (This should be added to the collection of *Murphy's Law* sayings.)

Overcoming Mind Reading and Assumptions

At the beginning of the chapter we discussed the word *assumption* and its inherent dangers. Here are three more examples of assumptions that people sometimes make.

188

- "The other people don't want me to work with them."
- "My boss/co-worker/friend/whoever is mad at me."
- "I thought that was what you would have wanted."

Any of the above statements requires some actual verification before it can be accepted as fact. The most common questions to accomplish this are either, "How do/did you know?" or, "Have you asked that person?" We need hard, objective evidence to support the above-mentioned assumptions.

A very common problem associated with mind reading is the hurt feelings that regularly occur when someone says the equivalent of "She hurt my feelings" or, "He should have known better." Unfortunately, because of a variety of reasons, some people are very easily insulted. At the same time, most of the hurts that people experience in life are the result of something that occurs in their own minds. What they've chosen to feel hurt about didn't happen with the intention that was taken.

We often give the following advice: Since people very rarely insult someone intentionally, when you feel that you have been insulted, either ignore it, pretend that you heard a compliment, or ask them what they meant by the comment.

If you ignore it, chances are it will go away. If they actually meant it as an insult, he or she will try again. At the second occurrence, question them as to their intention. If you pretend that you heard it as a compliment, it will drive them crazy. If it were meant to be a neutral statement, then they will not correct you. If they meant it as an insult, they will try again. In both cases, assume that the statement was neutral in intent.

If you must question them, allow for the possibility that a miscommunication has occurred by saying something like, "I heard that last statement as potentially insulting. Was it your intention to insult me?" Or, "Is there something that I don't know? Your statement sounded like an insult." Again, the chances are that nothing was meant by it and now the individual will probably apologize and clarify what was actually meant. If, however, they indicate that it was an insult, then you can find out why and work to resolve any conflict that may exist. Of course, you should remember that they too may have misheard or misinterpreted something that they thought you said.

Often, it is not *what* was said, but *how* it was said. The inadvertent use of a poor tonality or inflection can turn a regular statement into an insulting one. We'll provide some examples of this in a subsequent exercise.

As a manager, as a professional communicator, you have it within your ability to control potentially explosive situations. The other person probably doesn't have the knowledge or the ability to do it. We have found that 99% of all such issues are immediately and easily resolved by clarifying and resolving potential misunderstandings before they escalate beyond repair.

All too often, people spend days or weeks fretting about some real or imagined insult. In our opinion, life is too short to waste that much time, effort, and energy on such trivial matters. It's easier said than done, but the effort you spend in educating your people about this approach can pay substantial dividends in improved employee relations.

Overgeneralization

"*Every* time I call, they give me a hard time. *Nobody* at the office *ever* lifts a hand to help me." These exaggerations seem true to the person who said them at the moment. When people are frustrated, it *does* seem like absolutely nothing is going right or will ever go right. All they can do is focus on the problem at hand. In addition, because of the very narrow focus and the feelings associated with the problem, they don't, and perhaps cannot, remember what normally happens.

If someone is giving you such a complaint, the easiest way to break the thought is by searching for the exception to their mental rule. For example, you could respond with either of these statements: "Do you mean that EVERY single time, without exception, they give you a difficult time?" or, "Not one single person in the entire office ever helped you out or gave you a hand?" If the person can come up with *even one* exception, the discussion will take on an entirely different tone. Yet, until you bring it to their attention with your question, they actually cannot see that they are involved in the exception rather than the rule. Of course, it could be true that, for whatever reason, this person's co-workers do not help him. If this is the situation, then you have a different problem to deal with. Normally though, because of your question, their hard-line statement no longer has its previous power over their feelings. More importantly, one or more of these questions will also usually lead the person into a mental state more conducive to logical discussion. (*Note:* Another technique, called *Fogging,* is specifically designed to neutralize anger very quickly and is presented in a separate chapter.)

Unraveling Beliefs that People Use to Rule Their Lives

Throughout our lives, we hear short statements that provide some truth or rule of thumb to live by. These adages serve the valid purpose of teaching children and providing a clear, concise statement which makes a particular point. "A penny saved is a penny earned," addresses thrift. "Never talk to strangers," and, "Don't speak unless spoken to," are sayings that would be decidedly disadvantageous to salespeople. Once one of these *statements of authority* is accepted by us as children, it can take on the power of a major belief that controls our behavior and feelings into adulthood.

Without involving ourselves with the therapeutic questions associated with this area, we will assume that you have already hired people who are not mentally programmed with the above statements of authority/beliefs which may rule their lives. Rather, let's concentrate on rules that are equivalent to adages that do have an effect on an office.

These are the unstated rules of the office which govern procedures and, often, office behavior. Sort of the *This Is the Way that it's Done* attitude. New ways are not searched for because the old ways are so entrenched. You know this is the situation when you hear definitive statements like, "This *is* how it is done!" or, "They say that. . . ." Who are *they* you might ask.

We know of one situation when a huge account would have been lost because a clerk refused to entertain the possibility that there might be an exception to the rule, and he basically set his heels in and refused to budge. Sometimes this is good, but in this situation it was in direct conflict with the manager's wishes. The clerk's bureaucratic attitude was not appreciated. In trying to determine why the clerk had been so rigid, the manager later found out that another clerk had lost his job for granting a similar request. The only thing that our clerk did not understand was that the clerk who lost his job did something on his own authority and in substantially different circumstances than was currently the case. However, the impact of someone getting fired instilled the equivalent of a phobic response in this one employee.

Whenever you hear someone say, "*They* say...", find out who's behind *they*. Whenever you hear a definitive statement about how something *should* be done, find out who issued the dictate. Usually, no one really knows.

Another way that these imperatives show up is through the use of statements that contain any of the following words or their equivalents: *should, ought to, must,* and *need to.* You will often see these words used when people are close to *burning out,* or when they are not performing according to expectations.

When burning out, most people have too many *shoulds* in their lives: They should cold call; they should be calling their clients; and, they should be getting more product knowledge. There can also be another dozen shoulds competing for equal attention. Such people literally pull themselves apart with all of the shoulds that they think they ought to be able to accomplish simultaneously. Unrealistic expectations? Absolutely! Something that you may have to deal with? Absolutely! These things are often outside the individual's conscious awareness.

Employees who are not performing to expectations may be burning out, but they may also be involved in some internal conflict. For example: We know of many people in the financial services industry who want to do a good job and put in the necessary hours to bring in the production, but they also want to spend time with their families, enjoy themselves, and exercise. Both parts of their lives are demanding attention, causing the conflict we discussed.

Throughout our lives we have been taught that we should be able to balance all the aspects of our lives. We've also been taught that we have an obligation to our job/career, our family, our religion, our country, and all of the other things that we ought to be doing to demonstrate that we are successful and otherwise good people.

You might have to address this issue during coaching and counseling sessions with employees. You may also have to be the one to raise the issue because it is often outside of their awareness. Once you've suggested to them that they *list all of their shoulds,* they can then *prioritize them* (sometimes with your help). Then they can negotiate with themselves to *sort out* which ones really need attention and which ones can be temporarily or permanently postponed or eliminated. After all, a person can only do so much.

One of the questions that you or they need to ask is, "Who or what gave you the rule that you should do such-and-such?" More often than not, they won't be able to give you an answer. Yet, for years they may have been running their lives by these unconscious rules.

It is important to realize that you are *not* giving psychiatric counseling. Leave that for a trained professional. You are, however, asking a few key questions that will often help people to get out of their own way. These internal imperatives and internal conflicts are often the causes of personal conflict and poor performance.

A final commentary regarding the *shoulds:* These beliefs create a whole series of expectations that often determine how we react to the world in general and other people in particular. Virtually every personal conflict is based upon some should that the other person has violated. One key question to always ask yourself and teach others to ask is, "What do you/I *expect?*" **We get angry, upset, distressed, or anything else only when our expectations are NOT met.** However, most of us have several expectations which are totally unreasonable. Once this is brought to light, they become easier to handle.

Breaking Down Associations

"*Associations*" are very important when working on motivational issues and job satisfaction. To a large degree, they are more fully dealt with in the chapters devoted to motivation because, in the sense that we will employ them here, they establish a decided correlation between certain actions and meanings. An often-used example in therapy would be, "If he loved me, he would give me flowers." Somehow, for that individual, flowers equal love. Her partner or spouse could do all of the other things that *other people* would equate with love, but she would need flowers. Unless she tells him, or he magically figures it out, he's basically caught between a rock and a hard place. Ironically, she *expects* him to know that she equates flowers with love.

It is much the same in business. Some people need a public pat on the back, while a private verbal recognition may be enough for others. The chances are that these psychological rewards would be powerful persuaders or motivators for a variety of people in your office. The question is: "What motivates an individual?" The answer often depends largely on what form of reward an individual associates with personal success. As we discussed in the various chapters dealing with psychological profiling and personal motivations, if you know what to search for it becomes quite easy to pick and choose your reward system so that it matches the needs of the individual and motivates him toward further accomplishment. Despite your best intentions, however, if you randomly select a reward and it fails to match the individual's association, you will not have motivated him and could be thought of as not caring.

Summary

The techniques we've presented here try to point out the importance of saying "Huh" more often than you may be used to; of course, we've also pointed out more sophisticated ways of saying "Huh." If you follow this method, you'll find that problems become more easily resolved and that you know your people more completely. You'll become more effective in your job and your employees will work harder and with more satisfaction (assuming that you apply some of the motivational techniques presented in other chapters).

Chapter 21

Dealing with Angry People

All of us have dealt with angry or upset people. Regardless of the cause of their emotional state, it was probably very difficult to deal with them effectively. How do you calm down an angry and upset person so that he will listen to reason, and work with you to solve whatever problems is bothering him? The purpose of this chapter is to provide a series of steps that can be used when dealing with angry individuals.

Of course, the first thing to remember is that you cannot control the situation unless you are in control of yourself. Unfortunately, this is often easier said than done, because almost everyone becomes a little defensive when approached by someone who is angry or aggressive. That's because we tend to take personally those feelings that are directed at us. However, as a branch manager, you are a professional; one who always does your best for your customers, your employees and your superiors. As a result, regardless of the underlying problem, *you* have no need to take it personally or to become defensive. By remaining in control of yourself, you will easily be able to gain control of the situation. To do this, follow the steps outlined below.

Establish Rapport

Regardless of the relationship or the nature of the interaction in which you are involved, *always* establish rapport before taking any other action. Of course, this does not mean that you should respond symmetrically, by getting angry in return. (*Note:* Remember, symmetrical interactions are those in which both parties respond in the same way; both friendly, both hostile, etc.) All that results in is a round of escalating anger that may lead to a breakdown in the relationship. (See Chapters 14 and 15.)

In the case of angry individuals, establishing rapport consists of matching their energy level and their speed and intensity of speech. Once you have matched them and established rapport, begin to lead them into a calmer state using the *leading technique* (presented in Chapter 14), or by using the highly specialized questioning process about to be introduced.

Speak Their Language

Remember, most arguments and hurt feelings are the result of simple misunderstandings. This occasionally results when two people speak to each other using two different predicate (sensory-oriented) systems. Make sure that you match their system. If they are visual, use visual terms with them. If they are auditory, use auditory terms, and so on. (See Chapter 16).

Questioning

Misunderstandings and angry/hurt feelings also occur because of unmet expectations. Most of us simply assume that everyone else assigns the same meanings to words and actions that we do. This may be because the circle of family and friends with whom we grew up with did. However, we rarely work with the same people into adulthood. As a result, the people we meet as adults often have different meanings for words and different behavior expectations.

When you become involved with angry or hurt individuals, it is important to discover both the exact cause of their current state and the specific circumstances necessary to alleviate it. Without this information, it is not only difficult to keep them calm, it will be impossible to avoid a repetition.

In Chapter 24, we discuss a program of questioning that will enable you to elicit the specific information that you desire by focusing on vague expectations, deletions, etc. Once you've established rapport, begin to question them, using the meta model questioning program, even before they have become completely calm. We'll discuss clarifying techniques in more detail after the next subsection.

Break the Pattern

Angry disagreements almost always follow a recognizable pattern of symmetrical (similar responses) or complimentary (opposite responses) interaction. One individual, in a Dictator style, approaches the other in a hostile, aggressive manner. At that point, the recipient of all that hostility and aggression responds either complimentarily (submits and tries to withdraw), or symmetrically (with anger and aggression of his own). If you have ever watched such a situation develop, you already know that neither response works because both lead to a trap.

If you respond to all angry aggression by giving in, you will establish a habitual complimentary pattern of relating that can be very hard to break. At that point, both you and the other person know that all he need do is become angry or aggressive and you will submit to his desires. This is an unhealthy win-lose situation that is very much how the classic school yard bully accomplishes his ends. Once he has established his dominant position, it is almost never challenged. This is bad enough when dealing with childhood bullies, but it is intolerable when dealing with customers, employees or peers, or superiors.

However, if you always respond symmetrically, with your own hostility and aggression, you establish a power struggle that must continue until one of you submits, creating another win-lose situation. It is important to recognize that **no one ever wins a power struggle**, or any other win-lose situation. If you (the manager) win, you risk losing a customer, a good employee, or a future law suit, depending upon the nature of the struggle. In every case, you lose the relationship. If that relationship is important to you, you may find out too late that your victory cost more than it was worth.

Use your rapport, communications, and questioning skills to maintain a flexible, parallel style of relating that disarms your opponents without increasing either your hostility or theirs. As you demonstrate your genuine interest in them and their concerns, it will become increasingly difficult for them to maintain their anger.

The Dictator

As we mentioned above, regardless of an individual's normal mode of relating, when he becomes hostile and aggressive he is entering the realm of the *Dictator*. Remember the needs of the Dictator when dealing with him:

- The need to be *special*. Regardless of how thoughtful we may normally be of others, when we are angry or hurt our only interest becomes the meeting of *our* own needs. Put other agendas aside and be certain that you give them your undivided attention.

- The need to be *better than others*. Another variant of being special, this need is manifest in hostile language, sarcasm, and insulting others. When we are angry or hurt, we become defensive, and may manifest that defensiveness by verbally striking out at others. Avoid placating or responding in a hostile manner. These responses will only result in your falling into the traps discussed previously. Use the *CLAPping technique* discussed in the next main subsection.

- The covert *need for security*. Most people are actually a little threatened by their own hostility and aggressiveness and secretly wish that someone would take control of the situation before it escalates beyond repair. By remaining in control of the situation and your own feelings, you fulfill that need.

- As mentioned above, most people tend to become angry when their *reasonable* expectations aren't met. As a result, their trust is violated. As you establish rapport and demonstrate a sincere desire to understand their needs and requirements, you will also help to re-establish that trust. By using the specialized questioning techniques of the meta model, in combination with CLAPping, you will be able to determine the specific criteria that must be fulfilled in order to complete that process.

198

Why So Hot?

As you question an angry individual regarding the causes of his anger and the nature of the remedy that he requires, you will also obtain information regarding his motivational criteria. That is, what specific factors make him angry, and what specific factors will remove that anger. We've already mentioned this several times and it may appear that we are only repeating ourselves. However, the concept of what causes anger and what is necessary to remove it must be looked at from several perspectives.

When we look at effectively selling something to a customer, we examine every aspect of the way the customer thinks, feels, and makes decisions so that we can match him completely. Hence, we look at:

- His psychological profile/emotional needs;
- his sensory orientation (i.e., visual, auditory, or kinesthetic); and,
- his buying motivational criteria.

When you begin to work with an angry individual, it is just as important to obtain the same information about him if you are to successfully *sell* him on the concept of calming down and working with you. Hence, the apparent redundancy of criteria-type questions.

Examples of questions that you might ask an angry individual are provided below. However, use the CLAPping technique first in order to validate your understanding of the individual and his anger. Also, remember that validating someone's anger, or even his right to be angry, is not the same as agreeing with his anger regarding the cause.

- "Well, I can see you're upset. Tell me what will provide what you need."
- "It's obvious you really mean that. In your opinion, how should it have been done differently?"
- "If I understand you correctly, you feel that you've been treated unfairly. Is that right?" (response) "I think I understand. What specific things will improve the situation?"

Each of these questions is designed to help you to maintain control of the situation while eliciting the criteria necessary to eliminate the other's anger.

CLAPping:

To overcome someone's anger and aggression, or even his resistance to a desired action, there are four easy steps which should be followed before even attempting to respond to the individual's position. After these four steps have been followed, you can respond to his concern and, if appropriate, return to your own agenda. They are as follows:

1. C (clarify),

2. L (legitimize),

3. A (acknowledge), and

4. P (probe).

Clarify

Before attempting to overcome someone's anger or negative attitude it is important to be sure that you are dealing with the real source of his concern. It is easy to begin to respond to what we think he wants without checking first to see if we are on track. However, doing this can complicate your efforts to deal with his resistance by trying to deal with something other than the real problem. This might happen in either of two ways:

- First, sometimes an individual will act angrily or aggressively because he doesn't understand something that is being done which affects him. Often this is the result of a breakdown in communication. He may even have difficult in explaining exactly what is upsetting him.

  In such cases, it is important for you to patiently help him to explore the cause of his discomfort until he can identify it and discuss it. Attempting to overcome the anger and resistance without doing so first will inevitably result in resentment on his part. **Remember to match intensity and rate of speech.** The questions will lead the individual from an emotionally charged state to an intellectual state.

- Second, sometimes the cause of the anger first shared by the individual is not the real reason for his anger (e.g., a customer may say that he is upset with his FC for calling only when he has something to sell, when in reality he may be too embarrassed to admit that he's really angry because he feels that his FC doesn't take him seriously).

For this reason, it is very important to persist in your efforts to *clarify* and not to quit until *all* of the causes of the individual's anger and resistance have been uncovered and dealt with. What follows is a sample of a *clarifying* discussion between a manager (you) and a client.

Client: I'm not sure that yours is the right firm for me. My FC seems to call only when he has something he wants me to buy, and then he's very high pressure. The next thing I know, I've bought something I don't really want and I have to pay a large commission on top.

You: (PROBING) Are there any other areas of concern for you?

Client: Not really. I'm just tired of constantly being hounded to buy something.

You: (CLARIFYING) So, your primary concern is that you feel constantly pressured to buy things you don't really want, and then end up paying a high commission to do it. Is that right?

Client: Sure.

You: Are there any other areas of concern for you? Anything else that has upset you?

Client: No. That's it.

Simply put, you are asking, "Are there any other areas of concern for you, Mr. Customer?" However, you will still wish to further clarify the specifics of what he *wants* to make him more comfortable. Use our questioning techniques here.

Once you have *clarified* the nature and cause of his anger and resistance, you must communicate to him that you both *acknowledge* and understand his concern, and that you also accept it as *legitimate* (an individual's feelings and concerns are *always* legitimate, even when they are unfounded). **Remember: Failure to legitimize someone's anger or concern is the same as telling him that you don't consider it (or him) to be very important.**

Legitimize and Acknowledge

When someone is angry with us, it is frequently because he has concerns, or *anxieties* that we haven't relieved. Unfortunately, before we can respond to his feelings, we must successfully communicate to him that we understand them and that it is all right for him to be angry or anxious (i.e., we are not threatened by his feelings). We'll continue our previous example:

You: (LEGITIMIZE and ACKNOWLEDGE) I can certainly understand why you might feel angry if you really believe that we are only interested in making commissions off you. I think *anyone* would be upset if they *had* felt that way. (Continue to CLARIFY) So, Bill (the FC) has *never* called you except to ask you to buy something? (PROBE) Not even once?

Note: This does not mean that you agree with him, only that you acknowledge and understand his concern and legitimize it. It is here that many people try to *tell* an individual that they understand without first demonstrating their understanding. In so doing, they appear defensive and will certainly cause the client to become defensive. Always remember that as a professional, you will *never* need to be defensive because you will *always* do the best possible job for your customers, employees, and superiors. Hence, if one is upset, it won't be because of your performance. Please also note the use of the past tense "*had*" in the sentence, "I think anyone would be upset if they *had* felt that way." By using the past tense, you subtly imply that the concern existed in the past but does not exist *now*.

Client: Well, maybe not never. But almost never. And the commissions are way too high. The no-frills brokers charge only about half of what you do.

You: (CLARIFY) It sounds as though you feel that it's not fair to have to pay twice as much commission to us as to a no-frills broker for the same trade. (PROBE) Is that basically correct?

Client: That's right.

You: (Further CLARIFY) It must have been very frustrating, Mr. Jones. If we could resolve those two problems, would everything else be all right? (PROBE) Or are there other concerns?

Client: No. That's it.

Probe

Having communicated your understanding and acceptance of the individual's concern, you must *probe* to determine if you have been accurate in your assessment. You've noted that we probed after every clarifying, legitimizing, and acknowledging remark in the preceding examples. Even if you were incorrect, you will have gained in two areas:

- First, you will have demonstrated your interest to him.
- Second, you will know that you are on the wrong track and will be able to go back and try again until you are correct. This prevents wasting time and risking your relationship with the individual by becoming frustrated over trying to solve the wrong problem. The worst that can happen is that he will appreciate your efforts to understand him and he will try again.
- However, if you are correct in your assessment of the problem, you not only improve your level of rapport with him, you also lower his resistance and now know that you and he are on the right track in terms of meeting his needs. Even if the nature of the problem is such that your agenda is not completed, you have completed the conversation with an improved client/manager relationship.

Paraphrasing

Perhaps the easiest way to CLAP is through the use of *paraphrasing*. When the someone becomes angry or brings up a concern, paraphrase that concern back to him in your own words and probe to see if you are correct (this is effectively the same thing as using a *summary probe*). In so doing, you simultaneously *clarify* the nature of his concern, *acknowledge* and *legitimize* it, and demonstrate your understanding, or at least your desire to understand, and verify the correctness of your understanding.

Client: The interest from my CD hasn't been credited to my account yet and I've been waiting six weeks for my new check books. I tell you, I'm not going to put up with it any longer!

You: Let me make sure I've got this right, Mrs. Jones. The interest from your CD is overdue and you still haven't received your new checkbooks, after six weeks. Is that right?

Once you have demonstrated your understanding to the individual, it is safe to tell him that you understand and then respond to his concern.

Responding

Having successfully determined the cause of the individual's anger or the nature of his complaint, you must now respond to it. It should be remembered that overly long answers tend to be given by individuals who are nervous and unsure of themselves, so use the *KISS* principle—Keep It Short and Sweet. If you appear nervous or defensive to him, he may interpret that as evasiveness or weakness and become even angrier. This can quickly undermine the rapport you have just built through CLAPping.

You can always expand upon an answer, but it is very hard to take back information that may end up confusing your listener or increasing his discomfort.

> Remember the case of the little boy who asked his mother where he came from. His mother became acutely embarrassed and provided a detailed answer that included a complete description of how babies are conceived and born. The boy looked increasingly confused throughout the discussion and his mother became increasingly uncomfortable as her "lecture" progressed. Finally, when it was over and she "probed" to see if he were satisfied, he said, "Gee, Mom, that's wild! Johnny comes from Chicago."

Also, when someone is angry or negative, you must remain positive. Turn potential frustrations into successes by *reframing* what he has said into something else you can use.

Client: I don't know about this, Bill. The economist, on TV, says that the market looks very weak right now.

You: It sounds like you're worried that he might be right. Is that it?

Client: Yeah.

You: I can understand that. I can't tell you what a pleasure it is to finally have a client who is interested enough in his investments to really look into the market and the economy. Bob, you know that our analysts have been highly regarded on Wall Street for years. Would you like me to send you some information on what they think that the market will be doing over the next six months?

Client: Sure.

You: Good. I'll do that today. Then, after you've had a chance to look over what the various experts say, we'll chat again. If you're still uncomfortable with the market, we'll look for alternatives. How does that sound?

Probe Again

Once you have dealt with the client's objections, it is important to probe again to determine, first, if he has *understood* and *accepted* your response and, second, if he has any further questions or concerns. Once this has been accomplished, you may return to your agenda and the remainder of your presentation if you feel that it is still appropriate.

Client: Brokers have gotten very bad press coverage lately. How do I know that I can trust your firm? *(Concern)*

You: It sounds as though you are worried about how honest we'll be. Is that right? *(CLAP with summary probe)*

Client: Well, yes. *(Response)*

You: I can understand that. The press has raised doubts about the integrity of the securities industry in the minds of many people. I guess it's a little like the bad press doctors get sometimes. A very small number cheat. But that doesn't make all, or even most, doctors dishonest. It's the same with us. Mrs. Jones, what would you need to feel comfortable working with us? *(Response)* *(Probe to elicit criteria)*

Client: I like to see who's handling my money, and what kind of place it is. I can usually tell by someone's face if he's honest. *(Response)*

You: It sounds like you'd like to come into the office to meet us and see how we work. If that right? *(Probe)*

Client: Yes.

You:	That sounds like a great idea. I always enjoy meeting our clients face-to-face, and this will give us an opportunity to discuss your needs. I can introduce you to your FC at the same time. Do you have any other concerns or questions?	*(Response)* *(Probe)*
Client:	Not right now.	
You:	That's fine. If you think of any more, you can bring them up when we meet.	

Summary

As a professional who always does your best for your customers, employees, and superiors, you need never become defensive in the face of someone's anger. Use the techniques discussed in Chapters 20 and 21 on creating a state of excellence in order to practice these effective ways of dealing with angry people. Then, anchor this new state to situations in which you commonly face in others.

Chapter 22

Counseling Employees About Performance Issues

It is a rare employee who consistently rates *Far Exceeded Expectations* on his or her performance review. It is rarer still for any company to have more than 20% of their employees rated so favorably. This is normally true for line and staff positions, from laborers to members of upper management. What happened to the other 80%?

Numerous studies on employee performance have concluded that most employees can retain their job by performing at 20%–30% of their individual capabilities and capacities. They further concluded that people can consistently perform at 80%–90% of capacity if motivated to do so. The gray area between 30% and 80% can be positively affected by proper motivation.

Most courses on, and approaches, to this concern have dealt with managers appropriately motivating their subordinates (of course this assumes that managers are already self-motivated and have their own acts together!). However, have you, or anyone you know, ever had a day in which everything went absolutely right? You know, where you were great, motivated, on target? Alternatively, has anyone you know ever had a day in which they just didn't get things done right? Most of us have these days. However, for most of us, they pass rather quickly and we return to our normal productive state. For others, the poor days can stretch into weeks or months (longer term symptomatic behavior is characterized by different terms—*burn out, depression, demotivation, attitude problems,* etc.).

Besides liking one mental state and disliking the other, what are the thinking differences between when you get into the good state or the other? The answer isn't in the conscious awareness. If it were, we would always have good days. Yet, by definition, there is a difference.

In most organizations, the majority of the people perform at the lower end of the productivity spectrum. Within these organizations there are usually also a few key personnel who are not quite maximizing their contributions to the firm. How much productivity, how many ideas, how much money is lost because of these partial contributors? The amount is incalculable. Yet, which organization can afford to allow this to occur?

Before discussing how to deal with substandard performance, it might be useful to explore its causes. When you think about it, failure to perform according to expectations can only be the result of a combination of any of three factors: First, does the individual really *want to* perform; second, does he know *how to;* and, third, does he have the *change to?* (See Chapter 17.)

Want To

An individual usually has conscious choice in deciding whether she wants to do a particular thing. Yet, we all know of the situation where a person *wants* to do what's expected, but something stops her from doing it. Assuming that there are no environmental factors (outside influences actually preventing the action), that something comes from the unconscious mind. This may take the form of some fear, a competing desire, a belief, and so forth. For whatever reason, a conflict is present.

Therefore, even if people want to perform actions to keep their job performance at peak levels, they might not be able to because of the internal conflict. The conflict might take the form of "damned if I do; damned if I don't." "If I work harder I'll accomplish more, but if I do work harder I may be given more responsibilities and fail at those." Logical analysis is great—sometimes. But, logic doesn't seem to work when an emotional conflict is present.

Often, an individual's performance problem is simply a matter of motivation. If we, as managers, know how to motivate someone effectively, they will "want to" perform most tasks satisfactorily. Where motivation is the case, use the skills that you have already developed in communications, psychological profiling and motivation to move them in the desired direction. If you uncover a concern that good performance will result in ever increasing demands, or eventual "failure," deal with it. However, if it appears that a deeper conflict is present, you may wish to consider other options.

How To

Sometimes, the individual in question really wants to do a good job. However, if she is missing certain background information she may not be able to do it even though she would like to. Usually, a book, a training course, observing others, asking questions etc., will resolve this situation. That's how most people learn.

Unfortunately, sometimes the person is too embarrassed to ask or to search for information that cannot be obtained in a book. (Note: this may be similar to an internal conflict which needs resolution.) Also, sometimes the information is just not available from standard sources; such as, precisely how to communicate effectively with someone else or how to become creative.

When you first hired this individual, did you adequately explain your expectations and how she would be evaluated? Was the training she received adequate for the demands of her current task? Often, job descriptions change and expand, and the initial training becomes inadequate for the new requirements.

Finally, you already know that failure to match someone's thinking process (e.g., their sensory orientation) can result in confusion, rather than the desired understanding. When she was oriented and trained, were explanations provided in a "language" that she could relate to and understand? Were adequate checks made of her understanding? If not, the substandard performance of your employee may be your fault, not hers.

Chance To

If environmental factors actually prevent the person from doing the job (e.g., paperwork from another department arriving too late, parts delivered late, covert sabotage, etc.) then those environmental factors must be identified and remedied. If they cannot be remedied, then job responsibilities should be changed to allow for those factors.

Now What?

Once a so-called subaverage performer is identified, there are only a limited number of possible actions. They are:

- Transferring the individual.
- Demoting the employee.
- Modifying (redefining) his job responsibilities.
- Terminating and replacing the individual.
- Providing additional training and hope for the best.
- Coaching and counseling him.

With the exception of the last two alternatives, such actions necessitate the replacement of that person with someone who is more qualified. This replacement requires the expenditure of additional time and money until he proves himself and fully assumes his new responsibilities. The last two choices will **potentially** work. However, a certain amount of time must be allowed for the training or counseling to take effect. During the transition period, the subperforming individual is still not making a full contribution. If the individual responds positively, great! If not, you're back to the original four choices. Before we examine ways of counseling employees who give mediocre performances, let's briefly discuss each choice more fully.

210

Transferring the Individual

This is frequently a viable solution because people are often promoted to their level of incompetence (the *Peter Principle*). The most common example seems to be the star salesperson who is promoted to manager, but who doesn't have the requisite skills to manage effectively. Or, sometimes an effective employee or manager is transferred from one department to another and loses his effectiveness. It may not always be possible to return this person to his previous position. (*Note:* This may be construed as a demotion, but would probably retain the employee within the organization.) However, if you do send someone back to his old position, he has to be replaced by someone else (hopefully by using a modified selection process). Unfortunately, the transition period for the newly appointed manager costs the company money in terms of unrealized loss of productivity. Yet, in this situation, perhaps, it can't be helped.

Modifying (Redefining) His Job Responsibilities

There are times when it just isn't practical to either transfer someone or fire him. When this occurs, it is often possible to reach a compromise wherein you redefine a person's job responsibilities to meet his abilities and level of functioning. Needless to say, this is far from an ideal solution and results in virtually validating a substandard performance. However, sometimes the individual in question is performing below standard because of stress problems. When this is the case, temporarily modifying (or even reducing) this person's responsibilities may be all that is required to help him regain control of his work and return to full effectiveness.

Demoting Him

Most people tend to take demotions personally, usually resulting in their looking for other employment. This results in lower morale and poorer production. In addition, when someone is demoted, not only is there temporary loss of productivity as he assumes his new, lower responsibilities, but he will also require a replacement after he leaves. Hence, at least two positions have lost productivity. (As a rule of thumb, it is safe to assume that the replacement cost of any individual is usually twice his annual salary).

Terminating and Replacing Him

Terminating an employee is far more complicated than just firing him. Today, laws protect most people's jobs to the extent that you may be required to counsel with them several times regarding their job performance before you can fire them without running the risk of a law suit. You may also risk a law suit or action by the Office of Economic Opportunity if the individual you terminate is female or a member of a designated minority group (see Chapter 25, *Recruitment, Selection, Development, and Retention of Minority Financial Consultants.*

In addition, depending upon the employee's position, he may require out-placement services, termination pay, etc. Then, a replacement must be found, trained, and given a chance to grow into the new job. This can be very expensive (the average cost to replace a relatively key person in an organization has been estimated at approximately three times that person's annual salary).

Providing Additional Training

During the period of time that they are being retrained, employees are not able to maximize their performance. Assuming that the training is effective, then the company may have effectively salvaged a key person. At this point, however, it is important to consider the underlying reasons for the poor performance. If the person was not motivated to do the job, or if he had some sort of family crisis, all the training in the world may not be effective.

Coaching and Counseling Him

When you first recognize that an employee isn't fulfilling his job responsibilities, it is important to call the person in and determine the cause. Remember, essentially all performance problems can be reduced to "Want To, How To, Chance To" (the questioning techniques described earlier in this chapter). Regardless of the cause of his sub-standard performance, you will have to counsel him regarding that performance and your expectations for the future. Always remember that the most important message that you wish your listener to hear is that you *care* about him. If this feeling doesn't come across, you will only confirm his worst fears and you may destroy what motivation and self-confidence he has left. People often become defensive when they are counseled and you can never guarantee that the person you counsel will do what you wish. However, there are several things that you can do to minimize that person's defensiveness and increase his motivation to change. Here is a list of 12 rules of thumb for counseling an employee:

Rules of Thumb

1. Be sure to *choose an appropriate time and place* before you begin to counsel. A good rule of thumb is: **Praise in public, rebuke in private.** In addition, it is generally unwise to respond to someone when one or both of you is angry or upset. Wait for a calm time.

2. *Always establish rapport* before you begin to counsel. Do this whether he has come to you or you have gone to him. It's the surest way to communicate that "I care" message.

3. After you listen to what someone has said, use paraphrasing to make sure that you understand what he means and, especially, what he feels. Remember, if you're going to work from their point of view, you need to be sure that you understand what it is. For example:

   You: Don, it sounds as though you're feeling a little frustrated over this new operations policy. Is that right?

4. Always discuss the individual's *behavior* rather than the *individual*. For example:

   You: Sally, it's important to be back from lunch by one o'clock so the others can go. (Effective)
   Not: Sally, I understand that you have developed the bad habit of coming back late from lunch. (Ineffective)

5. Share your *observations* rather than trying to *read the individual's mind* regarding why he did something. **If you don't know what someone is thinking or feeling, don't guess, ASK!** Mind reading builds barriers. For example:

   You: Bill, you have arrived later three times in the last week. Is everything all right? (Effective—opens further communications)

Not: Bill, it's obvious that you don't care enough about your work to even come in on time. (Ineffective—promotes immediate defensiveness)

6. Describe what you feel and what you have experienced rather than making judgments about the other person or his actions. Judgmental statements make people defensive and closes lines of communication instead of opening them. For example:

You: Harry, I'm concerned about the number of hours that you spent prospecting for new business last week. (Effective)

Not: Harry, with your prospecting record, you must be the laziest salesman in the branch. (Ineffective)

7. Don't deal in extremes or generalities. In other words, don't label people and remember that no one is all good or all bad. Avoid words like *always* and never. Once we label someone, we paint him into a corner that leaves him little room to improve. After all, if you think that he is *always* late, why would he bother to try to improve? You probably wouldn't give him credit for it anyway. For example:

You: Jane, you were late with your prospecting statistics three times this month. Is there anything I can do to help?" (Effective)

Not: Jane, you're *always* late! You *never* have your prospecting statistics on time! Why can't you get with the program? (Ineffective)

8. Avoid giving advice. Whether the advice is good or bad, it changes the nature of your relationship. If your advice is bad (or improperly followed) and fails, your FC may blame you instead of taking responsibility for the outcome himself. If your advice is good and it works, you will have gained a dependent who will be tempted to come to you to solve all of his problems instead of doing it himself.

Of course, there will be times when it may be necessary for you to go beyond giving advice by giving the employee an order. As a rule, however, aid your employee (especially an FC) in *his* exploration of alternatives until he feels comfortable in making a decision for himself. Even if you have a better solution, let him try his and experience the consequences—either good or bad—unless they are illegal or unethical and/or will endanger his health or the branch.

9. Before you release your emotions, ask yourself why you are communicating to begin with. Are you trying to help her to be a better salesperson, or just to blow off steam. Remember, your emotional release may make you feel better but may also cost you both the relationship and the employee's confidence. What value do you wish your communication to have for her?

10. Give the person you're counseling only as much feedback as she can handle. Most of us have many habits or failings that we could afford to improve, but when someone shares all of them with us at once, they can be a little overwhelming.

   In most cases, it's best to comment on only one or two behaviors in a given meeting. More than that can be hard to remember and be discouraging. Once progress has been made in those areas, praise her for his progress, then go on to the next area for improvement.

11. Determine your FC's psychological profile at the time that you begin counseling him and be prepared to deal with the emotional needs that underlie his profile. For example: An individual who is a *Dictator* needs to be reminded that she is special and that you have high expectations of her performance because of her great talents. Motivating her to do her job may be as easy as reminding her that it's the kind of job that you would only give to a few individuals. On the other hand, that kind of approach might be very threatening to a *Bureaucrat* or a *Socialite*.

12. Finally, remember to *speak her language*. If she has a visual orientation, use visual terms. Auditory words may only confuse her.

Setting Goals in Coaching

When you sit down with an employee to discuss his progress or concerns, help him to establish meaningful goals using the steps provided in the goal setting chapter. By doing so, you will help him to organize his thoughts about both his concern and its solution in a way that will improve the chances that he will follow through on it. Remember the requirements for establishing a goal:

- The goal must be stated in positives. What he does want, *not* what doesn't he want.
- The goal must be in his control. This means that if there is something you want him to do, he must be convinced that he wants it as well. Otherwise, it is your goal and it is *not* in your control.
- The goal must maintain any positive aspects (positive from his point of view) of his current situation. For example: If a positive aspect of too much time spent socializing with other employees is the attention he gets, then you must be sure that he gets additional attention from you and others when he does a good job prospecting, or selling, etc.
- The goal must be *ecological*; that is, it must not cost more than it is worth. If an employee sets a goal of prospecting for 40 hours a week but damages his health in the process, it's not worth it.
- Finally, the goal must be testable. As you work with him to select performance goals, be sure that you both understand how his performance and progress toward achieving those goals will be measured.

Summary

Increased productivity (getting the person from performing at 20%–30% of capacity to performing nearer to 80%–90% of capacity) is the goal of most businesses. Usually, the reliance on traditional methods of motivation will produce some of the results. But, the traditional methods are limited.

Rather than employing the traditional solutions to continued underachievement (firing, demoting, etc.), you can now salvage those employees who have the potential for making significant contributions to your branch. Using the counseling techniques described in this and other chapters, the expenditure of relatively minor amounts of time will enable you to more fully realize the full potential of those whom you employ. After all, the alternatives are far too costly and impractical for the long term.

After you have determined whether a performance problem is the result of *Want To, How To, Chance To,* make the necessary decisions regarding how you will deal with the problem. In most cases, you'll find that simple counseling will do the trick. Then use the 12 rules of thumb for counseling provided in this chapter to establish new performance goals.

Chapter *23*

Putting Yourself and Others in a State of Excellence

Recently, there has been an increasing emphasis on helping employees and managers achieve states of personal excellence in their work and individual lives. The techniques introduced have ranged from meditation to jogging and have been vaunted as the key to personal growth and productivity. Yet, despite all of the magazine articles and "pop psych" attention that the concept of heightened performance has attained, few seem to really understand what it is or how to achieve it.

Perhaps the best way to define a *State of Excellence* is by saying it is a combination of psychological and physical states that enables us to perform at optimum levels. These peak performances are often remembered as times when we approached our maximum performance in a situation—when everything just clicked and we had the world as our oyster.

The difference between average or even good performers and the *superstars* of any profession is that the superstars achieve and maintain a state of excellence on a regular basis. In a word, they have a higher batting average. Their performances are *consistently* excellent rather than just occasionally, or randomly, so. For them, maximum or near maximum performance is a way of life. These people have an unconscious mental program for efficiency and effectiveness which is habitually employed.

The purpose of this chapter is to provide you with a method of 1) accessing memories of previous *successes*; 2) capturing the unconscious *mental attributes* of the physical and psychological states associated with those successes; and 3) creating an *automatic response* to specific future situations which will include these ideal mental and physical states.

Although this may seem to be a large order to fill in a limited number of pages, it is actually quite easy. The techniques that you are about to learn are derived from applications of cognitive psychology.

Possible Uses for the State of Excellence

The techniques we will present have helped FCs achieve outstanding results in a wide variety of activities. For example:

- An *Olympic swimmer* uses this mental conditioning process to prepare for swimming meets. She has conditioned herself to automatically feel great as she leaves the locker room and approaches the pool. Her results have become so much more consistent that the coach is having this process taught to the other team members. The same technique is used in other sports.

- *Salespeople* automatically feel motivated, confident, enthusiastic, etc. when beginning a sales presentation. As a result, their sales ratios are consistently high, and off days have become a thing of the past.

- Broadway *actors and actresses* use this technique to recreate their best performances each time they go on the stage.

- An *advertising executive* now considers this knowledge to be his secret weapon which keeps him one step ahead of the competition.

- A successful *attorney* we know uses this technique to access a state of excellence before walking into the courtroom.

These people have trained their minds to automatically tap into mental and physical resources that will enable them to maximize their performances. In addition, each person has carefully predetermined when, where, and under what specific circumstances these states of excellence will occur. The balance of this chapter will provide you with the skills to effectively create your own personal state of excellence.

A summary of this process is provided here to enable you to understand how the various concepts and techniques fit together. Although helpful, it is unnecessary to read the entire chapter before doing the various exercises. There are three broad steps:

1. Determine when and where you want your State of Excellence.

2. Decide what mental attributes/resources would be most useful and then ensure that these mental resources will automatically occur when you need them.

3. Use the procedures that combine all of the previously taught techniques to achieve your own state of excellence.

In order to obtain maximum benefits, you are encouraged to follow the directions precisely. Try all of the suggested experiments and answer the various questions. The highly sophisticated and efficient techniques presented will allow you to obtain precisely what you want. The results you obtain will depend upon careful and thorough progress through each recommended step.

Before you begin, it is very important to carefully consider exactly what a state of excellence means to you. Each of us has our own unique definition. This becomes particularly important because, like any goal, achieving a state of excellence has to be specifically meaningful to you.

Take a moment and think of a situation in which you would like to consistently be at your best and write it down on a separate piece of paper, or on the line below. For reasons that will be given later, it is important to determine precisely where and when a *particular* state of excellence would be useful.

A situation/time in which I would like to be more effective is:

_____ .

Associated with times of peak performance are specific mental and emotional states. For example: The Olympic swimmer needs to simultaneously have confidence, eager anticipation (which she describes as "good butterflies"), and enthusiasm. She also perceives the race itself and her competition in a certain way when she thinks of them. These mental and emotional states are necessary ingredients for *her* state of excellence.

Considering the situation which you indicated above, what mental states or resources (confidence, motivation, relaxation, enthusiasm, etc.) are needed or would be useful for this situation? Write them down on a separate piece of paper, or on the lines provided.

1. _____   5. _____

2. _____   6. _____

3. _____   7. _____

4. _____   8. _____

More Completely Defining the Resources Needed

The next question is very, very important because your state of excellence will be partly a result of the answers you provide. What does each of the words you listed on the resources list mean to you as an individual? In a moment we'll provide you with a series of questions to ask about each feeling that should help to more clearly define their meaning to you.

As you take a moment to consider the meaning of each of the resources that you've chosen, make note of a particular time in your life when you experienced that particular feeling very strongly. Be as specific as you can and answer each of the following questions in as much detail as possible. Remember, this is essential because it will allow you to capture the essential components of the resources you've selected and incorporate them into the state of excellence that you wish to achieve. During the process, you will be working with and *installing* each individual resource feeling so that, when they are fully combined, their collective power will be felt. By carefully recalling and defining the essential physical, mental, and emotional aspects of the listed resources now, you will be assured that you can access it correctly later. *Lack of specificity will lead to poor results.*

222

Coaching and Counseling

Use a separate sheet of paper for each of the resources you've listed as necessary or useful for attaining the specific state of excellence you wish to achieve.

Resource wanted: _____

How do you know when you have achieved it? How do you stand, sit, hold your body? Recreate the exact physiology. If you stand/sit like that right now, is that feeling recaptured? If not, what else must be done to capture the feeling?

How do you look? _____

How do you sound? What, if anything, are you saying to yourself?

How do you feel? How would you describe the feeling to someone else with enough detail so that they could replicate all the nuances of the feeling in themselves? _____

How do you differentiate this feeling from other feelings? _____
_____

How do you know that you are having this particular feeling and not another? Briefly describe a past situation/event when you had this feeling:

_____

_____

Now that you've determined which resources would be the most appropriate and useful, as well as defined the specific aspects of each resource selected, it will be useful to explore additional exercises to further assist you.

Components of Thoughts, Memories, and Experiences

Everything that we experience comes to us through our five senses—sight, sound, feeling, taste, and smell. We process information (think and remember) by using mental equivalents or representations of those five senses; that is, most of us think by using pictures and/or sounds and/or feelings. For instance, before you read any further, take a moment to remember, or to re-experience, one of the situations from your past that you listed as a representation of a resource state. Close your eyes and remember it now.

What aspect of the memory did you recall first? Did a scene flash into your mind first? Or, was it a sound or a feeling/sensation? Perhaps even a pleasant odor, or a taste. Were you aware of all the visual, auditory, and feeling components? Or, was one aspect not immediately available to you? Think about something at the office or at school. Replay it in your mind. Which aspect—sight, sound, feeling, smell, or taste—were you first aware of? Which aspect were you most aware of? Least aware of? This experiment demonstrates three things:

1. Thoughts are composed of sensory components. Psychologists call these sensory components *modalities;*

2. our minds tend to recall one particular modality first; and,

3. even though most experiences contain all five sensory components, certain components may be initially unavailable to our conscious mind.

As you further review our experiment, did you notice that each sensory component could be broken down into further subcomponents? For example: The visual sensory component/modality could easily be broken down into various subcomponents such as color, focus, pitch, and rhythm. These subcomponents are called *submodalities.* There are two very important things about submodalities:

They can have a tremendous effect upon the impact of feelings that we associate with memories or experiences; and, it is possible to consciously control them.

However, before we discuss submodalities any further, we'd like to take you through a brief exercise which will demonstrate your ability to control your feelings by modifying the submodalities you associate with a given memory. In this experiential exercise we'd like to figuratively take you for a ride. Take your time with this next exercise to experience its results as fully as possible. We think you'll enjoy it.

> **Directions:** Review one of the *winning* memories you wrote on your 3″ × 5″ index card to deal with stress and mentally pretend that you are *watching yourself on a television screen.* Be aware of your feelings as you observe yourself going through the experience and the changes in your feelings as you try the various suggestions. *Note:* At this point the important idea is whether your feelings change in intensity, not whether the changes are more or less pleasurable. Now:

- Make the television screen the size of a large movie screen. Did your feelings change as the picture became larger?

- Imagine that you are sitting very far from the screen so that it is no larger than a postage stamp? Does that affect your feelings?

- Now return the picture to the original size and make the picture very bright, then very dark. Again, was there a change in the intensity of your feelings?

- What if you make the memory a single snapshot or a moving picture? How does each act on your part change the intensity of your feelings?

- This time, try changing the components of sound by making any sounds much louder, then much softer; then shut off the volume entirely. Were there any changes in the feelings attached to this memory?

  Now try stepping through the screen and into yourself in the picture and *relive* the experience as if it were happening to you right at this moment—see it now, hear it now, and feel those feelings again. Re-experience it as fully as possible.

  What was the difference in your feelings' intensity between watching yourself on television and reliving the experience? For most of us, the intensity of experiences tends to increase as we relive (become *associated* with) a memory. The *dissociated* state (watching oneself on television) tends to be less intense for most people. Remember, the differentiations in the pictures or sounds (light/dark, near/far, etc.) are called *submodalities.*

  In a moment we'll ask you to step into the past and make another series of submodality changes as you relive a pleasant memory. Once again, the purpose is to verify, within your own personal experiences, that certain submodality changes result in a change in the intensity of feeling. These simple changes should be made in the midst of the experience (making modifications of what you saw or heard); that is, you will be changing the components of a memory. Finally, for each modification, be aware that a change in the intensity of feeling may occur.

Directions: Recall a **pleasant** experience, perhaps a particularly enjoyable conversation with someone you enjoy being with, or one of the happy memories from your *stress card*.

Visual changes in the remembered experience: Be aware of feeling-intensity changes as you go through each of these.

- Make what you are seeing much darker, then much brighter.
- Make certain aspects more or less focused.
- Try zooming in on a part of the scene, then zooming out.
- Make the movie much faster, then much slower.
- Make any visually oriented variation you choose.

Auditory changes in the remembered experience: Be aware of any feeling-intensity changes as you do each of these.

- Make any sounds much louder, then much lower.
- Change the direction that the sounds are coming from—in front, behind, from the left, then the right.
- Change the tempo so that it is much faster, then much slower.
- Make any further auditory variation you choose.

Feeling changes in the physically (or *kinesthetically*) remembered aspects of the experience: Be aware of any feeling-intensity changes as you do each of these.

- Make the environment much warmer, then colder.
- Have the entire feeling be located in only one part of your body, then have it spread throughout your entire body.
- Become more aware of any tactile aspects, then less aware.
- For the sake of simplicity, we'll include taste and smell within the kinesthetic aspects. Are you aware of any odors or tastes associated

Coaching and Counseling

with the memory? Strengthen, weaken, or change them and notice the change in feeling-intensity. *Note:* Smells associated with memories often have an extremely powerful effect on the feeling-intensity of a memory.

● Make any kinesthetically oriented (physically oriented) variation you choose.

Having gone through this phase of the exercise, you were almost certainly able to change the intensity of the experience as you made some of the suggested changes. **The key point to realize is that you can change your feelings by changing the way you remember (or anticipate) events. To a very large degree** *many of your feelings are subject to your conscious control!!*

The final aspect of this exercise is to relive the experience one more time making a series of changes which will enhance the pleasure of the experience. A brief listing of some of the submodality changes is provided in Table 23-1. Remember, you can take this or any other pleasant experience and make the memory much better and more intensely pleasurable. Vary each of the components and, as you vary it, leave it at the point where it gives you the best feeling. *Note:* Some of the variations will result in large intensity changes while others will provide no conscious effect. Interestingly, in the future, whenever you recall a memory that you have modified, you will recall it in its modified rather than its original state.

The submodality listing in Table 23-1 represents only a few of the more than 50 variations that can be made. Variations of these techniques can allow you to *neutralize unpleasant memories* and associations.

TABLE 23-1. *Submodality Changes.*

Visual	Auditory	Feelings
color	volume	temperature
focus	pitch	location
speed	direction	pulse
contrast	rhythm	pressure
brightness	tempo	texture
distance	tone	intensity
clarity	frequency	movement

By modifying how you remember something you change the feelings associated with it. This alone can give you more control over your performance.

Before going further, try this experiment which will be explained later. For the moment, think of your enhanced winning experience while simultaneously carefully looking at the box immediately below:

$$\boxed{\#1}$$

Defining Your Outcome(s):

These techniques are effective and powerful when correctly employed. Because of their power, it may be worth briefly repeating the legend of King Midas. King Midas loved gold and prayed to the gods that everything he touched would be turned to gold. He was granted his wish and, as is often the situation in life, got more than he bargained for. Everything he touched turned to gold—including his wife, children, and food.

The old adage "Be careful of what you wish for, you may get it," applies here. Your outcome(s) from this procedure should be very carefully defined because *you will get exactly and precisely what you want.*

As a result, it is important to examine just how your state of excellence should be contextualized. When do you want it and when would it be inappropriate or undesirable? After all, think how much better off King Midas would have been if he could have turned his golden gift on and off as needed. Hence, it is usually wise to play devil's advocate with yourself and really think about the times when this particular state of mind would be inadvisable or undesirable.

As you carefully define your desired outcome, remember the rules of thumb for goal setting that we discussed in chapter 3. Carefully consider, and ask yourself each of the following questions, then write the answer down on a separate piece of paper or in the space provided, below.

- **What do I want to do, achieve, be?** (How would I like to be different?)
- **Is my outcome stated in positives so that there is something specific to move toward, rather than simply something I don't**

want For example: "I want to be more enthusiastic" rather than "I don't want to be bored."

- **Is the outcome within my control?** (Is it something that I can individually accomplish? It should not require the actions of somebody else.)
- **How will I look, sound, and feel once I have achieved my outcome?** For example: I'll stand tall with my shoulders back. My voice will sound confident. I'll feel good about myself when I'm like this.

  —How will I look: _____.

  —How will I sound: _____.

  —Howw will I feel: _____.

- **When, where, and with whom do I want this outcome behavior?**

  —When: _____.

  —Where: _____.

  —With whom: _____.

- **Under what circumstances:** _____
  _____

- **When would I NOT want this outcome? When would it be inappropriate?** There are almost always circumstances or situations when a particular behavior would work to your disadvantage. *Think carefully about this.*

- **How will I know for sure that I have achieved it? What will be the proof that I have it?** Be certain that you have defined your outcome specifically. Very often people will say "I want X," but if you haven't defined what that means, how are you going to know when you have achieved it?

- **How will getting this outcome affect other areas of my life?**

  —Social: _____.

  —Mental: _____.

  —Emotional: _____.

  —Spiritual: _____.

  —Family: _____.

  —Professional: _____.

- **Will getting this outcome help me achieve other things in my life?**
- **Is this outcome really worth getting?**

Having defined your outcome, please review the personal resources you listed earlier in this chapter and add or subtract mental resources that would help you achieve that outcome. Remember, you will need to define them precisely on visual, auditory, kinesthetic, and psychological levels because of the way that the mind and body work together. You have already experienced this as you completed the above-mentioned exercises. In addition, these exercises have prepared you to easily and effectively implement the final set of procedures which will culminate in your specific state of excellence.

However, there is one more component for you to understand before establishing your state of excellence. Look carefully at the box below and remember what it represents:

$$\boxed{\#1}$$

As you looked at the symbol, did a certain pleasant experience almost immediately come to mind (perhaps only fleetingly) with a few pleasant associations? If so, you've just experienced what psychologists call *anchoring*.

Anchors

An *anchor* is a term which represents the stimulus in a conditioned response. To be technical, it's similar to the Stimulus–Response (S → R) phenomenon of the behavioral schools of psychology. Perhaps the easiest way to think of an anchor is as being similar to a reminder bell (or wrist alarm) for thoughts or feelings. Setting the wrist alarm reminds us to do something, or feel something, whenever the alarm goes off. Once we have set the alarm, we go on to complete other tasks until the alarm goes off. Whether it be minutes, hours, or weeks later, the sounding of the alarm triggers a memory of what needs to be done. If we really thought about the item when we set the alarm, that alarm will remind us of the task.

Similarly, an anchor acts as a reminder of a particular thought or emotional state. Once established (installed), an association occurs between the outside stimulus (the symbol or anchor) and the memory or feeling. When it is set-off (triggered) the memory, or a mini representation of it, is automatically played back. Consequently, an anchor allows us to capture, virtually at will, the essence of a memory.

A feeling which occurs in one context of your life can become associated with another situation. For example, we might anchor a time when a person was unusually efficient in doing a task. Then, attach the efficiency-anchor to a situation which requires additional efficiency. In this way the situation itself triggers the desired mental state associated with efficiency. That *state of efficiency* causes a higher level of effectiveness to occur in that new context.

You will be using anchors to create your state of excellence. Instead of a symbol, we'll be using a key word or phrase as the anchor. To do this, we'll use anchor words associated with times when you demonstrated the desired resources in the past. Then we'll significantly intensify these resource states through manipulating their submodalities and by actually adopting the posture, tone, physiology, and psychology that you associated with each resource.

At this point it would be useful to review the resources that you want to have and prepare a separate index card or sheet of paper for each of the resources that you list. The format is repeated for your convenience. This time, however, pay particular attention to the event in your life when you really had that specific resource available to you. It is very helpful to recall events that have had a similar context to the one you are about to work with. That is, if you want more enthusiasm in a business situation, try to remember any previous time when you were enthusiastic in a business context. If no specific instance comes to mind, remember any time when you were enthusiastic, perhaps about reading a book, an idea you had, etc.

Desired State Questions

Resource wanted: _____

- How do I know when I have it?
- How do I look?
- How do I sound?
- How do I feel? (If I were to describe the feeling to someone else with enough detail so that he could replicate all the nuances of the feeling himself, how would I describe it to him?)

- How is this differentiated from other feelings? What in me enables me to tell that I am having this particular feeling and not another?
- Name a past situation/event when I had it.
- Specify a key word/phrase that I can use to recall this situation or event.

Establishing Your Mental Resources

For each of the past situations where you had this resource, enhance the memory as much as possible using submodalities. Take your time with this. As you enhance the resource memory so that you feel even better about it, think of, and mentally listen to, the key word or phrase which represents that event. This key word/phrase will itself become an anchor for the enhanced feelings. Finally, these anchors of key resources will be used in developing your state of excellence.

Summary

You have just completed the preliminary work for creating, enhancing, and anchoring a new state of excellence in your life. In the next chapter you will learn how to install this state so that it may enhance your functioning in any desired situation.

Chapter *24*

Installing Your State of Excellence

Now that you've completed the preliminary work, you are ready to *install* your state of excellence. To do this, we'll utilize a two-step process that will give you added behavioral flexibility and resources in specific future situations.

The Behavior Generator

The *Behavior Generator* is a technique which allows us to predetermine how we will act in an anticipated future situation. It ensures that our automatic responses will be the ones that are most appropriate and beneficial in that context. Here is a broad summary of the process.

- First, review your answers to the *Defining My Outcome* questions in Chapter 23 so that you are clear about the times and places when you want the new responses to occur.

233

- Now, mentally try out the new behaviors by imagining how you would look and sound with your new behavior as you act in this different way.
- Add any resources that would be useful.
- Finally, once you determine the new behaviors you desire, mentally rehearse how you will react with a certain person, or rehearse a performance, or be the absolutely best you can be in that situation.

Follow the directions precisely in order to receive full benefit. Only when you have completed each of the preliminary exercises will the *Behavior Generator* ensure that your state of excellence becomes a reality.

The Behavior Generator is divided into three primary actions:

1. Determine how you would like to act in a given situation;

2. modify the new behavior until you are completely satisfied; and

3. install the future behavior.

Because this procedure creates an automatic response, it is very important to thoroughly consider the potential side effects of your behavior—something already done by answering the *Defining My Outcome* questions. As you generate the desired new behavior, you'll automatically also create a set of alternative responses which will enable you to appropriately react to variations of the selected circumstances. This is because your new behavior will be flexible and adaptive, rather than carved in stone.

The procedure for the Behavior Generator is as follows: (Note: Please read the following steps thoroughly before you begin so that you will be familiar with the terminology and the procedures and can then utilize the process effectively.)

1. **Determine what behavior(s) you would like to experience** and review for yourself the *Defining My Outcome* questions. These are very important because it will ensure that you obtain precise results at the needed time.

2. **Determine whether you know that to do or how to act in the situation.** If you know exactly how you would like to act, then

go to step 3. If you're not too sure exactly how you would like to act, you might wish to model or emulate someone. If so, go to step 2a.

2a. **Choose a person that you would like to model or emulate.** That is, think of someone who already elegantly demonstrates whatever behavior you are trying to learn. For example: Many people model themselves after a TV or movie personality. Remember, the person you select should elegantly demonstrate the behavior you would like to add to your repertoire.

2b. **Create a mental movie** and watch and listen to the individual you've selected to emulate on a mental screen as he performs the desired behavior. At this point you are his understudy. Carefully memorize how your mentor acts and/or reacts to the situation you have selected.

2c. **Decide whether or not you would like to act in this manner.** If so, then go to step 3. If not, redirect the scene or decide upon another model and recycle to step 2a. *Note:* This recycling procedure is part of the checks and balances built into the process to further assure its effectiveness.

3. **Create a mental screen on which you may *watch and listen to yourself*** try out the experimental behaviors that you've selected. It is important that you be able to watch yourself role playing in this mental movie (that is, you must be dissociated while trying out the new behaviors).

4. While observing yourself on this screen, watch **and listen to the movie carefully.** Do you like your actions? Feel free to modify your actions, reactions, responses, etc. Experiment. Enjoy the process.

In addition to modifying your own actions, posture, and statements, modify the movie effects. (That is, modify the visual and auditory submodalities of the imagined experience until you are completely satisfied.) Review the list of submodalities (Table 23-1) already provided for additional ideas.

Change any of the components that would make your movie script look or sound better. Make note of which changes cause a positive or negative reaction and retain the effects that you feel are beneficial.

If you had previously determined that certain additional personal resources would be helpful, add them now, one at a time, by looking at the key word or phrase on the index card, thereby triggering the anchor. Be aware of any changes in your feelings as you do this. Also, be aware of changes in your posture and/or speech pattern as you add these new resources.

If you are less than totally satisfied or slightly uncomfortable watching and listening to your image, then change the script by recycling to step 4, adding additional resources, modifying your physiology, and making additional submodality changes. You might also decide that you would like to see how someone else might do it by recycling to step 2 and further observing the same or a different role model.

5. **When totally satisfied with the TV/movie script, mentally step into the picture so that you are momentarily living the movie.** The purpose of this is to determine whether or not the new behavior actually feels good; in other words, whether or not you really like the new behavior. You'll get a positive or negative feeling at this point. If it feels good, then you have a potential new behavior and can go on to step 6. If not, then step out of the picture and return to watching yourself on the screen again. Then recycle to step 4 and make any necessary additional modifications. (*Note:* At this point, you might wish to concentrate on the effects and additional resources.)

6. Having found one or more alternative behaviors, it is important to *future-pace* yourself. To do this, imagine a time in the future when you will be in that situation or a similar situation. (*Note:* This is sort of a mental rehearsal in which you condition yourself to employ the new responses or behaviors at the time that you want it.) Imagine yourself on the mental screen in that future situation. If it still feels good, go to step 6a. If something doesn't look, sound, or feel right, return to step 4.

6a. Now, **imagine what it would look, sound, and feel like if you were living it** (the new behavior) **now:** seeing through your own eyes, hearing through your own ears, and being aware of your feelings. If you like your new responses, especially the feelings, continue to the next step. If not, it is important to return to step 4.

6b. If you are fully satisfied with step 6a, **mentally rehearse your new behaviors in at least two additional future situations**—that is, repeat step 6 for additional future-pacing for times or situations when you want these new behaviors. This ensures automatic implementation of the new actions at the appropriate times.

7. Congratulations! You have completed the process and have installed additional behavioral responses. This process can be continued with additional refinements as your needs change. *Because we cannot control other people and their actions and reactions, it is wise to work on different scenarios so that you have a variety of responses.* This technique can be applied to many areas of your life. While the technique may at first seem somewhat complicated, thousands of people have found that they can change their lives by simply following the procedures exactly as they have been provided. If you later decide to make modifications or enhancements to a behavior, merely repeat the process.

The Behavior Generator can be utilized for virtually any situation in which you would like to perform more elegantly and comfortably. *The key is to modify the script until you are completely satisfied with the entire performance.* A thorough reading of the previous material will allow you to easily follow this summarized procedure.

Summary of the Behavior Generator

1. Decide what you want.

2. Do you wish to model someone?
   a. If not, go to step 3.
   b. If Yes, a) choose the person, b) see yourself as the understudy for that person, c) decide if you like what he or she does and either go on to step 3, or choose someone else to model.

3. Observe yourself on a mental screen.

4. Change the script, the submodality effects and add resources until totally satisfied, or choose another model and recycle to step 2a.

5. Momentarily live in the movie. Check your feelings. Continue or recycle to step 4.

6. Imagine three future situations by first observing yourself and then living it. If satisfied, you have completed the procedure. If not, recycle to step 4 and continue till satisfied.

It is important to note that you can now exercise conscious control over reactions that were previously automatic. You can now mentally program personal excellence with this process.

Stepping Into a State of Excellence

This is the final process required for establishing your state of excellence. This process is made up of five easy steps in which you will use the results of all of the exercises that you have completed thus far.

1. You have already created a series of resource anchors and placed them upon index cards. Next, you must determine what external stimulus you wish to use as a trigger-anchor for your state of excellence. A golfer might choose picking up a club at the first tee; a salesperson may choose putting the phone to his ear; a musician might choose the first note used to verify the key in which he is playing; while another person might choose the doorway of an office or another location as the thing which triggers the state of excellence. Since you already know the situations in which you want this state, choose something that you would definitely see or hear to serve as the anchor.

2. After choosing the anchor, mentally pretend that you are about to enter into the situation—in fact, it is just one step away from you. As you mentally see, hear or feel that anchor, look at each of the index cards carefully and allow the resource anchors to be triggered. Take your time. Add in the resources one at a time, feeling yourself become even more excellent.

Just as the intensity of each anchor is being felt, say the word *excellence* out loud in voice tones and qualities that represent how wonderful you feel. The word excellence then becomes an anchor for the combined resources.

3. After you have mentally revved up, physically step past the imagined initiating anchor while mentally repeating the word excellence using the exact voice tones and qualities that you had just finished using. That physical step is a representation of you stepping into your excellent state and has been found to be an excellent enhancement to the state.

4. As you make that step, allow the feelings of excellence to swell up within you.

5. After a minute or so, repeat the physical step procedure. Do this for a minimum of three times. Essentially, you are training your mind to automatically recreate this state of excellence whenever you step into the anticipated situation.

CONGRATULATIONS!!! You have completed the process and now have ensured that a state of excellence occurs at the time desired. You have learned to direct your mind in such a way as to ensure that you are regularly using more of your inherent potential. Welcome to the ranks of the habitual star performers.

Summary

In this chapter, you have literally learned the secret used by so many of the world's most successful business people, performers, and athletes to achieve consistent, outstanding performance. By practicing it, you can virtually guarantee that your performance during sales meetings, with customers, and with your superiors will be superlative. You'll increase the effectiveness with which you utilize your current resources, as well as add the additional resources you need to make it to the top.

(*Note:* During these two chapters, you first completed a thorough process of preparation before stepping into your new state of excellence. It is imperative that anyone who attempts to install such a state complete each of the outlined steps and precisely define things for themselves. These skills are also provided in our tapes and workbooks.)

Section VI

Personnel Challenges

Branch managers in the financial services industry face a series of personnel challenges that other managers in their own company do not have. These challenges stem from several sources. For example:

- In many areas of the industry, the branch manager has nearly complete autonomy in hiring for his or her branch. This means that he must abide by the EEO requirements which are normally handled by the Human Resources Development Department.

- As with any manager, branch leaders must manage the flow of communications not only to their revenue producers, but also to the support staff if morale and efficiency are to be maintained.

- In addition to sales and office personnel, many branches also have an operations staff that processes securities trades, new accounts, insurance applications, deposits, etc.

241

- While many larger financial services companies provide some form of central training for personnel, the branch manager is responsible for orienting both the FCs and the staff to the branch and the company. This includes initial training of some form.

- Finally, most branch managers are faced with the challenge of dealing with a diverse sales force; the manager must channel and maintain the enthusiasm of the new FC, and rekindle the enthusiasm of the experienced FC who has reached a comfort level. In addition, the manager must support the superstar in a way that both improves his production and also makes use of him as perhaps the branch's greatest asset.

The chapters in this section will address each of these challenges and provide innovative solutions to each.

Chapter 25

Recruitment, Selection, Development, and Retention of Minority Financial Consultants

Marilyn Pearson

Immigration, changes in birth rates, women in the work force, and the aging of America are just a few of the factors which are changing the ethnic, racial, and sexual composition of the labor force. The cumulative impact of this changing ethnic and racial composition of the labor force will be to create:

- a net smaller growth of workers, and
- a workplace dominated by women, blacks, and immigrants, in which white males account for only 15% of the new entrants.

Therefore, the rapid integration of minorities into the financial services industry has become a necessary goal. Each delay in dealing with this basic problem of exclusion of minorities and cultural insensitivity will make the job of recruiting minorities much more difficult.

243

While many banking and insurance firms are far ahead of the securities industry in the recruitment and retaining of minority FCs, they still have a long way to go. All financial service companies must establish themselves as legitimate equal opportunity employers in order to attract and develop the work force of the future. This is the only way companies can remain competitive as we enter the 21st century.

In the pursuit of attaining Equal Employment Opportunity (EEO) goals, the recruitment of FCs among women and minorities has been previously focused primarily upon hiring guidelines rather than on retention. To some extent, hiring minority and female FCs has been viewed as an EEO concern rather than as part of a unified selection, development, and retention process. The cost to any firm of poor selection and development of minorities is staggering.

This chapter will cover several key problem areas and present actionable recommendations. As these situations did not develop overnight, it will take time to reach the ultimate goals. Change is never easy. However, in this case it is imperative for companies to become committed to this challenge now in order to have a competitive edge in the 1990s and beyond. There are four major areas which contribute to minority turnover:

- A negative mindset on the part of some office managers;
- poor recruitment and selection of minorities;
- inadequate development of minorities; and,
- lack of ongoing support of minorities.

Each area will be considered separately in the sections which follow.

In some areas of the financial services industry, minority FCs have been labeled as poor producers. Such labeling raises two questions:

1. Are minorities given enough time and support in order to become good producers?

2. Are their support and development needs somewhat different?

While there are exceptions, poor selection, development, and management support have generally all contributed to the lower average production and higher average turnover of minority FCs. In the next subsection we will consider how these factors operate.

The Mindset of Office Managers

For some managers high turnover and low production among minorities reinforce pre-existing negative expectations. These managers might have the point of view that a minority who is terminated after two years of low production proves that minorities as a group are not good in the financial services industry. In addition, because successful minorities are small in number and frequently have very low visibility inside their firms, many managers are never exposed to positive images.

Most managers are unaware of some of the unique challenges that minorities face, such as customer resistance and prejudice. Minority FCs frequently experience problems in gaining or retaining the trust and confidence of their customers. Many cases have been cited wherein a minority FC loses, or experiences sudden dormancy in accounts of nonminority customers, after an in-person meeting occurs. Minorities who try to communicate with their managers about these challenges sometimes get unsympathetic responses, largely because nonminority managers have never experienced these types of problems during their production careers.

Recruiting Superior Candidates

Judging from the experiences of current and former minorities in the industry, some managers may have sacrificed quality for quantity in hiring minorities; i.e., a manager whose primary concern is to fill an EEO quota is often less concerned about the quality of a minority candidate he chooses than about simply hiring a qualified candidate who happens to be a minority. A branch office manager may resent what he perceives as EEO quotas and may indeed be pressured into hiring a certain number of minorities within a specific time frame. In addition, because the emphasis is on hiring and not on retention, the manager may feel compelled to hire a questionable candidate just to meet his quote. When this individual fails, rather than see it as a result of a faulty selection decision, the manager interprets the failure as a sign that minorities just are not good hires.

Part of the problem lies in recruitment. Sources of qualified minority candidates may be difficult to locate. There may be very few minorities in a particular local area, and fewer still who would want to commute or relocate to a predominantly white area. Companies may not have a presence in the local minority communities. Hence, prospective candidates are often unaware that opportunities even exist. Managers may also be looking in the wrong places, such as by recruiting at college instead of targeting minority sales people in other industries.

Another piece of the problem is selection. Many managers have difficulty in assessing minority candidates relative to the attributes necessary for success within the financial services industry.

Successfully Developing Minority FCs

The third major factor contributing to the turnover of minorities is the failure of many branch office managers to successfully develop minorities. While many managers hire minorities, they often fail to take into account that, because of some customer attitudes, it frequently takes longer for a minority to achieve the same level of success as a nonminority in the same position. These managers don't realize how crucial their support is to the overall success of that individual. Often, minorities feel that they have not been given sufficient time to develop relationships with their customers.

In addition, working in predominantly white offices often makes it difficult for minorities to fit in. They feel isolated from their peers and often don't have the same access to the best prospects in the local area. For example: If a big producer opens an account that is smaller than what he normally handles, the FC usually passes the account along to another FC in the office. Minorities often feel that they are left out of this referral loop because they are not always part of the inner circle. If this is the case, the manager needs to be aware of the situation and actively support that individual.

Many minority FCs have also reported that customers are less tolerant of mistakes. Hence, they feel greater pressure to perform well for clients. While it is important for any FC to do his best to perform well, too much concern in this area can result in a decrease rather than an increase in performance. *Note:* See chapters on motivation, fogging, and counseling for more details on how performance demands that are too high can lead to burnout. Within the brokerage industry, these FCs feel that their stock selections and timing must be impeccable and that they must be able to answer all questions accurately and immediately, without having time to consult with product coordinators or marketing representatives when necessary. This pressure to perform creates anxiety and fear of failure on the part of the minority and makes the consequences of failure seem more serious. This often results in minority performance that is poorer than that of the nonminority FC and, because of this, most minority FCs tend to be terminated much earlier in their production careers than their nonminority counterparts.

Minorities have also found it more difficult to target appropriate prospects, and their managers often don't counsel them in this area. Since only a very small percentage of the households earning $50,000 or more is a minority one (264,000 out of 10,000,000), minorities must prospect nonminority clients to be successful. New hires are likely to spend a good deal of time prospecting in the minority community, where the chances of locating qualified prospects are much lower. In addition, even when accounts are opened within the minority community, many minority FCs find it harder to pursue large orders and to ask for additional business because they come from modest socioeconomic backgrounds and have not been exposed to financial dealing at this level. They're working from a different mindset.

Adding to the isolation that minority FCs sometimes feel in the office is the fact that success often further distances them from their peers. That is, the more a minority FC produces, frequently the less willing other FCs are to help him or her continue that success. This is exacerbated when the minority FC also feels unable to communicate with his or her manager or feels that the manager does not understand that a minority FC has to work harder and longer to earn his clients' trust.

The author of this chapter, for example, interviewed a young black woman who left a firm after less than one year of service. She cited her lack of preparedness for the position in sales and poor managerial support as the reasons for her termination. She stressed that minorities, in general, do not have the cultural framework for feeling comfortable in the language of the financial services industry and in the world of the affluent customer. They need support, additional training, and direction from their managers in order to overcome some of these cultural handicaps. A special two-month orientation program for any prospective candidate, regardless of race or sex, might be developed to help those who have the raw skills, but lack the cultural and experiential framework needed to hit the ground running.

Providing Ongoing Support

The last major contributor to minority turnover is the lack of ongoing support programs that address their special needs. Many of the people I spoke to said they had no idea who the successful minority FCs were. Trainees in particular wanted to know what strategies successful minority FCs used and what advice they would give to those just starting out.

Formal, in-house departments offering a peer support network and a centrally available source of information are needed. A good example of such organizations is the newly formed National Association of Securities Professionals (NASP). This group was established in April 1985 to promote professional excellence and equal employment opportunity for blacks and Hispanics in the securities industry. The association aims to increase public awareness, particularly among minorities, of career opportunities in the securities field; to foster the growth of minorities and minority-controlled organizations in the industry; and to enhance the communication and professionalism among its members.

In addition, it might be very helpful to establish an informal network with other minorities during the hiring process. More experienced minorities should be available in local areas where new hires can contact them for support, guidance, and advice.

Recommendations

Create a Positive Mindset

Because many managers view the hiring of minorities as an *EEO problem*, they need to be made aware that turnover is a *business problem* that affects the bottom line. Branch office managers should be educated regarding the high costs of turnover and should be encouraged to take a more active role in supporting and developing minori-

ties, not for EEO reasons, but because it can pay off in higher production and lower turnover. Firms should also ensure that minority FCs are
featured in a professional capacity in internal video network produc-
tions.

Although there is clearly not much that can be done to change
irrational customer objections, it is possible to underscore support for
the professionalism and excellent training of all minority FCs through
print and media advertising campaigns.

Recruit Superior Candidates

When recruiting brochures are designed, minorities should be
pictured in the financial services role along with whites. Videotapes
also could be made to show to prospective minority candidates. The
tapes might show a panel of successful minorities describing the job and
what it takes to be successful.

To specifically help with the recruitment and selection of minorities, two actions can be taken:

1. Increase the pool of qualified candidates.

2. Improve the care managers take in hiring minorities.

To increase the pool of qualified candidates, managers should communicate with each other about minority candidates. When no open-
ings exist in an office where a qualified candidate has applied or is
being considered, other managers in the general area should receive
the paperwork on the candidate for consideration. Also, internal
sources of minority candidates should be considered.

In addition, managers should also be encouraged to take steps to
develop local community awareness of the opportunities available in
their companies. For example: A manager could create a marketing
team aimed at minority markets and organizations in order to recruit
minorities while conducting sales campaigns. Such a team might be
coupled with the support of appropriate business units. Managers
could also start college intern programs and make special efforts to
attract minority students to work in the local branch office during
winter breaks, spring vacations, and summer vacations. Finally, managers should look for candidates from minorities who are in sales in
other industries.

To improve the care managers take when they hire minorities, a firm's sales management development program should include some awareness training for sales managers to make them more sensitive to the unique challenges facing minority FCs and their greater need for support. In addition, there are several characteristics that managers might look for when recruiting minorities, such as:

- maturity and self-confidence,
- prior sales experience,
- knowledge of the financial services industry,
- knowledge about the details of an FC's job—prospecting, commission selling, intra-office and interoffice competition, etc.,
- the ability to verbalize their skills and expressly state how those skills correlate with the requirements of the job,
- the ability to express their thoughts in concise, succinct statements,
- the ability to interact in business settings in which the candidate is in a racial and/or sexual minority, and
- the willingness to commit the time and energy necessary to become successful.

Awareness and Commitment by the Industry

With a strong commitment from your firm, you will be able to achieve those goals. As the industry continues in its efforts to focus on this issue, a change for the better will be inevitable.

1. *Involvement on a Regional Level:*
   a. Provide education regarding the minority issue and related problems.
   b. Determine how many minorities each region must hire.
   c. Evaluate financial loss due to previous hiring/lack of retaining minorities.
   d. Find the highest concentration of minorities in each region (breakdown by city).
   e. Define the role of minority FCs in meeting regional goals.
   f. Develop a minority network.

g. Follow up with managers on minority progress along the
   way.

   h. Inform new hires of the company's Minority Network
   and other local organization chapters for support.

   i. Provide coaching and counseling to minority FCs.

2. *Publicize (Internally) the Firm's Commitment to Minority Issues:*

   a. Publish an article in the company's internal newspaper
   discussing the company's commitment to minority hiring, development, and retention.

   b. Periodically provide ongoing and follow-up articles that
   show the achievements of minorities.

3. *Reward Office/Regional Managers for meeting minority hiring reten-*
   tion and production goals.

4. *Recruitment:*

   –Develop a minority source directory for your geographical
   area. Set up contracts with firms that are exclusively involved in minority recruiting.

   –Another source for recruiting is the *Black Enterprise Maga-*
   zine recruitment fair. Fairs have previously been scheduled
   in Boston, St. Louis, New York, Los Angeles, Oakland/San
   Francisco, and Philadelphia.

   –Recruitment Conventions sponsored by the National Pan-
   Helenic Counsel.

   –Develop a minority apprentice program. Hire these employees using the same strict standards that you apply when
   hiring any new minority. The individuals could be young
   college graduates hired and assigned to work with a successful senior minority FC. The apprenticeship could last approximately 18 months to two years. It is hoped that such an
   approach will ensure job retention for these particular minority individuals.

Finally, it is important to stress the benefits of pro-active minority recruiting to managers. Visibly recognize the efforts of managers
who successfully recruit minorities. This would underscore a company's commitment to hiring qualified minority FCs.

Summary

The face of the American labor force is changing. The 1990s will experience a sharp reduction in the number of qualified white males who enter the work force. In addition, the recruitment and retention of minority FCs in the financial services industry lags far behind that of other major industries. However, through recognition of the problem and aggressive intervention, steps can be taken *now* which will ensure the availability of qualified minority FCs for the industry.

Chapter 26

The Art of Managing Diverse Personnel

Robert J. Miesionczek

Successfully managing a sales office is one of the most difficult challenges in the art of management.

Many managers will lay claim to the same judgment about their own management roles. Only in a sales office, however, do you have to integrate on a constant basis the diverse elements of sales and operations. This is the subject of the chapter you are now reading. We'll focus on the different needs of your sales and support staff, how to balance those diverse needs and maintain a high level of motivation for your combined office staff.

Our tools to do this will be a straightforward leadership model and a simple formula for motivation. We'll apply these tools to profile the different—and often conflicting—roles of sales and operations. We'll then look at ways to balance these roles that will result in a more efficient and motivated staff and a more productive office.

253

Management and Leadership

There are many definitions of the term *leadership* and many explanations for why people become *leaders*. Since it is ephemeral and intangible, a perfect definition and explanation is as easy to find as the pot of gold at the end of the rainbow. However, if you turn the argument around and view leadership from the point of view of *why followers follow*, there are some interesting insights to gather about motivation. There are also interesting implications for managing an office of diverse functions—such as sales and operations.

The next section in this chapter describes the leadership model. This model doesn't look at *styles* of leadership. It focuses on the *messages* that are conveyed by leaders through the way they communicate and conduct their business. People in management and leadership roles send many messages about themselves and what they view as important. The model provided is designed to focus on the *primary message* that followers will connect with. These *primary messages* create a *psychological contract* that forms the basis of a relationship that followers have with leaders.

A great manager also must be a leader. So you can also consider these psychological contracts as fundamental in a quality manager—subordinate relationship and a productive office.

The Leadership Message Model

Note: This model is adapted from William Bridges' book, *Surviving Corporate Transitions*. It differs in that this model represents leadership from the point of view of the message that the leader conveys, to his followers as opposed to just leadership typing. This leadership message model can be broken down into four distinct *wavelengths:*

- *Conceptual Message:* For the *conceptual leader* the *message* is "You can realize your greater potential." At the same time, his *focus* is on the *big picture*, the greater or deeper meanings in all things. His style is inspirational and can be summarized as, "You can do things that you haven't even dreamed of." Finally, his *hook* comes at the emotional, or feeling, level.

254

- *Relational Message:* For the *Relational leader,* the *message* is, "We should work together." His *focus* is on *team membership and teamwork.* His style stems from a sense of unity, summarized in "We'll work better if we work together." Like the conceptual leader, his *hook* is on the emotional, or feeling, level. The emphasis is on partnering with co-workers.

- *Catalytic Message:* For the *catalytic leader,* the *message* is, "You can solve the problem(s) that stand in your way," (organizational/technical) or "You can overcome these obstacles," and so on. His *focus* is on *solutions* or ways to get things done. Essentially, his style is *entrepreneurial,* summarized in, "Find the best way," and his *hook* is at the logic, or thinking, level. This message differs from the conceptual in that it clearly defines obstacles and generates solutions. Conceptual messages are more general and less solution-oriented.

- *Structural Message:* For the *structural leader,* the *message* is, "There is a structure that we should work in," or "There are ways that things should be done." His *focus* is on *order and facts or structure and procedure.* His style is based upon a sense of order, summarized in, "We'll do things the right way." As with the catalytic leader, his *hook* is at the logic, or thinking, level.

Consider this model from the perspective of those who are *followers.* Most motivation theory says that people do things because it is in their best interest to do so. If this is true, then followers are motivated by the messages that a leader sends which most meets their needs. For example: If an individual is looking to overcome obstacles, he is going to buy into the message of the *catalytic leader* very easily. On the other hand, if he needs a sense of order and structure, then the message conveyed by the *structural leader* will be powerful to him.

Individuals are motivated by a complex of ever-changing needs. However, at this point let's put aside individual and personal needs and, instead, *focus on the pattern of needs that are a consequence of a particular function or job.* Different jobs have different measures for success. Hence, each job creates a different set of needs (i.e., *Job Needs*). When combined with the proper leadership message, these needs can have a significant impact upon the leadership and motivation of employees.

Leadership and Motivation

Leadership and motivation can be represented by the formula:

> Job Needs × Psychological Contract =
> Leadership or Followership

Remember, the Job Needs represent the fundamental *needs* of the individual as driven by the *job* for which he is accountable. In a sense, *job needs* represents the needs of the individual in doing his job well.

If a leader/manager sends a message which complements the job needs the follower/subordinate will establish a *psychological contract* with that leader/manager. Hence, knowing what people's needs are and sending a message that will meet those needs is represented as:

Job Needs × Psychological Contract

Recognizing and connecting with people's needs will place you in an *informal leadership role*. You don't have to be a manager to be a leader. You can see this in the patterns of relationships between subordinates as some seem to naturally follow the lead of one of their peers. (*Note:* This informal leadership role can be positive or negative for one who manages groups that include such relationships.)

The *formal* leader/manager role, combined with the job needs and the psychological contract, determines the criteria for the effective leader and manager. Hence, an excellent manager could be characterized by the following formula:

> (Job needs × psychological contract) +
> formal leader role = the excellent manager

The excellent manager, represented by this formula, is one who is able to:

- Read the needs of subordinates in doing their jobs;

256

- create a contract that says you can help people meet those needs; and

- formally and effectively manage.

Remember, we're not viewing leadership or management from the point of view of the individual. Instead, we're viewing leadership/management from the perspective of the job to be accomplished. In short:

"What do I need to get my job done?"

Sales and operations have very different job needs. Knowing this and creating psychological contracts that match each job function by redefining the message you send is fundamental to successfully managing a sales office. We'll look at this in more depth by focusing first on the needs of sales and then on those of operations.

The Sales Match

Which message will be most powerful to sales people? In most cases, they respond best to the message of the *catalyst* or *conceptualizer*. This is because detail and accuracy are very important to successful salespeople, but these needs are subordinate to their primary need—the need *to produce*. Most consistently successful salespeople delegate their detail work to clerical or operations staff. (*Note:* This does not refer to the details involved in profiling clients or determining a sales strategy. Those "details" should be done by the salesperson.) That is, successful salespeople maintain overall knowledge and control of the details—but they have their support staff do the work (if support staff are available).

The successful salesperson's *job need* is sales growth, production, and fulfilling potential. As defined by the leadership message model, the primary message a manager should send such individuals would be one spurring achievement, not setting limits. In general, managers who run offices that have a relatively seasoned sales staff should send messages that are either catalytic or conceptual. Their sales staff should be thinking, "You're helping me go as far as I can," or "You're an ally in removing obstacles to doing my business," when they communicate with him.

Let's try out these ideas. Below are profiles of the sales staffs of two distinct sales offices. Read each profile and then predict the primary job need for each. Write your prediction on the line labeled *predicted job needs*. Choose your prediction from one of the leadership message types described earlier in the leadership message model.

Retail Office Profiles

The East Side Office

- Total of 20 retail sales staff members.
- Average sales experience is eight years.
- About 80% worked for the competition in the past.
- Age range: Late 20s to mid-50s.
- One trainee.
- Production average: $250,000/annual.
- Production range: $170,000 − $750,000.
  Predicted job needs _____.

The West Side Office

- Total of 12 retail sales staff members.
- Average sales experience is one year.
- All are new to the business.
- Age range: Early 20s to mid-30s.
- Seven novice sales people (one year plus experience).
- Five trainees.
- Production range: new − $190,000.
- Production average: $60,000.
  Predicted job needs _____.

Clearly, the East Side Office is more established. Both offices are working toward the same goal—sales production. Their job needs, however, should be different.

For the East Side Office we would predict *catalytic (or conceptual)* leadership, while for the west side office, *structural or relational (with conceptual)* leadership. Why would these be different?

Since the East Side Office is established, we would expect most

258

of the sales staff to have their own sense of direction or purpose. They won't need it from their manager. Hence, a conceptual message probably would not be the most powerful. Also, if business is doing well (for the sake of argument, let's assume that this is the case), structure (structural) and teamwork (relational) messages will not be as effective or powerful as the catalyst. That leaves us with the catalyst's message. Clearly the message required here is, "I'll help break down the barriers; you do the business."

The West Side Office is a different story. The general business environment here is good as well. However, most of the staff is new and have to be seasoned in how to develop and do their business. This staff would most powerfully respond to a message that offers structure (structural message) within which they can grow and learn. Teamwork (relational message) may also be important because of the latent question, "Will I be able to do it?" and the fact that people find comfort in groups.

In addition, the manager of this office will be looked upon as one who can help his sales staff realize their greater potential (conceptual message). The message of the catalytic leader would probably not be as powerful since new staff don't generally see barriers as clearly as their more experienced peers. Therefore, a structural message (with catalyst and relational variations) would be most effective.

There are implications here for office manager selection as well. Let's look at a profile of two office managers. Just like the prediction you made of the job needs for our two offices, try to predict each manager's potential *primary message* or his psychological contract.

Toni

- Bottom-line oriented. Focus is on maximizing revenues.
- Competition: Focus on a similar office within the firm.
- Message: Do more business.
- Few staff meetings.
- Not noted for expansive explanations. Terse and business focused.
- Not noted for management by walking around (MBWA).
- Procedures are guidelines.
- Approachability: If business focused and important, yes.

Probable Psychological Contract: _____
(Refer to message model on pages 254–255.)

Bill

- Bottom-line oriented. Focus is on minimizing expenses.
- Competition: Focus on doing your business well, getting better at what you do.
- Message: "Do business well."
- Frequent staff meetings.
- Presents in-depth the best ways to do your business and shows examples.
- Noted for walking around and asking how things are going.
- Procedures are there to follow.
- Approachable at any time, just "Come on in."

Probable psychological contract: _____
(Refer to message model on pages 254–255.)

Toni would be strongly characterized by a catalytic message such as "Find the best way," or "You can solve these problems." Clearly, there is an entrepreneurial focus, with teamwork and structure subordinate. Therefore, her psychological contract would probably also be *catalytic* and she would be most successfully matched with the east side office.

Bill, on the other hand, is more on the structural/relational side of the message model. The primary messages he conveys are: "I can help you do business well," and "We can do it together." Hence, his psychological contract would probably also be *structural/relational* and he would be most successfully matched with the west side office.

It is important to remember that people, as individuals, will have different personal job needs. For example: The manager may have already considered that the one trainee in the east side office needs to follow a different message than that of his peers. That's fine; you can use this model to contract (psychological contract) with individuals as well as groups.

However, for our purposes, we are focusing on the patterns of common needs (job needs) created by the job. Even though both office examples profiled sales staff with a common final goal, the realities of their job—one staff needs a catalyst's message, while the other staff needs a structural message—mean that they will contract with managers who send different, though appropriate, messages.

Are You Locked-in by Your Message?

Not at all. You can send many messages without having to change who you are. All you need to do is to read the job needs of your staff (either individually or as a group) and create the appropriate message. We all have a combination of needs that can be related to the model, so you can talk (send) any message. All that's necessary is to expand your *managerial envelope*. You have to be able to read the job needs and to develop the responses that can create an effective psychological contract to meet any need. *No one sends only one message—at least no one who is going to be successful in the long term.* Conditions change, and so will your message—if you're going to be effective.

Motivating a Diverse Staff

So far, we've looked at our model primarily from the point of view of you as a manager of sales staff, but what about the message to your operations staff? First, remember that it is important to focus on the job needs that are created by the demands of different job functions. Looked at this way, it is apparent that the primary job needs of the operations staff are quite a bit different from the needs of your sales staff. For example:

- Operations personnel must be very detail oriented. It is their job to make sure all the i's are dotted and the t's are crossed.
- In addition, they are not measured by office or individual sales production, but by how many errors they have.
- Finally, they may also be measured by how promptly and courteously they deal with customer service issues.

Given this reality, consider how effectively (or ineffectively) the leadership message you convey to your sales staff meets the job needs of the operations staff. What is the primary message to which the operations staff will respond? It will most probably be either relational or structural. This is easy to understand given that the operations staff need to work together to get the job done. Their job involves dealing with procedure, order, and facts.

This shouldn't be interpreted as suggesting that good salespeople don't need structure or teamwork, or that good operations people don't need to see the bigger picture or have an ally in meeting their accountabilities. It is meant to suggest that a balance of messages has to be sent by the branch/sales manager if he wants to maximize the performance of the office and maintain a motivated staff that functions at full capacity.

The Operations Job Needed

Below, are some typical accountabilities that fall (by design or by accident) into the job of operations:

- Tracking payment date for a sale.
- Entering sales orders quickly and correctly.
- Maintaining check disbursement schedules.
- Reviewing documentation for completeness and accuracy.
- Implementing special instruction items (like a federal wire transfer of funds).
- Requesting and tracking payment extensions.
- Providing courteous and efficient customer service.
- Processing trades.
- Bookkeeping accounts (keeping client accounts balanced).
- Handling legal documentation.

What is the message (psychological contract) that will be most effective to someone with these accountabilities? Clearly, the sense of order found in the structural message—using (not abusing) procedures, and maintaining schedules and documentation—will be most powerful. Since, for operations staff, getting things done involves working with a lot of people, the relational message (i.e., a sense of unity or teamwork) will also be powerful.

Do you send these messages to the operations staff in your office? If you don't, it is possible that your operations staff is unable to function at its optimal capacity. Try these messages and see how they effect the overall efficiency and effectiveness of your operations staff.

(*Note:* This does not mean that your primary message to your sales staff should change to accommodate your operations staff's needs.)

Consider the following ideas to bolster your structural/relational message:

- *Support procedural and policy requirements* that the operations staff must fulfill.
- *Enlighten the sales staff* to the basic requirements of the operations staff (i.e., operations personnel are measured by accuracy as well as speed).
- *Limit exceptions* to the rules.
- *If the rules impair production,* work with the operations staff to remedy them. (This doesn't mean reversing firm or legal policy. Rather, *find the most efficient way to work within the rules.*)
- *Maintain a positive sense of purpose with operations staff.* They are not there as an afterthought or as a barrier. They are one of your greatest assets in doing your business cleanly and efficiently.
- *Make sure the sales staff maintains its responsibility for detail.* Are orders written up correctly? Does the sales staff take time to do things correctly? Do they rely on operations too much to act as the backstop.
- *Maintain the operations domain.* Don't allow sales staff to intrude arbitrarily when the operations staff is busy. (For example: FCs are not supposed to be in the wire room, make sure that they are not.)

Your Office Leadership

We've looked at management from the point of view of leadership messages to which followers respond. It also pays to examine the perceptions that your staff may have of you.

Think about the typical issues you speak about with sales and operations staff. The issues you discuss will give you a good picture of the demands of different functions and the needs (job needs) that have to be considered. The responses you observe from your staff will give you a clue as to how well you are meeting those needs.

- What leadership message do you send to your sales staff? To your support staff?
- Does your message match their job needs? (Do you have a psychological contract?)

Do you encounter resistance or receive verbal or nonverbal signals that all is not well? Try to determine whether you are sending the proper message or a mixed message. At this point, you may have an individual in mind whom you feel isn't performing in his job. Don't jump to conclusions yet. Perhaps you haven't considered his needs clearly enough. Maybe you're really considering your own needs, instead. Try to take a dispassionate view first.

Since you're the manager, his failure is your failure! This is a disquieting thought. You either fouled up the hire or committed management malpractice.

Management Savvy

If you agree with what you've already read, being a *savvy* manager (i.e., one who is a leader for many constituencies) should be easy. We assume that you've probably moved up the management ranks because you are perceived as effective and competent. Your message has been appropriate for the group you've led. This *was* your formula for success.

However, *whenever you move up in management ranks, you don't add more work to your job, you add more constituencies (i.e., people with diverse job needs). Savvy managers recognize new constituencies and adapt accordingly.* They don't change their primary message, but rather become more flexible and adaptable. This is why management was described as an art at the beginning of this chapter.

A manager who fails to acknowledge new constituencies will be prey to the *Peter Principle.* According to this principle, a manager will rise to his or her level of incompetence. If you become locked in by your success (that is, send leadership messages that were appropriate for where you came from and don't adapt to where you are now), you can become a *Peter Principle* statistic.

Conclusion

Try out the ideas we've explored. Read the job needs of your staff. Then read and respond to your own job needs. In essence, run your office efficiently. Maintain a sense of organization and defined purpose. Balance the diverse job needs of the different elements of your office. Find the middle group that will allow you to conduct business cleanly, efficiently, and productively for all of your constituents. This is why the job you have is unique in management and potentially so rewarding.

Chapter 27

Internal Branch Communications

Victor T. Ehre, Jr.

Are there traits common to branch or regional offices? Branch offices vary in size, shape and function, depending upon the industry and purpose of their operation. Some branches are primarily service centers of limited scope, with most of their processing functions transmitted electronically or otherwise to another, more centralized location.

Yet for all of their variety, each branch office contains extremely divergent positions and skill levels. For example: In the typical insurance company branch office, positions range from the highly professional roles of underwriting, claims handling, and marketing to the less technical roles of filing, data entry, typing, and rating.

In such an environment, it is easy for a manager to focus a great deal, if not all, of his attention on the higher profile positions for which he is responsible. This is true whether those are the positions which generate the most revenues or those which appear to be in the most need of attention. Unfortunately, this often means that other areas are ignored until a problem occurs.

However, an important responsibility of any branch manager is to create an attitude among all levels that each and every position is essential to the effective running of the branch and that each member of the staff brings value to the organization. They must, or why would the positions exist? It is imperative that the manager attend to every function and the individuals who are an integral part of the operation, even if they are neither a problem nor a source of immediate revenue. This is particularly true of those positions which are considered unimportant or unglamorous by most people because they don't have the usual public recognition of their work as a typical motivator. However, if you want to see an operation grind to a halt, try to operate without the typing pool or the filing department for a few days!

The bottom line: In a properly structured organization, *every* position is important. Remove one department or function from the loop, ignore it, or fail to educate or motivate that group and you create conditions that will guarantee declining performance or, even worse, revolving door turnover problems in that department. If you doubt this, consider your secretary, sales assistant, or even the receptionist. None are paid well and few receive any real career incentives. Yet, how well do you function when they are absent for more than a day?

The point is that a branch office is a working system, not just a group of individuals who share space. Like any system, every part affects and is affected by every other part of the system. Hence, every position is reliant upon the actions and activities of others. As a result, any problem that affects even one member of the staff will inevitable cause ripple effects that will eventually reach every member of the branch, and may have a detrimental effect on service to customers.

Similarly, below-average performance in one area reduces the overall effectiveness and service of the entire branch. While this may seem very obvious, it is appalling how often branch managers ignore the very basic needs of a large portion of the branch in favor of the high profile individuals mentioned earlier. Often, the only people in the branch who are really informed about major policy changes, the company's primary goals for the next five years, etc., are the revenue producers. This not only leaves the support staff feeling unimportant and unmotivated, it also makes them uninformed outsiders who may have no idea of your goals and needs beyond their own immediate job description.

Ideally, the objective of every branch manager should be to involve *every* employee in the operation of the branch, at least to the extent of gaining an understanding of the branch's goals and how they affect the branch's operation. Unfortunately, every manager faces the problem that not every employee holds the same commitment to the branch and his job. Certainly, employees show up every day and do their job but the levels of energy and enthusiasm we would like to see just aren't always there. Despite all that you do, there will always be a few poorly motivated individuals. However, it is your responsibility to minimize the size of this group, while encouraging all to view their contribution to the branch in a positive light.

Communications

While the managerial and professional personnel in a branch may have an understanding of their roles and the goals of the company and branch, the support personnel often do not. This may be a result of management's belief that these individuals either would not or could not understand the issues. It could also merely be due to inadequate communication between management and staff. Look at your own branch and ask yourself if either of these is the case. If the former is true, in all likelihood you've sold your staff short. If the latter is true, you need to increase the quantity and the quality of your communication with your support staff.

The issue of management to support staff communications goes beyond any employee's understanding of your branch, region, and company goals and objectives. It extends to, and should focus on, the very basics of each individual's position and the role that he plays within the organization. How often have you overheard an individual comment on some problem in the branch and say, "Well, it's not my problem. It doesn't affect me." The fact is that the more individuals understand about their own duties and how those duties mesh with those of everyone around them, the more they will understand how the issues and problems facing the branch ultimately relate to them and their jobs. Communication at a number of levels is necessary for:

1. An individual's desire to understand what he is doing.

2. An individual's desire to know how his job affects other departments within the branch.

3. An individual's desire to understand how her job affects the company's relationship with its customers.

4. An individual's desire to know how the company is doing.

5. An individual's desire to learn about other things that might have an effect on him, such as products, programs, or problems that are developing within the company's competitive environment.

6. Other things that might enrich her understanding of the industry of which she is a member.

Let's take a closer look at each of these areas.

The Employees' Understanding of Their Job

Note that we use the concept of *understanding* what they are doing rather than *knowing* what they are doing. There is a very important distinction to be made here. We can train our employees to perform the functions necessary to get the job done. We can hand them manuals, set standards and procedures, and oversee their day-to-day activity to assure that they know their job. However, unless we add *understanding* to knowledge, we have created production machines in human form.

For example, in the insurance industry, there are a number of functions in the rating department which are very technical in nature. These functions are also critical to the proper pricing of our product. While our rating personnel know that it is important that the policies be rated correctly, all the members may not understand the meaning or purpose of the individual components of their duties.

In one instance, I observed a rater feverishly entering data into the appropriate blocks in her computer. The blocks had jargon labels such as BI, PD, MED PAY, PHYS DAM, etc. At one point, she turned to me and asked if I knew what the abbreviations stood for! Here was an individual who had been doing this same job for years, and no one had taken the time to explain the very basics of what she was doing in simple terms so that she could have some greater level of understanding. The kinds of errors that can be generated through such a lack of basic understanding stagger the imagination. People *do* wish to know *and* understand what it is that they are doing. Managers must be cognizant of that need and respond appropriately to it.

> Employees want to know and understand what they are doing.

Interdepartmental Relationships

As managers, we are all keenly aware of the flow of paper within our operation and how each department can and does affect the other. Do all of our employees have the same understanding, or at least some understanding, of how their job fits within the production chain?

Our industry is terribly reliant upon paper flow. Yet, the work of many of our employees seems to almost magically appear on their desks in the morning and, just as mysteriously, disappear in the evening. Many are not only unaware of the real importance of their work, but they are also unaware of how that work affects others within the company or how the consequences of a delay on their end could have an impact on other areas. Therefore, it is incumbent upon you, the branch manager, to work with his direct reports and supervisory staff to educate the support staff on how their activities interrelate with those around them.

Customer Relations

If you were to ask your employees if good customer relations are important, you would undoubtedly receive a resounding "absolutely" from everyone. The problem in almost every business is that this response is seldom translated into each employee's daily work activities. One reason this is true is that most employees are sufficiently removed from direct contact with customers that there is no obvious connection in terms of how their activity could possibly have an impact upon the customer.

A file clerk may not make the connection that prompt locating of files for the underwriter will mean that a response to the customer will be accomplished more quickly. A typist, though he knows that fewer errors are better, may not carry that understanding forward to how errors cost the branch money and reflect upon the reputation of the company in the eyes of customers.

Yet, because service and quality are the major means by which the public and others can differentiate companies, it is essential that everyone, at every level, understand how their activity affects our commitment to service. The consequences of failing to educate everyone in this area are potentially devastating.

Company Results

How would you like to work for a company that never shared its goals and objectives with you? It is very important that everyone be exposed to what we are trying to accomplish. Several benefits are achieved by doing so.

- First, employees are more committed to the company and their job when they have some understanding of what the company is trying to accomplish.
- Second, when coupled with an understanding of how their job affects, and is affected by, those around them, they gain a broader picture of how their activities contribute toward reaching those company goals.
- Third, when people understand what we are trying to achieve, they can contribute in other ways such as offering suggestions that could improve the bottom line.

There are also costs for not sharing the goals, objectives, and results of the branch and company with your staff. The ever present rumor mill is one offshoot of a lack of communication. This append-age, found in every business, can be one of the most insidious and disruptive forces within any organization. It undermines morale and injects suspicion into nearly every activity in the office. Further, rumors can cause abnormal resistance to new programs that you may wish to institute. While the rumor mill can not be completely elimi-nated, its impact can be reduced.

The disruptive influence of the rumor mill is inversely propor-tional to the amount of information that you share. It is critical, therefore, that management take care not to feed the machinery by failing to communicate. Complete information, distributed in a timely manner, is the only way to reduce the repercussions of the rumor mill.

Recently, rumors of possible lay offs were circulating around our office. I can think of no more damaging issue in a workplace than this. Because our operation is a growing one, these rumors were totally groundless. How do you handle such a situation? Many might decide that because the rumor is so ludicrous, no response is needed. Here is where it's important to remember that our employees are not always in possession of all of the information. Since they are not, it is up to us to take the steps to inform them of the true state of affairs when they are contrary to the facts. Failure to do so will continue the disruptive and costly influences associated with such rumors.

Another cost associated with a failure to share objectives and goals can be increased turnover. Every year, thousands of people leave their current positions for other companies. While many leave for more money or greater perceived opportunities, many others leave because they feel that they are not informed or treated as a resource. It is difficult for any one to feel satisfied about what they are doing when they have no understanding of how they fit into the bigger picture of the operation. As managers, we must give them the benefit of timely, effective information about the company. Let's not sell our people short.

Environmental Issues

Going hand-in-hand with the philosophy of sharing company and branch goals and results with the entire office, is the need to share information about outside forces that affect and shape the company's direction. I know of no industry in which the business climate is not changing at a furious pace. The competitive pressures mount with each passing day as individual firms attempt to develop and exploit niches that will consolidate their position with existing customers and expand their influence with potential clients. As the environment continues to change, branch management is constantly challenged to respond. Often overlooked is the fact that many of our employees would also like to know what is going on as well.

While it goes without saying that an informed staff is an important asset, all too often communication is limited to a handful of critical personnel. There seems to be a feeling that most employees would either not understand or have no desire to know what goes on beyond their own duties.

Again, such an attitude sells your staff short. No doubt there are a number of people who will fail to grasp all of the intricacies of what is happening in the marketplace. Still, it is their job, and the place they spend 33% of their work week. Why not give them the benefit of the doubt? Overall, studies have demonstrated that the more employees know about their job, company, and the factors which influence them, the more committed they become to their work.

Since many employees also have direct contact with the customer, it makes good business sense to raise your staff's understanding of the issues facing your industry. While it is unrealistic to expect most employees to be able to articulate these issues in depth, providing them with a basic background can help to position the branch a little better than your competition in your customers' minds. One never knows. At our office, I share with all my employees not only our results, but also a little of what is happening in the industry at large on a monthly and quarterly basis. In so doing, I am trying to say to them that I feel these issues are important, and that I want everyone to be aware of them. So far, it has worked very well.

Other Activities of the Company

Communication can also take place through other issues. If the company has contributed in some fashion to a community activity, it is important to share this with your staff. We all like to feel good about what we are doing and what our company is doing. Give your employees every chance to brag about your company.

Summary

Business is a people-oriented activity. Unfortunately, many managers focus outwardly. While the customer is king, there are a number of things we all should be doing on the inside to bring stability, knowledge, and understanding to our operations. Your greatest resource is your employees. They are the ones who can literally make or break your results. For the most part, they want to have an understanding of their role. Enrich their understanding of their jobs, the goals of the company, the environment and other activities, and you will enrich your results as well. Ignore them and you run the risk of mediocre performance, higher turnover, and poor service.

Chapter 28

Let Me Teach You How to Fish

Robert Clark

"Give a man a fish, feed him for a day, teach him how to fish, feed him for a lifetime." At one time in your career you may have stumbled upon this old adage. Over the years we have come to repeat it frequently in the Greater Princeton Agency since it perhaps best characterizes our agency training philosophy.

From the explorer participating in our career sample, to the fledgling new agent, through the ranks to the veteran of 30 years, a well-orchestrated training system has been one of our unswerving goals.

My exposure to the Agency Management Training Course (AMTC) further enhanced a conviction I had long ago embraced as a high school teacher. A well-designed and consistently well-executed training program, both on a formal and informal level, combined with strong supervision, can have a profound impact on the success or failure of our organization in terms of candidate attraction and selection, agent retention, agency morale, and total productivity.

What AMTC says is true! Without training a good agent will achieve good results, but an average agent will achieve only fair results. However, with training an average agent will achieve good results, and a good agent will achieve superior results.

We can recruit and select good people, give them creative ideas, and put good tools into their hands, but unless we train them to use the ideas and tools *regularly* neither of us are likely to achieve the results we both seek.

And what are the results we both should seek? The major objective of our Agency Training Program is and should be to produce results by increasing both the quantity and quality of the business produced through well-trained agents.

Where does quality agency training begin? First and foremost, it begins with a well-trained general manager or agent. This does not mean improving technical knowledge, such as Chartered Life Underwriter (CLU) or Chartered Financial Consultant (ChFC), but rather by mastering the skills of *how to train* and *how to train others to train*, particularly assistant management and agency specialists. The ability to teach others to train has to be a primary ingredient of a general agent or manager's success in the area of agency training. A general agent or manager cannot accomplish the training task alone, but must rely heavily on a well-trained staff. In the Greater Princeton Agency, we devote much time to the development of assistant management and agency specialist training skills.

Before describing how we train our agents, perhaps a brief picture of our marketing territory is in order. For many the name *Princeton* conjures up thoughts of a quiet, farming community surrounding a prestigious Ivy League University. Although much of this picture still remains, within the last 10 years Princeton has emerged as the epicenter of tremendous growth and development.

Where fields of corn once basked, financial and hi-tech corporate centers characteristic of some of the Fortune 500's best now stand. Along with the corporate growth has come the development of many new upscale homes, condominium and town house communities, shopping centers, malls, and various small businesses. Thus, the market we now serve encompasses not only the stately Princeton of old but also the new entrepreneur, the growing middle class, and the young, upwardly mobile executive. In addition, the large metropolitan markets of New York City and Philadelphia are within an hour's commute of downtown Princeton. The "new" Princeton demands a high calibre, well-trained agent to bring quality products and services to a highly sophisticated and competitive market.

The Career Sample: Selection and Training

"In a few years, you will have the agents you deserve." This short statement packs a lot of truth! Within a brief period of time an agency becomes a direct reflection of the people it recruits and how they are trained.

Quality training begins with the correct selection of candidates. Unless we attract candidates with the required level of learning ability, all training becomes tedious and meaningless for both the trainer and trainee. It is here that we often find the root of manager burnout and agency failure. Poor selection can easily lead to an eventual lack of enthusiasm for good training, while good selection can accelerate the desire for more and better training. Since selection is so integral to our career sample training program, let me briefly explain our selection process.

Selection begins with an initial interview that is generally conducted by our agency recruiter, whom we hired a little over a year ago as part of our continuing evolution toward total agency functionalization. The person we hired came to us with a professional degree and background in recruiting, a real bonus which has not only increased the number of candidates we interview, but also the quality of those candidates.

It's the recruiter's responsibility to conduct a brief fact-finding interview, a career presentation, and administer Prudential's Career Profile Exam which measures the candidate's math and verbal ability as well as sales aptitude. Because we currently require a candidate to pass the Series 6 exam as well as New Jersey's stiff life and health exam prior to giving a full-time contract, high math and verbal scores are a prerequisite.

Candidates who survive the initial interview are subsequently invited to return to the agency for a panel interview conducted by myself and, usually, two functional managers. Each panel member queries the candidate on a series of preassigned career-related questions while the other panel members observe and listen.

Following the interview, panel members meet to discuss the candidate's responses and their observations. We believe the panel interview technique to be superior to our former one-on-one second interview technique. Often, in a one-on-one interview, the interviewer, while recording certain data, may actually miss pertinent observations and nuances of certain responses. The panel interview technique appears to solve that problem and allows for a better selection based on a more complete and refined data gathering system.

Once a candidate passes the scrutiny of the panel, he or she is again invited to the agency to further discuss a career with one or more agents who are in various stages of their careers. We also show the candidate several career-oriented video tapes, and begin the referencing process which we learned from Bernie Rosen through AMTC. Where applicable, we also conduct a spousal interview. Lastly, I once again meet privately with the candidate to discuss my observations and to respond to any of the candidate's concerns.

At this point, if I feel comfortable with the candidate, I extend an invitation to join our career sample. We prefer the term *career sample* rather than *temporary contract* or *precontract* because we want the candidate to understand that the selection process is still ongoing.

Both verbally and in writing we communicate to the candidate the various prospecting, sales, and academic goals that must be achieved during the career sample. Generally our career sample lasts three to four months.

Although a candidate must achieve prospecting and sales goals, it's very possible for us not to offer a candidate a full-time contract for failure to meet out academic goals. As our business has become more complex, we find that the ability to comprehend and learn is of crucial importance to long-term survival and success. Therefore, the ability to learn and receptivity to training are integral parts of selection within our career sample.

Before any training takes place, we assign each candidate to a primary trainer, usually one of our functional managers. It is the primary trainer's responsibility to supervise and coordinate the candidate's training so that by the end of the career sample all training is administered (of course, he may not necessarily personally administer every aspect of the training). The primary trainer ultimately assists me in evaluating the candidate's ability to learn.

Although some overlap exists, we can divide our career sample training into three distinct areas: 1) academic, 2) prospecting and sales skills, and 3) field work.

Academic training consists of a variety of topics. The first is life and health licensing training which we conduct classroom-style as required by the state law. NASD (National Association of Securities Dealers) training is also completed in the classroom with some individual instruction. We also utilize Prudential's Agent Career Path Program Phase 1 (ACPP 1), as a well-composed and well-organized self-directed learning program. The candidate completes all phases of the program on his own under the guidance and supervision of the primary trainer.

The ACPP 1 covers a variety of topics that are important to validate a life underwriter's career sample. Among some of the topics addressed are Application Completion, Project 100, Pioneer Prospecting, Target Marketing, The One Card System, Prudential's Life Portfolio, and so forth. We grade candidates on how accurately and thoroughly they complete the material. All grades are recorded.

We conduct almost all prospecting and sales skills training in the classroom; much of it involves on-camera roleplaying. As I learned in AMTC and have come to more fully appreciate over the years, there is little better substitute for strong skill development than repetitive on-camera roleplaying. We supply each candidate with his or her own videotape for class and individual use.

Classes take place every Saturday morning from 9:00 A.M. until 12:00 P.M. We religiously follow a well-designed lesson plan for each class modeled on the *pesos formula* (prepare, explain, show, observe, and supervise). A variety of topics are addressed and roleplayed, including: the sales process from pre-approach to close, Tom Wolf's Financial Needs Analysis, sundry phone tracks, and a basic lesson in life insurance.

We are convinced that on-camera roleplaying has opened several important opportunities for us, including a window to evaluate a candidate's potential abilities:

- to absorb, and subsequently, to animate abstract concepts;
- to interact with others;
- to close a sale; and also
- to hone a candidate's skills in these areas.

This is where we actually begin to teach a person *how to fish.*

The candidate's primary trainer generally assists and evaluates his prospecting ability. Furthermore, the functional manager, or one of the field supervisors, accompanies the candidate on sales interviews. The first several interviews are entirely handled by the functional manager or field supervisor, with the candidate as an observer. Ultimately, we reverse the roles.

At the end of the three- to four-month career sample, we evaluate the candidate on all of the training that has occurred and make a decision whether or not to offer the candidate a full-time contract. The career sample has been both a selection tool and a springboard to the full-time contract.

New Agent Training

Our major training goal for the new agent is quite simple—to build on the basics established during the career sample. Our training methodology, therefore, does not vary a great deal. We all know that successful producers are those who consistently perform the basics time and time again and, thus, become the most proficient at using them!

Our new agent training program is conducted principally by myself, the management team, and agency specialists. We require all first-year agents to attend a weekly Monday morning class structured mainly upon Prudential's Agent Career Path Program Phase 2 (ACPP 2). The program's purpose is to enhance an agent's product knowledge and sales and the prospecting skills learned during the career sample. On-camera roleplay continues to be an integral part of ACPP2.

We also conduct Friday morning classes on a bimonthly basis for all agents with less than five years experience. These classes are devoted to a variety of more advanced topics. They are often conducted by either one of our agency specialists, e.g., our pension specialist, business insurance specialist, estate planning specialist, or an outside speaker.

In addition, we require enrollment in at least one Life Underwriter Training Council (LUTC) course for agents with less than three years experience and CLU or ChFC for those over three years. Our training system is simple, yet effective. Continuous application and supervision are key.

Middle Agent Training

Because a general manager or agent is often heavily absorbed by recruiting and new agent training and retention, associates who have survived into what I call the *middle years* of their career, five years and over, find their training needs often neglected. Many plateau in their development or even regress. This was exactly the situation we found our agency about six years ago; we decided to do something about it.

In 1982 we formed the *Senior Agent Skill Development Program* designed for agents with five or more years experience. The purpose of the program basically was, and is, to pay attention to the training needs of these agents and to enhance and develop their skills and knowledge as well as productivity. In general, the program has been a tremendous success. Several of the participants have become perennial Million Dollar Round Table (MDRT) qualifiers as well as qualifiers of Prudential's President's Club. Others have moved up to at least the Regional Business Conference qualifier level.

By design, the program's moderator is required to be a perennial MDRT and President's Club qualifier who leads by example. Our present moderator, Agent Roy Hudson, CLU, does the job admirably. The approximate 11-member group meets monthly to discuss and review a variety of insurance-related topics from prospecting to pensions, to clerical support training. In addition, the moderator meets with each agent individually once a month to review any progress made toward goals and to discuss whatever is on the agent's mind. I receive a written progress report from the moderator following each session. In conclusion, sometimes it seems just simply paying attention to an agent can spell the difference between success and failure.

Advanced Agent Training

Much of our advanced agent training is usually accomplished in a variety of ways. Some is accomplished on an individual basis, while the remainder may be on a more formal level through study groups, attendance at CLU institutes, MDRT and CLU seminars, and home office training. We have also begun to utilize Prudential's newly developed Agent Career Path Program Phase 3 (ACPP 3) which is designed for more advanced agent training. The program covers such topics as Executive Compensation, Split Dollar, 162 Bonus Plans and Pensions, etc. As we continue to grow, we expect to expand in this area.

Although we are quite proud of our very formalized training system, we feel the glue that really holds it together is the agency's high morale. We have a generous spirit of sharing among all agency associates. Basically, we all want to see each other succeed and make the whole greater than the sum of its parts.

Summary

Over the last seven years, the Greater Princeton Agency has invested much time and effort in developing strong selection and training systems. We feel our efforts have been well rewarded, as is evidenced by the fact that our agency has won a number of our firm's President's Citations and continues to rank among its leading ordinary agencies.

As a management team, we are committed to quality selection and the continuous evaluation and refinement of our training systems. We find the right anglers and train them on how to fish properly. In this way, we know we will reap a bountiful catch.

Chapter *29*

Handling of New, Old, and Great FCs

Three Kinds of FCs

Among the FCs in your office, you probably have a mixture of rookies (less than two to three years in production), experienced FCs (more than two to three years) who are doing fairly well, and star performers (who have both experience, usually at least five years, *and* good production). Each group should be thought of as separate and distinct from the others. Each has different needs and understandings and requires different types/levels of ongoing training and motivation. (*Note:* We realize that some FCs will fall into more than one group and recommend that you group them according to their primary performance attributes.)

As with almost anything, you or your designate will spend the majority of time working with the people who have the least production, that is, your new FCs. They require the greatest amount of supervision and training, they have the most questions, and they have the highest probability of failing. Hence, your work with them will require several years before you realize a fully satisfying return on investment.

The more experienced FCs with medium production levels are often a manager's greatest frustration because they could probably be doing substantially more with their careers and their lives. Some of them are obviously progressing. For these people, you may want to speed up the process. Unfortunately, too many FCs in this group are probably going nowhere quickly. Some of them have simply become locked in a comfort zone and do not extend themselves. They are often the most difficult to work with, yet will give you the greatest immediate and long-term return on investment.

We'll call the final group the *stars* of the office. We realize that they are not necessarily stars within the industry, but they are the big fish in your pond. Whether they act like prima donnas or busy executives, these people need to be handled with kid gloves, and treated with respect. They need you to smooth the way for them and to resolve day-to-day problems. Since this small percentage of the office is probably generating the majority of the revenue, assisting them in any way possible is always a good idea. However, they also need additional education and need you to work with them. The leverage that they can provide you will manifest itself throughout the office.

Given this broad overview of the needs of the three groups, the balance of the chapter will discuss the approaches that you might take with each group.

We assume that you really wish to develop your FCs and to maximize their potentials. Then everybody wins. Unfortunately, there are many firms with the philosophy that everybody should just either sink or swim. We suggest that you teach everyone possible how to swim. As you do, some of those who might have otherwise drowned will now stay afloat, and some of those who may have been poor swimmers may now have the opportunity to swim like champions.

Why FCs Fail

Everyday, hundreds of FCs who entered the financial services industry with boundless enthusiasm drop out or are fired for failing to make the grade. The reasons given for failure are many. The actual list may be enormous, but there are a number that occur with a great degree of frequency. They include:

- Cold calling is too hard.
- Can't take the rejection.
- Can't take the responsibility for handling money.
- Can't make decisions.
- Hours are too long.
- Pressure is too much.
- Found another job.
- Market is too high/low/volatile, etc.
- Lack of production.
- Put all eggs in one basket and they broke.
- Put all hope in one egg and it went bad.
- Not enough sales support (as if it were really necessary).
- Move to another firm ("grass is greener" belief).
- Compliance problems.
- Stress.

Selling is a very stressful job. FCs get it from their clients. They get it from the managers. None of these people started off intending to do poorly. Something went wrong and the next thing you hear is another excuse.

While the excuses are infinite, the excuses/rationales—real or imagined—usually fall into one of three categories: They don't know *HOW TO*; they don't have the *CHANCE TO*; they don't *WANT TO*; or some combination of the three.

How To

Training is the normal response. If a person does not know how to do the job, then an educational program is needed. Many rookies have never learned the basic communication skills that are so important. A lack of product knowledge can limit the potential of even excellent communicators. Although some people can sell ice to an Eskimo, they will probably find themselves in a compliance problem unless they have product knowledge and ethics. There are books to read, courses to take, and people to emulate in order to address these *How To* issues. It is important to take such training one step at a time so that the FCs can actually absorb all that they need to learn.

Lack of knowledge is also a problem for intermediate FCs who may not have advanced their knowledge level to the degree that they should have. They may or may not realize it, and if they do realize it, they might not always admit it.

The *stars* usually have a substantial amount of know how. However, even the most knowledgeable FCs don't know it all. In addition, because of their influence within the office—whether or not they actually want it—their pursuit of knowledge will stimulate the others to do the same. Finally, because of the number of clients they have, they will be able to maximize their use of any new knowledge, translating it into commission revenue.

Chance To

Many FCs are actually prevented from doing their job because of barriers to effective performance. These barriers can include lack of phone coverage, lack of secretarial help, handling too many trivial client problems, or too much paperwork. Often, people prevent themselves from doing anything because they are too disorganized and spend all their time planning while actually accomplishing nothing of value.

The *Chance To* issue is a problem for all FCs, regardless of their level. Each has daily problems that he must contend with, and each runs the risk of allowing those problems to either rule or overwhelm. As the manager, it is your responsibility to get things out of your FC's way as well as to sometimes assist him in getting out of his own way.

Want To

People may have all the knowledge and opportunity in the world, but without the basic desire or motivation they will go absolutely nowhere. This lack of desire can take many forms, including:

- Fear of failure.
- Fear of success.
- Stress.
- Illness—physical, emotional, or mental.
- Family conflicts.
- Personal internal conflict(s).

286

- Office politics and affiliations.
- Fear of taking risks (personal or market).
- Fear of pain (rejection, being wrong, etc.).
- Incompatible goals.
- Want something different (hidden agenda).

You can have a positive effect on many of these *Want To* issues by working with people, providing advice and motivation, and counseling. Other problems, such as family conflicts and illnesses, are outside of your control, but you may still be able to influence them. As the branch manager and chief role model, you have tremendous persuasive abilities if you choose to use them. In fact, your leadership abilities may be the determining factor when it comes to which of your employees make it in this world and which do not.

As we explore the things you may consider doing with each of the three groups of FCs, you will find that you are often dealing with issues involving either *How To, Want To,* or *Chance To.* (This concept was more fully discussed in Chapter 3.) As we identify the needs of each group, we'll provide a variety of ideas that you may wish to implement. We hope that they will spark additional ideas which may be even more helpful for your particular office situation. (*Note:* If you have any special methods which you feel would be worth mentioning, please let us know and we will credit you with them in future editions.)

Trainees and Beginners

Some of them just might make it. Most of them won't. Some of those who otherwise wouldn't may have a chance IF you provide the help and direction they need. This help and direction can take many forms, including emulation of the star producers, what behaviors you choose to reward, how you react to them and others, as well as any training that they receive.

Basically, new FCs need direction and guidance just like any other new employee. Most new people are a bundle of energy that is seemingly going in all directions at once. While a pleasure to watch, this unbridled energy can also be dangerous if left without proper direction. In their enthusiasm, new FCs will often try almost anything that looks as though it will work, without thinking of the consequences to the customer of the firm. Remember that new FCs may not be completely familiar with ethical and business regulations and their application to sales. They can also dissipate their enthusiasm by becoming bogged down in activities that do not move them toward their goals. If you allow them to do this for too long, you can waste that energy before they achieve success.

One way of channeling their energy is by acclimating them to the company and its culture. The philosophy that you expound and the approaches that you suggest will form much of their foundation. By identifying the character traits you desire, the personal attributes you admire, and your philosophy of doing business, you set the frame in which these people work.

Since talk is cheap, it is incumbent upon you to actively demonstrate your beliefs through your day-to-day interactions with these and other employees. (This has already been discussed in Chapter 2 on character—Reflections of You: Developing Star Traits—and its development.) Your philosophy of doing business will pervade the entire office. Yet, the new employee will soon be faced with any contradictions that may exist and will certainly have to deal with the office *assassins* and malcontents. Any idealism can quickly wear off unless treated with regular doses of reinforcement.

Fortunately, reinforcement can take many forms, from your own enthusiasm to regular personal progress reviews. We believe that new FCs need regular performance and goal reviews. They may have goals that are too simple and easy to attain and require upgrading. This is often the case when they first start production and fail to establish more meaningful goals after a few months. They may accomplish the easier goal but end up bored and frustrated. On the other hand, their initial goals may be too strenuous. This often leads to burnout problems. In either situation, the FC *is not performing to expectations* and, because of the nature of the problem, *cannot perform to expectations.*

A periodic review of prospecting and selling skills is also important. Once an FC gets on the phone for awhile, it becomes easy to accumulate, maintain, and accentuate poor verbal patterns. Force of habit takes over and the FC no longer hears his own mistakes. He may be able to sell things, but he is probably not as efficient or as effective as he could be. This review can take the form of having a mentor listen to some conversations, periodic peer reviews, or outside training courses.

288

Help from peers and/or from an assigned mentor is often invaluable. It can alleviate a host of pressures and provide a learning and motivational tool. People sometimes feel stranded and alone; being a member of a group in which everyone is experiencing the same thing is comforting. The group members can get into mini sales contests with each other and can often motivate each other to higher levels of performance.

A mentor often accomplishes the same purpose. Here, a more successful producer, who knows the tricks of the trade, can provide knowledge based on years of experience. In addition, the mentor can really understand the problems that new FCs face. This is usually NOT true of the FC's family and friends. The mentor can often also provide helpful solutions by saying, "I've faced that problem in the past and this is how I've solved it." Finally, mentors have more product knowledge and can be an additional role model for the rookie. (*Note:* Of course, you have to make it worthwhile for the star to provide even a limited amount of time. This will be discussed later.)

Motivation is ultimately something that is the responsibility of the individual FC. Support from peers and a mentor will be major influences, but the additional support of family and friends can often make all the difference in the world. Suggest that your FCs bring their friends and families by the office. This is important because most people like to be recognized as someone important, especially by spouse and children. After all, the FCs will be spending many evenings at the office, away from them. Their families need to understand and be supportive; otherwise conflicts can occur which will distract the FC from the job at hand. By bringing family members into the process, you can often obtain their active support by helping them to understand that those nights at the office are for their benefit.

When you speak to an FC regarding goals, ask about what benefits the family will receive. Try to have the FC set goals with his family. This will enable him to work harder and handle the stresses of the job more effectively. Chapter 17, *Stress and Motivation*, identifies the negative results of mishandling work-related pressures.

Family members of FCs tend to respond favorably to information about any career tracks that may be available for those who do well in the business. The heavy price for success paid now may pay off in the future, and many families are willing to make sacrifices provided they know why they're making those sacrifices. Alternative discussions could occur at the home of a successful FC who throws a party for the rookies. The rookie's family members realize that such a lifestyle can be theirs if Dad or mom is successful (more on this idea shortly).

Despite all of these long-term goals and the appreciation that hard work will result in the attainment of desires, the FC must still get down to work. Even great long-term goals often get lost in the midst of day-to-day hassles. The rejection associated with getting new customers is often very difficult to deal with. Ultimately, the FC must go it alone and make the daily effort. Here, too, you can help.

This is a motivational idea that many FCs have found very helpful. It involves a realization that each phone call that they make puts money in their pockets. That *prospecting is a numbers game* is well-known and intellectually appreciated by virtually every salesperson in the world. Why is it then that so few people act upon this knowledge and dial the phone much more often? Part of the reason is what we call *telephone-a-phobia*, which is addressed in another chapter. Another part is that they do not emotionally feel the need for a numbers game, nor do they feel good about being rejected.

The analogy that we use is simple. We pull out a roll of five dollar bills and then ask the FC to pick up the phone and pretend to dial a number. Not quite knowing what is going on, the FC picks up the phone and pretends to dial. In the middle of the dialing, we say, "No answer" and drop a $5 bill on the FCs' desk. "Pick up the phone again," we say. This time, as the FC dials we say, "Busy," and drop another $5 bill on the desk. This is done two or three more times while saying "Person not interested," or "Dial a Prayer," or "Person has no money." We then ask the FC how many phone calls he could make on a daily basis if each and every time he dialed, regardless of the response, or if he got through at all, we dropped five dollars on the desk. Most talk easily in terms of 200 to 400 phone calls per day. Motivation to call comes easily at five dollars per call. Who cares about the big "R" (rejection) at this rate? The point is well made.

We might ask, "How about if you were paid every hour on the hour? Could you do it then?" "Certainly," is always the reply. "How about at the end of each and every day?" Again, "Certainly," is the reply. We then tell the FC, "If you think about it, this is what your manager is really doing for you. But instead of hourly or daily, he lumps all of the payments into a weekly or biweekly check. What's the difference?" Its all in our perception or in our understanding of what the reality of the situation is.

As the manager, you must be able to provide FCs with the

290

important insight that *they pay themselves* every time they pick up the phone. This is relatively easy if you are also aware of their key motivations, the way they think, and their psychological profile (all of which are the subjects of other chapters).

Rookies need so many things that it becomes difficult to list them all. As in any other profession, their main lack is experience. But, whether or not they will be around long enough to gain it is very much up to you. Your help and motivational skills will often be determining factors. Hence, your awareness of their needs is also very important. Remember, as you work to empower others, you also derive major rewards since your performance is ultimately based upon the performance of your people.

The Middle or Intermediate FC

Intermediate FCs are quite different. They have different goals, desires, needs, and limitations. Let's consider the typical person that we have identified as the middle or the intermediate producer.

- They've been around for two to three years or more.
- Their production has seemingly leveled out.
- They have a good amount of product knowledge but are not maximizing their potential.
- If they were to extend themselves, they could probably double or triple their production.

They are the bane of most managers' existence. They are doing well enough to be left alone, but not well enough to be left entirely to their own devices. They are often difficult to deal with, but can provide you with great returns for your effort.

In essence there are a few things to do with this group. These include:

- Jump-starting their motors,
- moving them out of their *comfort zones,*
- encouraging them to continue their education,
- dealing with stress, and
- updating their goals.

When talking to managers about this group, we've run into the all too common attitude of, *If it ain't broke, don't fix it.* If you are *truly* happy with the overall production of this group, that's fine. But, if you really understand that this group has the greatest ability to significantly increase your branch's gross production, you may feel that the problem is worth fixing.

It has often been demonstrated that it is easier to move a $250,000 producer to $500,000 that it is to move a $50,000 producer to $100,000. The larger producers already have the know-how and the customer base to further expand their production. Unfortunately, they are often also more comfortable and willing to let their momentum carry them. They rarely seem to understand that if you are not going forward, you are going backward. Some don't fully appreciate that they will lose between 10%–20% of their clients during the next year through moving, dying, disenchantment, or being solicited away by a new FC at another firm who is actually cold calling. Hence, while they accept and follow up on referrals, they barely keep even with natural attrition.

The individual who is in a *comfort zone* is usually someone who has developed a customer base which provides him with the amount of income he wants without serious effort. One technique that has been successfully used in a variety of industries, and which can be very effective in motivating almost any mid-level FC who has reached his comfort level, is to increase his family's motivation to improve their standard of living.

We suggested to one sales manager that she sponsor a party to be given at the home of one of her star salespeople. She, and the star producer, invited all of the targeted FCs *and their families* to a pool party. A mini fashion show was part of the day in which a local couturier and a furrier exhibited some of their waves.

While walking around the pool enjoying the benefits of *the better life*, FCs and their families were realizing that it would only take a modest increase in family income for them to have a similar lifestyle. Of course, some were already thinking how they would do the living room differently and how they would prefer different landscaping. In sales parlance, they already *owned* it. The sales manager had at least one more surprise for the party. The local Mercedes-Benz, Jaguar, and Ferrari dealers had been requested to bring three or four demonstration cars to the party so that people could try them out.

Everything was done in good taste and the sales manager picked up the cost of the party. What was exciting was the fact that the lifestyle goals that were modeled were achievable, realistic, and within the reach of every FC at the party. But, they were *just outside of these FCs' comfort zone.*

The comfort zones of quite a few FCs were modified as a result of that party. Interestingly, an additional benefit of the party was an increased interest and involvement of several star producers with the rest of the office because they were equivalently-made role models. A couple of them even hosted their own parties.

This technique doesn't necessarily have such dramatic results with every participant. Some FCs need to attend two or three "parties" before they really hit home, and a few won't be affected at all. However, this kind of activity certainly generates interest. The same technique can be used with the new brokers. A very important consideration is to make sure that the goal can become achievable by putting in some additional effort. If they go to a party that is totally out of their league, then the distance between where they are and where they would like to be might seem insurmountable (which could be highly demotivating).

Performance, or lack thereof, is dependent upon a person's conscious and unconscious goals. It is a rare individual (3%—see *Goal Setting* in Chapter 3, *Hitting What You Aim At*) who consciously determines goals and objectives and writes them down, and it is an extraordinarily rare individual who periodically updates those goals. These individuals tend to become the leaders of the industry.

Goal updating is something that you, as a manager, are forced to do on a regular basis for business objectives. It is something that you regularly do for your FCs by assigning them yearly production goals. What really makes the difference is having the FCs make the goal their own and buy into it.

Sometimes you have to talk to them about inflation and the eroding value of their commission checks. Sometimes you'll need to discuss their performance relative to someone else in the group. Other times you'll need to promise them some sort of award. What will motivate them is largely determined by their psychological motivations which you will determine in other meetings. (See Chapters 14, 15, and 16 for specific information.)

One good thing about people is that they like to be respected and appreciated. Just as you made some of the stars into role models for the intermediates, you can make some of the intermediates into role models, or mentors, for the rookies. Role models tend to lead by example. They'll work harder and stay up longer so that they can show the correct face to the world.

There is almost a cause-effect relationship that if you increase a person's product knowledge and communication skills, you will get a resultant increase in productivity. Getting people to study during their leisure hours is not an easy task. Getting intermediate producers to actively practice their prospecting and selling skills on their own also has an extremely low probability factor. But, IF you get them to teach the rookies, THEN almost everyone's skills will be upgraded. It's relatively simple to initiate. It will take about six months to have the full results realized. The results will absolutely be worth the effort. Specific procedures are provided in Chapter 30.

There will be times when a coaching and counseling session will be required to really motivate a particular FC. Often, given the procedures we are suggesting, it is better to leave well enough alone since the upgrading of the entire office usually causes a ripple effect for most of the office personnel.

Sometimes, after you've done all that you can, you may have to make a decision regarding whether or not to continue an individual's employment. Remember that you would have had multiple meetings with someone prior to this point. If, after using all your skills, he still does nothing, he may become an energy drain on you and the rest of the office. If that happens, you just may not be able to afford that cost. In addition, if a person is not making it and has very little probability of making it, then he is probably in the wrong business. Trite as it may sound, you may actually be doing him a favor by firing him. Remember that people don't start off intending to do poorly. But, if they and you have really tried, it is usually best to let them do something else in which they can succeed.

Stress is a factor which must be taken into consideration when dealing with any FC who is not performing at his best. Since it is covered in numerous other sections, it is sufficient to simply make note of it here.

A final point, your intermediate FCs should realize that they don't have to be great to become star performers. They merely need to become very good. They need to realize that they can *choose to succeed.*

The Star Producer

Often, the greatest single asset of any branch is its *Star Producers*. As major sources of revenue for the branch, as role models for other FCs, and as sources of production ideas, these individuals can have a tremendous positive influence on any branch *if they are utilized effectively*. Begin by giving them the respect that their success has earned. At the same time, remember that respect does not mean adoration.

Recognize the reality that any FC can easily walk to your competition. In fact, the good ones are always being solicited and would certainly be welcomed (the odds are good that some of your best FCs did not begin their careers with your firm). Hence, avoid giving unnecessary offense by being overly rigid and demanding. Of course, even this must be balanced with their recognition that they are generally expected to abide by the same rules as everyone else. We know of many new office managers who started off setting down the law and lost good FCs unnecessarily, or were too lax and lost control of the branch. Establishing just the right level of control is always difficult but can be accomplished if you are prepared to be flexible as well as firm.

As a manager you must determine just what you wish to accomplish in the branch. As obvious as this question may appear on the surface, it goes far beyond simple production goals and the critical few requirements of senior management. What do you wish to accomplish in terms of the overall growth of the branch, yourself, and your employees? How are you going to accomplish your goal and what resources will you need? Whatever your goals, your employees are certainly your most important resource and helping them to clarify and achieve their goals will be one of the most effective ways to achieve your own.

The demands that star producers seem to make are usually items that can be negotiated. As you obtain this information, you will also discover their key motivational criteria as well as what they feel are the barriers that are preventing them from going even faster. Unfortunately, a few prima-donna superstars may not be as thoughtful in their dealings with you and their peers as they are with their customers and prospects. Fortunately, industrywide, these prima donnas are a relatively small percentage of the star performers. Most star performers are reasonable business people who work incredibly hard to actively juggle a million and one things at the same time.

As is true with all the groups, people like to be recognized. In our motivation chapter, three of the needs that are discussed are the needs for **Power** and/or **Affiliation** and/or **Achievement**. Depending upon the stars' motivation(s) you will be able to fulfill their psychological needs. With this and other information provided in the chapters on motivation and communication, you should be able to persuade most of the stars to participate in your office plans. This is important because you want some or all of them to be role models for the rest of the group, to host occasional parties, to become mentors for someone else, participate in group discussions, and to lend their expertise to other FCs. Remember, you'll be trying to accomplish this with a group of people who has little, if any, time to spare.

The first thing to do is to find out how you can help them to achieve their goals. Once you have assisted them in one or more items and you have more precisely determined their psychological needs and make-up, you'll be in a better position to ask for their help. They need to realize that by helping the office they are actually helping/rewarding themselves. Without going into any detail in this chapter, suffice it to say that the *power-oriented* person will obtain more influence with the rest of the staff; the *affiliation-oriented* person will have more pleasant interactions; and the *achievement-oriented* person will have some tangible awards for his efforts. Each will feel good about himself, the office, his co-workers, and his branch manager.

Research indicates that most star producers are unaware of the total amount of stress under which they work. They literally can't see the forest because of the trees. They would probably derive significant benefit from our section on how to deal with stress. One statistic from that section should capture your attention: The average million dollar producer who participated in a stress reduction program had productivity increases of 100% within one year; had substantially decreased the probability of heart failure; and felt much better about themselves and their work.

While the family members of the star producers are undoubtedly used to their work load and the attitudes that are brought home, that does not mean that they are happy with these things. Statistics clearly show that a divorce or family problems severely affect an FC's production level. In addition, stress appears to be the single greatest cause of those family problems and divorces. Intervene to reduce the stress before you lose a good producer.

296

Summary

Three types of FCs present three types of challenges. The new FC needs to be nurtured and carefully directed so that his boundless enthusiasm becomes a power that drives him to success and not self-destruction. The experienced FC who has reached his comfort level needs to be motivated to do even better. Finally, the star producer is an asset that needs to be carefully managed to provide the greatest leadership and support for the branch.

Since you set the tone for your office, you can initiate changes that will have dramatic effects on your bottom line. However, it is important to implement change slowly, evaluate the results, and give your staff time to adjust. Motivate and persuade people and they will do anything you wish. Since it is also for their benefit, everybody wins—and creating win-win situations is part of what management is all about.

Section VII

Training

The financial services industry has changed so much in the last 10 years that it has become almost a different industry for many people. The players have changed. Banks, securities dealers, and insurance companies are now all functioning in all three areas. The proliferation of products and services alone is enough to require constant training updates if one is to stay current. More important, the market has changed.

Today's market is made up of individuals and companies that are far better informed about their financial needs than ever before. They expect and demand service. Old methods of selling will no longer bring success and many of them could even lead to law suits.

However, the domestic market is not the only one that is changing. More and more companies and their FCs are becoming involved with foreign customers. As we approach 1992 and the finalization of the European Economic Community, we must be ready to serve that community or lose significant market share (these issues will be dealt with in Section VIII). The following chapters will provide insights into the importance of training in each area of the financial services industry.

Chapter 30

One Product Per Week

Virtually every firm in the industry provides some level of formal training for its FCs. It begins with whatever study courses are available for any required licensing exams, and usually continues after the exam(s) with in-house training on procedures, products, and services. Some firms even provide a mentor program in which new FCs are assigned to work with experienced, successful members of the branch for their first three to 12 months. This is particularly helpful because of all the day-to-day procedures every new FC has to learn in order to work effectively in a branch office.

Needless to say, assigning a new FC to work with a mentor for her first few months can significantly speed up this assimilation process. However, even with formal in-house training and a mentor, most firms have many more products and services than can be formally presented. As a result, many new FCs find themselves a little overwhelmed in their efforts to obtain the product knowledge that they need. Simply put, they don't even know where to begin and which products and services to begin with. Yet, we know that the faster they become comfortable with the entire range of your company's products and services, the more effective your FCs will be in selling them. One way to encourage an FC to learn this material is through the use of study groups.

Obviously, getting FCs to study during their leisure hours is not an easy task. Neither is getting them to practice their prospecting and selling skills on their own. However, the peer review provided by a group can be a powerful motivator that can make the difference.

Installing a Product Presentation Program

Before you begin, let the FCs know that you are establishing a new program to enhance the professionalism of the FCs within the branch and that, eventually, all FCs will be expected to participate. Then, when each new FC is hired, explain the ongoing study requirements as part of their job description. At first, you may wish to begin with just the new FCs, and expand gradually until all FCs in the branch are involved. However, you may also wish to involve the more experienced FCs from the start. If so, you may ask for volunteers, or just select the FCs yourself and assign them. There are advantages and disadvantages to both approaches and you should use the one that you think will work best in your office.

Once you've dealt with the issue of attendance, establish a time early in the morning or late in the afternoon when they will be expected to meet. Once they've started, and have demonstrated a real commitment to the program, you may decide to be more flexible in their meeting arrangements.

Begin by dividing all of the participating FCs into study groups, or teams, of six. Then, on a rotational basis, assign one team member to learn as much as possible about a particular product or service. It will be her responsibility to present it to the other group members during a Monday morning team meeting. (*Note:* If you have morning sales/staff meetings, you may wish to have the teams meet during lunch or in the afternoons.) Using the formats suggested in Chapter 5, "How Running Effective Meetings/Sales Meetings," she should provide handouts, summaries, visual aids, and copies of any available literature on the product. Make sure that each team member knows her assignment two to three weeks in advance.

That person will then explain the features, benefits, and advantages of the assigned product or service to the other team members using layman's terms (as if they knew absolutely nothing about it). The use of layman's terms is important because it will enable team members to develop their own explanations of the product for clients who are also unfamiliar with its concepts and jargon. This presentation is then followed by a question and answer period, and by a group brainstorm on more effective ways of presenting the product to prospects and clients.

Once the team has completed brainstorming, each member should write a prospecting and/or sales script for the assigned product or service. Next, the team should break up into smaller groups of two or three people, and use their scripts to make trial presentations to each other. This will give them a chance to verbalize their own presentation once, and hear other presentations once or twice as well. At the end of each presentation, the other member(s) of the group should provide informal feedback on their reaction to the presentation. Such feedback can be most useful if it is given from a gut rather than just an academic response. For example:

- "Tom, I really liked your explanation of the new property and casualty insurance. It was easy to understand and I felt very comfortable with it." Or,

- "Jane, when you suggested that I had to make an immediate decision regarding the new program, it made me feel very pushed and uncomfortable. Up to that point I was very interested, but once you started pushing I wanted to back off."

That Monday Afternoon

Each person in the group is responsible for calling three or four friends, family members or information junkie customers who *cannot buy the product or service* and telling them about it. There is no possibility of an order, but there is a possibility of a referral. The key to these presentations is that they may be made in a *riskless environment* to people who want to assist. Have the FCs start with something like: "I just learned about a new product or service. Let me explain it to you."

That evening, once they've made their practice calls, all of the group members should get together and discuss the questions that they couldn't answer and share what worked and what didn't work.

Tuesday

Each FC should make four to five presentations to people who probably will *not* buy the product now but who may wish to purchase it sometime in the distant future. Because the FC does not expect the individual to buy, the presentations remain relatively riskless.

Wednesday

It is now time to make four to five presentations to people who can give the FCs a small order in the near future. By now, each FC has made anywhere between 10 to 15 presentations on the assigned product/service in both riskless and low-risk environments. In addition, each FC has by now developed both a good working knowledge of, and an increased comfort with, the product or service.

Thursday and Friday

Have each FC in the group make a dozen or more presentations to people who need the product (suitability) and can place an order now or in the immediate future. By this time, the FC has made over 30 presentations and has probably made a few sales. It becomes very easy to stay current on that product or service once it has been learned. The FC now has one more product to sell to her customers; one more tool to qualify people with; one more opportunity to gather and allocate assets.

On the following Monday, a different group member presents a new or related product or service and the process begins all over again. Just imagine what these people could be doing 52 weeks down the road. Allowing for delays and other priorities, they will probably have worked on 30 to 40 new products and services during that time frame. These FCs, regardless of their initial starting levels, will be well on their way to becoming extraordinarily knowledgable and sophisticated. (*Note:* It is important to avoid any tendency to rush the process. Allow for some flexibility and realize that there will be some overlapping. One year later, those people who have participated are probably going to be doing substantially better than those FCs who did not participate.)

If you originally selected participants on a volunteer basis, you may find at this point that those who elected not to join the group are now doing it on their own. Once they see how well it works, many FCs will really want to join the crowd. Make them earn their place and they will appreciate the opportunity.

Approaches and Benefits of Group Study

Now that we have presented the basic program, let's examine some of the approaches you can take, as well as some of the benefits that will be derived.

- At first you may want to initiate this program with a small pilot group, people who volunteer after hearing the idea presented in a larger sales meeting. Prior to this, it would be helpful to have preselected a team leader—other than yourself—who will act as the instructor.

  –For the skills portion, the instructor should be someone who has a recognized ability in prospecting or selling. This person will have to be willing to share some of her secrets by giving pragmatic solutions rather than vague generalizations. Ideally, it should be one of your star producers who would be willing to donate a bit of her time and effort to the development of the other FCs.

  –For the product knowledge portion, the instructor should be someone who can explain things on both a simple and a complex level. Usually, any FC who does a large business in a particular product will be a good candidate for this role. Realize, however, that a good salesperson is not necessarily a good instructor. You need a person who wants to develop her instructional abilities and presentation skills which can then be utilized in seminars.

- If you use the *one product per week* approach, you'll get maximum long-term benefit. This approach teaches people about products in a very effective and organized way. Within six months you will see dramatic results.

- The initial group members will regularly work with one another on skills and knowledge development. The intermediate FCs will teach the rookies and each other. The star FCs will teach everyone, including each other.

- After creating the positive responses you need by devoting additional time and effort to your pilot group, you can expand the concept to other FCs within your office. Some will jump at the opportunity to join the original group or to form a parallel group. Others will remain hesitant or uninterested—"Rome wasn't built in a day."

    —As new people come into the office they are automatically put into a group run by one of your more advanced rookies. Since this is introduced as a normal part of the job for these new people, you won't have to go through the transition period.

    The advanced rookie that teaches the course will increase his own presentation abilities while reinforcing his own knowledge.

    —Eventually, usually within the first six months, you'll want to bring in the FCs who elected not to participate. In an individual coaching and counseling session you can present the benefits in ways that will make them understand. See Section V for details.

Potential Problems

With any program there are always potential problems. Fortunately, each is easy to avoid if planned for in advance.

- There may be initial resentment at having to go to all these meetings. If the initial group consists of volunteers, this should not be an issue. Also, if the meetings are well planned and provide valuable information that meets the needs of the attendees, then the meetings will become valuable sessions for the group. We specifically included a chapter on how to organize and run a sales meeting for exactly this purpose.

- Some presenters may initially do a poor job. This is okay as long as you use this as an opportunity to teach effective presentation or platform skills. There are many good books on the subject. If you write to us for examples, we will be pleased to send you a few pages of techniques that we have written.

- The cooperation between FCs may vary until people get into the routine of helping each other.

- People may be unwilling or unable to provide objective, quality feedback in the initial weeks. (Comments on how to provide feedback follow shortly.)

- Some people (whether you use the volunteer method or not) may wish to drop out because of the extra work involved. Others may try to drop out after their first poor performance, especially if the feedback is viewed as criticism. This is often a result of performance anxiety.

- One or two people will really shine and may have a tendency to dominate the group and be used as the only models.

- Usually, one or two people will have very definite opinions on how things should be done. The need to hear as many ideas as possible must be emphasized to the group. There is no one right way. There are always many ways to accomplish any objective and you'll probably hear some very interesting innovations if you allow the creative processes to occur. This point needs to be constantly reiterated.

- Occasionally other priorities will make it necessary to change the meeting date. This is to be expected, and while the meeting should not be locked in stone, these self-developmental meetings should be considered a high priority item. Once FCs start noticing the increases in their own performance levels then *they* will make it a high priority.

- The meetings can have a tendency to turn into bull sessions rather than work sessions. How closely your supervise the sessions and the interest you demonstrate will have a large effect on this.

- Unless you have a good amount of diversity of topic presentation, the meetings can quickly become stale.

An Important Note on Feedback

It is important to teach people how to provide effective feedback. Please review Chapter 22, which provides a 12-point method of giving high quality feedback.

The participants should be offered the option of how they would like their feedback to be given to them as individuals. Some people prefer it laid on the line, while others need it sugar-coated. Some prefer comments with alternatives so that they have other choices. Of course, there are the very private people who will be totally unable to withstand any public commentary.

How to give feedback is important whether you are dealing with stand-up presentations or evaluations of sales calls. When feedback—not criticism—is given in the right way, the person receiving it can hear it and make use of it. If provided in the wrong way, it can be taken as criticism, and bring all the individual's defensive mechanisms into play.

Summary

No single training program can adequately prepare a new FC for the complex task of mastering all of the procedures, products, and services found in today's branch office. By establishing study groups, you can rapidly increase your FCs product knowledge as well as their selling and prospecting skills. These groups become particularly useful in the support they provide to their participants as well as the structured system they offer for disseminating information on new products and services.

Chapter 31

New Directions In Branch Management Training

The management of most companies today is made up of graduates of the country's many business schools. Harvard, Wharton, Stanford, and many others have turned out generations of highly trained managers, competent to analyze and run medium and large companies. However, with the possible exception of banking, few branch managers and sales managers in today's financial services industry hold an MBA. They have risen to their current rank from the sales force by being dynamic, successful, sales persons. As a result, they have not had the benefit of two years of graduate training in typical management skills and need to obtain such training if they are to function effectively in their current callings. Fortunately, branch management training in the financial services industry is undergoing a major renaissance and, when done correctly, can be an important element in raising the level of effectiveness of all managers within an organization.

This period in history has been well labeled as the *information age*. New products and services as well as new marketing techniques designed to cope with them are only a few of the challenges faced by today's manager. Add to that the continued blurring of the lines separating banks, brokers, and insurance firms and the increasing sophistication of customers and the difficulty of staying up to date approaches nightmare proportions. As a result, branch management training must be an ongoing process that includes all managers within the organization. In many ways, the company CEO and other senior managers have just as many learning needs as a new manager.

For a branch management training program to be successful it must have receptive, talented managers attending courses that are designed to meet their special managerial needs. Very few programs will be successful if those who attend arrive with a bad attitude. Failure is also guaranteed if the attendees are not suited to being a good manager, or if the program is not designed to meet their needs. Hence, manager selection as well as program development are crucial to any program's success.

In many ways, it is important to remember that the branch manager is, effectively, the CEO of his own little company. His needs, as well as the problems he faces, are often unique. For example, today's financial services branch manager is as wholly responsible for production, community marketing, sales and service, as if the president of the Chevrolet Division of General Motors. However, he does not have the support staff of Chevrolet's president. In addition, almost any employee in the branch can put that branch out of business and end the branch manager's career through a single costly act of dishonesty or incompetence. In some cases, a single unhappy sales person can leave the branch for another firm and serious affect the branch's overall earnings for that year.

As a result of these, and other challenges, focusing on the ongoing abilities of managers to expect, embrace, and effectively manage the process of organizational change, several features should be included in the development of management training programs. In the author's estimation, the following elements are necessary:

- *Internal Ownership*—Even when you use outside help in the development and delivery of a training program, identify and promote the program from its inception as part of your company's internal development policy. Too often, such programs end up appearing as a vehicle of the consultant.

- *Receptivity*—When putting together a training program, always think about your audience and their specific needs. Key questions you should ask include:

  –Which managers will be attending?

  –What are their developmental needs?

  –Ideally and realistically, how can we meet those needs?

  –What level of experience have they had?

  –What training have they requested?

  –Based on performance reviews, what training do they need?

  –What training have they had?

  –What training programs have been successful in the past? Why?

  –How can we make it easy for them to attend?

  –What administrative details are critical to your success?

  –What is in it for them to come to the program?

Always consider your target audience and ways to increase their level of receptivity to your program. Obviously, if they arrive with poor receptivity, you will have to waste energy and resources to raise it before you can really begin training. The need for this additional effort can be eliminated if you do everything you can to promote the program and its agenda in advance. Then all you have to do is deliver what you promised.

- *Results Orientation and Follow Up*—Central to your training philosophy should be the concept that all training should lead to measurable business results. Although that may seem obvious, it is apparent that far too many programs fall short of that mark. In order to accomplish the desired business outcomes, you must include within the program's design some type of follow up which will measure the effects of the training. This follow-up measurement can be simple or complex, but should never be overlooked.

  Typical of programs where results are hard to measure are those based upon the classic motivational speaker. Every year businesses pay large fees to speakers to motivate their sales/management force to strive harder to increase business, etc. Unfortunately, while business *may* increase slightly for one to two weeks following such programs, it tends to drop back to previous levels afterwards. In a word, no significant, permanent change has occurred. In fact, the participants have not obtained a demonstrable skill which will improve their ability to manage or to increase production. This is not to say that motivational speakers do not have their place. However, since the emotional high they are paid to engender is very temporary, they should play a supporting, rather than the leading role in the program.

- *Interaction among Business Units*—A program designed to actively support multiple business units should encourage participants to work with their peers from other business departments/units. This helps provide a common organizational culture while encouraging interdepartmental cooperation, enhancing managers' overall understanding of the business and facilitating follow ups. Today, with each area of the financial services industry overlapping, it is particularly important for the branch manager in one area to understand and relate effectively with his counterpart in the other areas. For example, the larger securities firms now provide many nonbank banking services and sell insurance in addition to their brokerage services. Bringing the managers of each of these areas together within a common training program can provide all of the benefits mentioned above.

- *Teamwork*—The heightened emphasis on teamwork as the way to build business in the 1990s should be an important component of all training programs. Granted, each of the sales personnel in a branch is effectively in competition with the rest of the sales force. However, branches where sales personnel help one another to close a sale tend to have larger production and employee job satisfaction than those where cut-throat competition is the name of the game. Managers who are effective at building and leading teams will also be the most sought-after managers of the 1990s.

The Audience

Certain audiences require special consideration when putting together training programs. Let's look at three different audiences starting with CEOs and senior management.

- CEOs: Even those employees in top management need to get away from the pressures and stresses they face on a daily basis. They also need to meet with other senior people from other businesses. They need open forums to discuss big picture items. However, CEOs also need to get specific training on technological capabilities, communications, goal and visioning skills, relationship building, and changes in the current business environment.

In addition, the CEO and top managers today must be in touch with their work force. They must demonstrate that they are real people who care about their employees. They need to articulate a clear direction and this direction must be one that people can get behind and support. This is why participation by regional and national officers is so important in branch management training (but only if they do some real listening in addition to any presentation they may make).

The job of senior management has changed from being the king or queen to being the team captain. Workers today are highly mobile and the best managers will be the ones who can gain commitment and loyalty and reduce turnover. Regional and national level managers must play a significant role in building loyalty and teamwork. Hence, training should play a significant role in helping senior management gain the skills necessary to perform effectively with the diverse work force of the 1990s.

• The biggest obstacle to senior management training is receptivity. Too often, senior management fails to recognize their own shortcomings and their need for training until a crisis occurs. As a result, training departments must work to raise senior managers' awareness of the benefits of ongoing education and encourage them to regularly attend both internal and external training programs. Suggested course ideas could include:

    —communication skills

    —effective presentation skills

    —working the room at social events

    —dealing with the press

    —running high-level meetings (including the Annual Meeting)

    —dealing with a senate hearing

    —setting goals and developing vision

    —quality service

    —building a company strategy

    —community relations.

- *Experienced Branch Managers:* Most experienced branch managers have already attended a number of different training courses. As a result, they may respond more positively if they are provided with a variety of courses that go beyond the standard subjects with which they are familiar. Because of their desire to emulate their leaders, any course provided to regional and national managers will probably find a receptive audience when given to experienced branch managers.

Branch managers should train jointly with regional and national management as much as possible for two reasons:

> –First, effective communication between these levels of management is critical. As branch and senior management train together, they will have an opportunity to relate to each other in a less threatening atmosphere than might be found in the field.

> –Second, everyone needs to be committed to the same goals and strategies. Working together during training programs can ensure that they are all working on the same plan.

Certain courses should be customized and offered to branch managers on a consistent basis. They include:

> –goal setting
>
> –coaching and counseling
>
> –presentation skills
>
> –negotiating skills
>
> –service management
>
> –hiring
>
> –motivation/morale building
>
> –retention
>
> –leadership
>
> –listening skills
>
> –stress/time management
>
> –problem solving
>
> –meeting management
>
> –creativity/innovation
>
> –computer skills

-accounting/budgeting

-community relations.

- *New Branch/Sales Managers:* Remember, with few exceptions, the new branch/sales manager has had no formal management training. Hence, at the very least, she should receive courses in such basics as: effective management techniques, administrative and legal issues, hiring skills, and time management.

Ideally the new manager should progress through a training program that lasts several years and combines on-the-job training with formal training. An example of such a program might look like the following:

Month 1: Two weeks of training in management skills, listening, leadership, presentation skills, hiring skills, and corporate culture.

Months 2–6: On-the-job training.

Month 7: One week of training in legal skills, administrative skills, budgeting, giving effective feedback, goal setting and communications skills.

Months 7–13: On-the-job training.

Month 14: One week of training in marketing, negotiation, advanced leadership, retention, and motivation skills.

Months 14–21: On-the-job training.

Month 22: One week of training on team building, problem solving, developing young professionals, quality service, building and communicating vision.

This type of training is expensive, but the managers who complete it are highly qualified to take over a more advanced assignment. This is especially true if they have already worked with a successful manager in a mentor relationship during their on-the-job experience. A key element to the new manager's training is that all of the formal courses should be tied into the company strategy and all new managers should be required to articulate this strategy.

Use Experts

It's important to use the experts available to you at all times. Usually, your best experts are right under your nose. They are the managers in your own company who get the great overall results you desire. Use them, recognize their achievements, and ask them to come into the training program to share their success techniques with other managers.

While outside experts can certainly be very useful for teaching specific technical skills, such as stress management, negotiation, motivation, and communications skills, they are less effective in teaching the problem-solving techniques needed to deal with the common branch problems which are unique to your company. Here, using your best managers can lead to immediate results. Remember, they've already solved those particular problems in their branches. So, avoid the mentality that you have to go outside to get all outstanding instruction.

Use Video

Whenever you have a skill-based program (presentation skills, interviewing skills, termination, coaching, etc.) use video feedback. Enabling an individual to see how he or she actually looks and sounds to others can foster effective behavior change. Video is extremely effective in demonstrating specifically which behaviors need to be changed. As a result, participants can quickly make significant behavior changes when they see themselves on video.

Summary

The process of training today's branch and sales managers is hardly an easy one. However, it need not be a daunting task. By establishing a training program which incorporates the right combination of skills training and senior management involvement, both new and experienced branch and sales managers can rise to the level of competence needed in today's financial services industry.

Chapter 32

Going Back to School

Joseph Ross

Do My People Need Continuing Education?

Most branch managers are not professional educators. In general, the financial services industry—at least in the insurance and brokerage segments—tends to promote successful salespersons to managerial ranks.

I thought it would be appropriate, therefore, to give a simple rule-of-thumb to determine whether or not a manager needs ongoing education for office personnel, or whether some other technique is needed. About a quarter of a century ago, Robert Mager gave a simple rule-of-thumb that is equally applicable today.

1. If a person couldn't do the job even if his life depended on it...he needs TRAINING;

317

2. If a person could do the job, but has forgotten...he needs RETRAINING;

3. If the person can do the job, but doesn't want to...he needs MOTIVATION.

If your experience is similar to mine, you have seen many managers call in motivational specialists, successful basketball coaches, and pop-psyche artists to talk to salespersons. Everyone had an afternoon or evening of feeling good and the outside speaker was a big hit. The problem was that no one really needed motivation. They *wanted to do the job—really they did—but they did not know how to* do the job. In other words, the manager chose the wrong remedy—a motivational talk when what was needed was training.

The insurance industry is leading both the brokerage and the banking industries in the requirement for continuing education credits to maintain professional standing for both life and health licensing. Whether or not banking and security brokerage will follow suit in the near future is problematical. On the other hand, one can say with a great degree of certainty that the typical manager has a training problem and needs continuing education as part of the solution to the problem.

Continuing Education Is a Function of Initial Training

If you are a newly appointed manager (and this would include a shift from one branch to another in the same firm), one of the first things you should do is to review the initial training of your sales personnel. Identifying sales personnel in a security brokerage or insurance office is easy; they are called salespeople. It is not so easy in the banking office because most of the personnel are reactive to customer needs; they are not *pro*-active in the sense that they prospect for clients.

To determine the need for continuing education, start with the initial training of your people. If this training is centralized, ask for a copy of the training kit or other printed material that is given to the typical trainee. Read it thoroughly. You'll be surprised at how much they are taught; you'll be equally surprised at how superficial the initial training is in terms, let's say, of what they should know at the end of year one, or year two, or some other benchmark.

If initial training is decentralized and, except for a few brochures and books from the home office, falls under your mandate, one of your first jobs should be to interview thoroughly the training personnel in your office. If there are not any formally assigned training personnel in your office, the problem is much bigger than you first imagined. In any event, use the same approach as was suggested above: Gauge what the persons know at the end of initial training and what they should know at the end of one or two years in the job.

The gap between what they know at the end of initial training and what they should know at the end of one or two years on the job is your principal area of continuing education. In all probability, you will have to get someone—either full time or part time—to assist you with the job of continuing education. You will need some planning, some record keeping, some curriculum design, and some form of *carrot and stick* to make sure that your personnel follow through on continuing education.

When you were appointed a manager you probably did not realize that you were also appointed a curriculum designer. You were, if you are to be a successful manager in the rapidly moving financial services industry of the 1990s. Basic curriculum design is not particularly difficult, so let's pursue that concept.

Establishing the Dos and Knows

Let's go back to the gap between what your people know at the end of initial training and what they should be able to do at the end of year one or two. Unless the individual is a true jack-of-all-trades, the person's job should be able to be divided into a succinct number of activities (the Dos) performed by the person. And, in order to do these activities, the person must KNOW certain things. Thus, in its basic format, designing the training comes down to a series of DOs and KNOWs.

Here, for example, are some basic DOs for a retail securities broker:

1. The broker must *pass* the registration examination.

2. The broker must *find* new clients for the firm and turn them into clients.

3. The broker must *list* the investment objectives of the firm's clients.

4. The broker must *make* suitable investment recommendations to buy and sell and must be able to *explain* these recommendations to clients.

5. The broker must *complete* and *enter* orders for securities products.

The list is not complete, but it is satisfactory for our purposes. As a basic curriculum designer for your people, you should make a list of the things you expect them to do at the end of year one or two. Ask your senior people to help you compile the list.

Note that in the list of DOs, all of the underlined words are:

- Transitive verbs; that is, action words that demand an object in order to be understood.
- Measurable in an objective sense. Thus, words like understand, appreciate, know, and similar subjective concepts are not acceptable as DOs.

Once you have established the DOs, establishing the KNOWs is relatively easy. What is not easy is the establishment of the order in which the various points should be made. The order and presentation is called *teaching,* and that is not an easy skill to acquire.

In any event, the KNOWs should be similar to the DOs in that they should be stated as *verbs* and should be *measurable.* Here, for example, is an expanded statement of the third DO cited previously.

The *broker must list the investment objectives of the firm's clients.* To this, the broker must know:

a. How to *identify* the firm's new account forms, and to *select* the form to be used.

b. How to *complete* the new account form.

c. How to *ask* the appropriate questions to get the information needed to respond to the questions on the form.

d. How to *distinguish* a client who wants income from one who wants growth, or a combination thereof.

This is sufficient. Your employees' needs for continuing education are determined by a thoughtful series of DOs and KNOWs. You may need help in the actual teaching of the DOs and KNOWs, but you should be able to determine what should be taught.

Now, let's turn to the next question: Who should do the teaching? Should you do it yourself; that is, within your branch? Should some forms of the training be centralized; that is, within a region or firmwide? Should you use outside extension or university courses where these are applicable? Here are some of the considerations in making the decision.

The Case for Branch Training

Probably the most important reason for branch training is that you, the manager, have direct control of the content of the training. This is particularly true if the training is to include *both* new content material *and* a review of prospecting and selling skills. Branch training is ideal for a combination of goals such as training and retraining in the same module.

Staff meetings, if properly organized, can be particularly well adapted to the dissemination of new information. For example, a meeting of the entire staff can be used to introduce a new product. Or, a meeting directed at the one- to two-year group in your office can be very helpful if you are trying to expand the product knowledge of this neophyte group.

One of the problems with staff meetings is that the staff expects to be *talked to* and the manager expects *to talk*. This is usually very dull and very poor teaching because it is not interactive and the participants contribute nothing except their presence.

It is not difficult to have a staff meeting in which the manager introduces the topic of the day, makes announcements, and then turns the meeting over to others for their contributions. Such contributions could be in the form of case studies. For example, the securities, banking, and insurance industries can profit from case studies:

- By life cycle needs; e.g., persons saving/investing for a home, for college educational needs, for retirement, and so forth.

- By product; e.g., universal life is much different in scope from whole life or term; or, in the banking industry, the difference between fixed rate and adjustable rate mortgages.
- By risk tolerance; e.g., the person who needs day-to-day liquidity versus the person who has a relatively large sum of money that will not be needed for two to 10 years or so.

Don't be afraid to ask your people to prepare a case study, to present possible solutions, and to open the floor to discussion. You'll be surprised at how enthusiastically your people will respond to this type of challenge. Witness the popularity of game shows on TV; people like to participate and to learn from one another. Professional staff members can pool their talents and present a joint presentation to the remainder of the office. The attention offered to peers as well as the feeling that they're one of us increases overall attention and participation.

Another advantage of the staff meeting is that it permits people to *stretch* their skills. Here are a few examples.

In general, the typical banker and securities broker (and in many cases the insurance broker) is not involved in taxation, estate planning, or advanced financial planning. On the other hand, some of your staff may be, or—better yet—some of your customers may be. **Most experts consider it an honor to be asked to participate in such learning experiences.** They will be glad to come to a staff meeting and answer specific questions on gift taxes, retirement planning, buy-sell agreements, and so forth.

Book reviews can be another form of stretching. Each of your serious salespersons wishes that he or she had the time to read all of the current books in their field, or parallel fields. With a bit of planning, you can get the people on your professional staff to read a book and give a brief review of the book at a meeting. Don't ask them to critique the book (that's a more advanced skill), but a summary of the highlights of the book would get your staff enthusiastic about staff meetings.

For example, a brief review of *Loving Trust,* by Esperti and Peterson, would have a dramatic impact on the securities brokerage, insurance brokerage, and banking staffs of any institution. However, **you need not limit reviews to books.** Magazine articles often lend themselves to review as part of an expanded educational horizon for your staff.

Again, on the local level, **much of the skills enhancement of your sales force lies in the effective use of the telephone.** Your telephone company is happy to provide its corporate users with skilled reviews of the proper use of the telephone. Call them. They may have an expert who will come to your office to review telephone use, telephone etiquette, or to suggest ways of enhancing the use of the telephone in your office.

Probably the most important aspect of the use of staff meetings, case studies, and *stretching* the financial horizons of your people is the attitude of the manager. If you, the manager, consider such ongoing education hokey, so will your people. If you consider such ongoing education as a simple extension of your role as manager and an endeavor to expand the professionalism of your staff, and it is conducted in a professional manner, your staff will embrace the idea wholeheartedly.

The principal negative feature of branch training is the lack of *economy of scale*. You are putting in a lot of effort for a relatively small number of people.

The Case for Centralized Training

These are probably the most important aspects of centralized training:

- People have an opportunity to get away from the day-to-day activities and retreat into a learning environment.
- People expect to learn and—guess what—they *do* learn!
- Teaching professionals can make a meld of teaching points that go across individual needs to meet group needs, firm marketing needs, compliance needs, and so forth.

The principal negative feature of centralized training is its cost. It simply costs a lot of money to move people to a centralized training facility, pay for hotel accommodations, and prepare a training program. Start with a minimum of $1,000 per participant and go up from there, depending on the length of the program and the average distance each participant has to travel.

Cost consciousness has caused a number of changes in the training industry in recent years. Centralized training is no longer considered the only way to give a uniform message to a group of people. Two recent innovations are particularly noteworthy:

1. Teleconferencing can be very effective if people have a common set of manuals to study and a specific time can be established for group testing and questioning. For example, I have probably taught more people face-to-face than anyone in the history of Wall Street. People now teach more by telephone than in person.

2. Computer-managed instruction is a method of testing the effectiveness of the learning process. Thus, the ordinary personal computer can be used, following a period of study from a training manual, to test the knowledge of the training participants. This can be done in such a way that it is nonthreatening and also gives the participant immediate feedback as to areas of weakness.

Again, your local telephone company will have information about teleconferencing, the kinds of equipment needed (it is not expensive), and some ideas on how to get started with a program of training that includes teleconferencing.

Teleconferencing is particularly valuable if you want to enhance telephone techniques in the area of prospecting and selling. With an expert available to coach and counsel, your staff can improve these basic skills. Teleconferencing also permits intraregional training between branches in the same region and thus takes away some of the artificiality of role playing in a typical telephone laboratory training situation.

The Case for Tuition Refund Programs

It takes a lot of training to justify a full-time training staff. Even a one-person staff with a modest classroom will come to $100,000 per year if you add salary, benefits, *bricks and mortar*, equipment, and supplies. Thus, if your operation is relatively small, there will be no economy of scale in hiring a full-time training person. Your training needs will be better served with staff meetings, a part-time training coordinator, intraregional teleconferencing, and the use of tuition assistance. Fortunately, there are a number of extension programs that can help the local manager with ongoing educational needs.

Bank managers have a wealth of resources. The American Institute of Banking, associated with the ABA, is the principal resource. Their BEN-line **(Banker's Educational Network)** can be particularly useful. The BEN-line can be used to get catalogs of books available, individual in-branch programs that are suited to continuing education needs, and the names and locations of schools that have ongoing education programs associated with banking. Their number is: 202-663-5430. In addition, many colleges and universities have individual courses in banking and allied subjects.

Managers of brokerage offices have a number of outside resources they can use for continuing education. On the general level, the **New York Institute of Finance** has been training Wall Street professionals for more than fifty years.

Their programs are given in the classroom (New York City only), in tailor-made programs developed for individual firms, and in correspondence courses. The New York Institute of Finance, which is a subsidiary of Simon & Schuster, also has an extensive library of professional books for the continuing education of both securities and commodities brokerage employees.

To reach the New York Institute of Finance for a syllabus of their offerings, the schedule of their courses, or a list of their publications, call: 212-344-2900.

For securities brokerage professionals who are interested in certification as financial planners, you may consider the **College for Financial Planning** located in Denver, Colorado. As a general rule, it takes about two years to complete their self-study course that leads to certification as a CFP (Certified Financial Planner).

The CFP course is composed of six segments, each of which has an examination administered by IBCFP **(International Board of Standards for Certified Financial Planners).** Completion of the examinations plus required business experiences will result in professional certification as a CFP. There is a continuing education requirement to maintain certification. Enrollment is not limited to brokerage employees; CPAs, LLBs, and registered investment advisors are also welcome. To reach the college, call 303-220-1200.

The College of Insurance, which is located in New York City, is a private college supported by more than 300 corporate sponsors. The college is accredited by the Middle States Association of Colleges and Schools.

In addition to professional development courses, the college offers both a graduate and undergraduate degree program for resident and nonresident students. The college offers several MBA programs. MBAs in insurance and finance are offered, and in 1990 two concentrations were offered: risk management and actuarial science.

The college also has extensive work-study programs whereby students attend school and work on an alternating semester basis. Resident students live in the dormitories on the top four floors of the school. To get information about the school, its programs and areas of professional development call 212-815-9237 for Admissions or 212-815-9201 for Professional Development.

We have provided the names and telephone numbers of four institutions that provide ongoing courses. There are many other organizations, some of which may be in your area, that offer excellent professional development courses. No slight is intended.

Record Keeping

Ours has become a very litigious society. Suits for damages caused by alleged failures to properly advise clients are increasing. And, the first thing the lawyer for the plaintiff does is subpoena the training materials of the employees in question.

Thus, a final word: If you use continuing education for your employees, be sure to keep a record of the training program, the name of the outside course, the time and place of the ongoing training, and so forth. It may save you a lot of money.

Chapter *33*

Continuing Education

Glenn W. Mitchell and E. Noel Gouldin

The financial markets have grown so complex that the once typical professional who got along by knowing a little bit about everything is fast becoming an anachronism. *Everything* encompasses too much now, with countless investments that didn't exist even a decade ago, as well as the non-too-subtle melding of once-separate fields such as banking, insurance, and the brokerage business. In addition, investors are poised to take advantage of this change whether financial professionals are ready or not. Today's investors are more sophisticated than ever before *and* they're better shoppers. No-load mutual funds and discount brokers give them bargaining power. To make things even harder, the media has unlocked the closed world of investing, and, not surprisingly in a litigious age, people have even less patience with sloppy work.

Being a good salesman isn't good enough anymore. Investors

want the kind of service that grows from increased knowledge. Hence, continuing education (c.e.) in the financial world is marked by a respect for rapidly changing markets, competent self-regulation, potential government intervention, turf wars, and technical innovation.

We'll look briefly at four industries' continuing education requirements and consider the pros and cons of future methods of c.e.

Insurance

Almost everyone in the insurance industry agrees that continuing education is critical. Suddenly, insurance agents are finding that they need to know about things that were once outside their experience. The *hitch*: No one can quite agree on how much c.e. is needed, what kind, or what it's worth. No national regulatory agency oversees the industry. Rather, it's in the hands of state insurance commissions. Only 22 states even require continuing education for insurance professionals (although there is a growing trend toward doing so for the projected 250,000 industry members expected by the mid-1990s). Among states that do require c.e., demands vary. Some states call for four or five hours of c.e. a year, while others demand 15 or 20. The identical course worth six hours in one state can be worth three in another or, in some cases, none. Some require proctored tests, others accept take-home exams with no supervision.

Approval of courses, according to one observer who offers courses for the industry, can be "whimsical." He also indicates that, "Each state's rules are forever changing. One day your program is right for certification, the next day it's not. It's a real nightmare; it's state's rights carried to the extreme. The state commissioners are just like czars and they couldn't care less about the public. They're just tools for the industry." Whether this reading of the situation is justified or not (one industry official said it's more likely that the states simply don't want the paperwork), it is true that the patchwork quality of requirements creates problems for practitioners who want to work in more than one state.

However, the inconsistencies of state commissions should not detract from the fact that the industry recognizes the importance of continuing education, an understanding typified by the **American College of Bryn Mawr,** Pennsylvania. The college offers courses leading to CLU or ChFC status (until recently, once earned, these designations were good for life). Today, the changing market and burgeoning product selection have led the college to decree that all graduates after June 1989 who wish to keep their CLU or ChFC status must now receive continuing education totaling 60 hours every two years. Individuals must take courses in such fields as wealth accumulation, risk tolerance, and estate, retirement and tax planning. Half the requirements may be fulfilled through classes from commercial vendors, universities, or the college itself, while the other half may be met through verifiable attendance at seminars, lectures, programs, etc.

Recognition of the market's demands has also led several thousand CLUs and ChFCs to voluntarily expose themselves to the rigors of continuing education through the American College's PACE program, even though there is no current requirement that they do so. The program calls for the same 60 hours of c.e. every two years that recent graduates must take. While only a tiny percentage of those active in the business have chosen the PACE route, one American College official sees it as the wave of the future, both for public respect and for self-preservation. "Originally, there was fear there would be a *super-CLU* or a *super-ChFC* if people flaunted their continuing education," he says. "But people changed their minds. It gives those who get it a more professional basis, and gives the public a better feeling about the industry."

Financial Planning

As with those in insurance, financial planners (FPs) have no national regulatory body. However, FPs are unregulated at the state level as well, although Washington state and Georgia require anyone using the title to be registered with the state insurance commission. This is partially true because *financial planner* is a title that, unlike CPA, CLU, or CFA, has no legal definition. Hence, the major stumbling block so far to state regulation of FPs is that no one can decide exactly what they are. (*Note:* A number of states have considered legislation, but voted it down.) That's why anyone can still hang out a shingle and call himself a financial planner. However, a certified financial planner (CFP) is something altogether different, and therein lies the setting for a turf war in alphabet soup.

The CFP designation is granted by the International Board of Standards and Practices for Certified Financial Planners (IBCFP). The

Board was established by the **College for Financial Planning** in order to separate the educational and policing functions of CFPs. The IBCFP monitors continuing education of 30 hours every two years in six specified areas: introduction to finance, insurance or risk management, investments, taxation and tax planning, employee benefits and retirement planning, and estate planning, with forty subtopics for each. By enforcing strict educational requirements, the IBCFP hopes to confer on the business a professional status which it has not always had.

The other major organization in the field is the **Association of Financial Planning** (IAFP). The IBCFP controls the CFP designation and requires members to pass their exam and maintain continuing education credits to remain in good standing; the IAFP is an open forum for both CFPs and anyone using the general *financial planner* title. The IBCFP and its alumni organization, the ICFP, maintain an education orientation, while the IAFP also deals with the marketing of products and services. This difference has led to a certain amount of friction between the organizations, although it is also true that both flourished in the early 1980s by selling tax shelters, and many FPs are affiliated with both organizations.

Recognition on the part of the IAFP of the importance of continuing education led to the formation of the Registry, a group within the IAFP whose standards for admission are rigid. These include:

- Thirty hours of continuing education each year for those who have been working CPAs, CLUs, ChFCs, CFPs, or CFAs for at least three years;
- practice case plans reviewed by a board of one's peers; and,
- a written exam.

There are fewer than 1,000 members and the Registry is open only to those who have demonstrated proficiency in practice.

Continuing education for financial planners may come from local professional meetings, regional conferences, national conventions, audio tapes with written tests, teaching, and from formal courses through universities or the College for Financial Planning. "Continuing education is a driving force," one industry veteran notes, "but it's hazy now on what's going to happen. Lots of it gets done just for the hours, but there's some good information in there. Still, the whole process for getting approval can be a significant inconvenience, because each organization's requirements are different." Or, as another observer put it, "capricious."

That *capriciousness* may ultimately become a thing of the past, however. Many industry experts believe that as the IBCFP becomes completely independent of The College for Financial Planning, it will acquire the status of guardian of the profession's standards. As now envisioned, the IBCFP will approve the financial planning curricula at institutions in addition to the college, as well as set requirements for continuing education. The result will be an industry norm accepted across the board within the profession and acknowledged by the public.

Stockbrokers

At present, there is no regulatory or self-regulatory requirement imposed on brokers for continuing education. The closest the industry comes to c.e. is in-house efforts pertaining to products or compliance, or requirements from allied fields for brokers who are also involved in financial planning or insurance.

In early 1990, however, a special committee of the National Association of Securities Dealers was formed to study the feasibility and worth of establishing c.e. requirements for members of the industry. At their most stringent, such rules would demand relicensing every three years, under either the aegis of the NASD or a similar organization.

Banking

The banking industry is also without any formal c.e. requirements. One explanation for this is that there is no way the diverse field of banking could be regulated by standards of competence or knowledge which would be applicable in any practical way (although certification for those in trust departments has become a possibility).

This is not to say that c.e. is ignored. Various colleges and universities, the Bank Securities Association, state banking associations, and numerous home study courses offer a variety of options for those whose advancement is often predicated on further study. The American Bankers Association's extensive Professional Development Program offers college credit for courses, and the American Institute of Banking conducts both beginning and intermediate classes. Continuing education for bankers is likely to become more critical than for any of the other professions considered so far. As the laws which once restricted bankers from dealing in a variety of financial operations are relaxed, their appetites for c.e. will grow for reasons other than just enlightened self-interest; it will grow as a matter of survival.

How to Obtain Continuing Education

Depending on the demands of the accrediting body, or one's own needs and wishes, continuing education for financial professionals can be found almost anywhere. Some options follow.

Schools

This can be for actual credit or for c.e. units. According to *The Independent Study Catalogue,* this means 10 hours of participation in "an organized continuing education experience under responsible sponsorship, capable direction and qualified instruction."

- One- or two-week **university classes** in such specialized fields as real estate law, investments, economics, appraisal and valuation, finance, banking investment, and securities at such universities as Columbia, Tennessee, and Pennsylvania. Costs range from $2,500 to $3,750.
- The **American College** or the *IBCFP* (already discussed).
- Independent vendors, such as the **New York Institute of Finance** ("Where Wall Street Goes to School"), either in New York or at programs offered elsewhere. NYIF covers basics like fundamentals of the securities industry or compliance, and advanced subjects, as well as new products. Pluses: No one questions the credits, one often has access to excellent teachers, and there is time to let the knowledge sink in. Minuses: Formal class work often takes time and money, and can call for travel that interrupts work.

Seminars

There are a million of them out there, good, bad and ugly, offered by everyone from university departments and top-flight independent trainers to self-appointed experts who arrive in a blaze of publicity and

332

leave on a highway slick with snake oil. Pluses: When seminars come to you, they're an easy way to get hours for c.e. monitoring, they're often specialized and can be responsive to changes in the industry. Minuses: If you have to go to them, they take time as well as money, and in any case, they're rarely cheap. You can only absorb so much, and information overload doesn't always stick, a factor exacerbated by an inability to apply it immediately. There's also a hint of ticket-punching while piling up hours for c.e. by attending less than challenging seminars or meetings.

Self-Education

Correspondence courses are available from many major universities or industry schools on subjects already mentioned. Pluses: You can work at your own pace, take time for things to sink in, and, from the high-quality products, you can really learn something. In addition, good tape courses offer the advantage of turning driving time into study time. Minuses: Many correspondence courses, on the other hand, are an unchallenging bore at best, a joke at worst. Often, the perception is never far away that using them is just an easy way to get the hours for c.e. requirements. And let's face it, there's almost never enough time to study on your own, unless of course the deadline suddenly looms and you're under intense pressure to get it done. You remember college, don't you? Computers tend to be useful for long-term training on subjects that don't change rapidly because it takes time to prepare the software. Self-education's fine for things like home repair, travel, and literacy, but it's not as effective for keeping up with new programs, products, etc.

Satellite Television

One portent of the future of c.e. is **Financial Satellite Network,** a subsidiary of Drossos Networks, founded in 1989. The network provides training primarily for brokers, as well as insurance and banking professionals. Programming is broadcast by satellite to subscribers' offices during business hours, and includes sales and marketing training, new products, compliance, financial planning, estate planning, options, and timely market-related interviews. Pluses: Current information with immediate applicability *narrowcast* for financial professionals, using recognized experts in each field. Economical, because to arrange personal instruction by all those who appear on the network would be prohibitively expensive, and useful because of the wide range of material covered. Small, easily absorbed doses can be recorded for replay. Minuses: Most shows have no audience interaction. There is no chance to follow-up questioning or informal conversation available at seminars or classes. Also, not economically feasible for small offices or for individuals.

Summary

Continuing education has become a must for any professional who wishes to even keep up, much less maintain an edge, in today's financial marketplace. The increasing complexity of products and services, as well as the advancing sophistication of the public, requires that each of us continue to expand our professional knowledge if we are to meet the growing needs of the customers we serve.

Chapter 34

The Changing Role of the Bank Branch Manager

Michael Saggese

Introduction

During the last 10 years, the financial marketplace and the regulations which have separated the functions of banking, insurance, and securities firms have undergone incredible changes, and continue to change everyday. As a result, the role of the typical bank branch manager is also changing significantly. Those banks and managers which are both prepared and able to keep up with these changes will flourish. Those who are unable or unwilling to change, will go under. This chapter will discuss what it meant to be a Branch Manager 10 years ago in the old commercial banks compared with what it means today.

Ten years ago, banks didn't do any sophisticated testing when they hired branch managers because managers didn't need to be salespeople. The manager just sat behind his desk. Today, banks expect their branch managers to go out and make a sale: that has tremendous significance in terms of changing responsibilities, and the added skills necessary to be successful in today's market. Today's branch manager also faces a host of problems surrounding manpower shortages, the complexities of back office support, and how to motivate a staff when you really have civil service.

Fish Out of Water

One of the most significant things that I've noticed, as the head of training for Midlantic, is that some of the branch managers who have been around for 10 and 20 years feel like a fish out of water. When you hired a branch manager 10 to 15 years ago, he was a member of the Kiwanis or the Rotary Club, he knew people in town. In fact, he knew everybody and, when people wanted to get a loan, they came to Joe and saw him at the bank and thought he was a good fellow. Both the manager, and the nature of the job, were essentially reactive.

Today, banks want an individual who's more professional, someone who's going to go out and actively prospect for business. In a word, that means we're looking for someone who is *pro-active*. Ten years ago prospecting was unnecessary. Today, like any other kind of salesperson, branch managers have a weekly or monthly quota. Each day, they've must make so many phone calls and, based on that, they'll set up so many interviews with companies and organizations. They've also got to contend with a dollar line—how much money they bring in to the firm. This is something really new to regional banking. Maybe some of the big commercial New York banks have done this in the past, but I think it's new to the branch managers that I talk to from regional banks. A couple of years ago, we acquired Heritage, which had a great reputation for bringing in customers. However, after the acquisition many of their managers did not stay with us because they found out that their role would be changing.

Day-to-Day Operations

Basically, the old branch manager's responsibility was to run the day-to-day operation of the bank. At the end of the day, he made sure that the tellers balanced, that the customer service reps balanced, and

336

that basic office facilities ran smoothly. Branch managers don't do much of that anymore. Today, they are really becoming new business development people and, from a hiring point of view, senior management is taking a long look at their overall skills—they're getting more sophisticated. We're actively looking for someone who is pro-active in a selling situation, probably external, or someone who is much more sensitive to customer needs.

Training Needs

We also need to train them to handle the increased level of product knowledge necessary in today's market. Ten to 15 years ago, we had maybe 13 products; now we have over 80.

Banks are finally starting to take the need for product knowledge training seriously. They're also starting to put some product information on the computer touch screens. Now, when a customer comes in, he can sit down with a customer service rep and, if he says, "I'm interested in a CD," the customer service rep can hit a dot on the screen that'll come up with a listing of the kinds of CDs available; the screen will even be able to walk the rep through the entire process. Products are becoming much more sophisticated and much more competitive. Some of the products that are offered now are the same kinds of products that have been offered by insurance companies and securities firms.

Changing Competition

One of the big changes affecting the branch manager of commercial banks, especially the superregional banks, is in the nature of the competition they must face to win customers. Ten to 15 years ago their biggest competitor was another regional or superregional bank. In the next 10 years, they're going to be competing against firms like Merrill Lynch, Prudential Insurance, or Xerox Financial.

For years, companies like Merrill Lynch have taken their sales personnel and put them through a five-week intensive training program. Compare this with the typical bank which puts its sales personnel and their branch managers through a three-day selling program and then sends them out and expects them to sell. What can you possibly learn in three days? How can this compare to what a Merrill Lynch or a

Paine Webber does, i.e., bring someone new in for training that includes up to three months of in-branch experience and special courses of study to prepare them for the general securities exam (and, increasingly, an insurance license), and then follows up with about three weeks of sales training and product knowledge. In addition, employees are brought back periodically for advanced courses and refresher courses. Whether he has an MBA or not, a branch manager with three days of training is at a real disadvantage when competing against someone from a securities firm who's had literally weeks or months of training.

Despite this discrepancy, banks put tremendous demands on their branch managers in terms of sales. Ironically, senior management now seems to be telling the branch manager that, "We don't care how well your branch is running. We want to know how much new business you brought in and what your deposit base is." This is despite the fact that he may not really have grasped, other than on a vague intellectual basis, what sales really is.

One of the other differences evidenced today is that some of the recent graduates of branch management trainee programs who are coming out of schools like Wharton, Villanova, Rutgers, and Seton Hall are much more professional, and have good communications skills. They tend to be much more aggressive and aware that their job is to sell. Everything else is secondary.

Changing Responsibilities

The responsibility of the branch manager is changing tremendously. Although she's responsible for the branch, she now has a second in command (the Operations Officer) who really runs the branch on a day-to-day basis. (*Note:* Some banks have set up regional lending offices and have regional lenders.) Any time the branch manager finds a potential prospect, she funnels it into the regional lenders. Other banks have individuals that they call *New Business Development People* who go out into their particular areas and represent more than one branch. For example, in Southern New Jersey, instead of having one person from Haddonfield, New Jersey, and someone else from Mt. Laurel all calling on the same businesses, the bank will have a regional business development specialist who works through the branch system and covers the entire region. He may come to you and discuss your business needs. He might say something like, "The Haddonfield, New Jersey, branch is nearest to your business. We'll set you up with an account there and open a credit line."

What many banks have done is to establish a *tier system*. They may have a head of Retail Banking who presides over two major divisions, a southern division and a northern division, each of which has an individual who manages them. Each one of those individuals, in turn, may have something like regional branch managers. This results in a pyramid structure which is typical of the classical organizational structures. Each regional manager would have a series of group managers under him and, of course, each group manager would cover five or six branches in the group. That's how the information gets filtered up the line and that's also how information gets disseminated down the line. That's how goals are set down the line. Today, your branch manager reports to a group manager who reports to the district who reports to the division, etc.

Quotas work the same way. Customers are going to expect different things from different branches depending on where they are. In the upwardly mobile suburbs, which contain a lot of professionals, a bank may offer different kinds of services and products designed to meet the needs of higher income families. At the same time, in the center of town, banks do a lot of corporate work. They have a lot of companies that come in and need check cashing; as a result, on Friday afternoons, the bank is a zoo because of all the employees who cash their checks.

Selling Skills

Perhaps the greatest area of changing responsibilities occurs in the area of selling skills. First and foremost, today's branch managers must be good salesmen and they've got to know how to prospect. They have to know how to go to Dunn and Bradstreet, or how to go to their local resources and find out which new businesses are coming into their area, who the heads of these businesses are and their needs.

We've recently started using a CIF—central information file— when prospecting. That's something relatively new at many banks. The CIF was developed to enable our branch managers and corporate lenders to obtain in-depth information about a prospective customer before prospecting them. For example, let's say that I'm going to the ABC Corporation. I can use the CIF to find out what kinds of accounts they have with us, who their principals are and what kind of accounts their principals have. That kind of information will enable me to approach any customer with a better understanding of what business they are currently doing, or not doing, with the bank. I can also find out something about the nature of their business and determine what products or services I have to offer that can make their company run more smoothly.

Another important change in the financial services market is the shift in emphasis to developing really effective communications skills. This has become very important in a competitive market that stresses consultative selling and personal relationships with customers. Ironically, branch managers in the old days were also expected to do relationship selling. But back then, they were expected to have the relationships before they were hired. Today, we expect them to have the skills to go out and develop the relationships.

We're finally beginning to realize the need to develop as many different kinds of accounts as possible with our customers. The more financial needs that we meet, the less likely they are to move their account(s) to a competitor. For the same reason, we want the personal accounts of the principals as well as their corporate accounts. Research indicates that there are two reasons for people leaving their bank: relocation and quality control. Let's face it, a bank manager has no control over a customer's relocation to a new town. Almost everyone wants to deal with a bank that is nearby. However, bank managers can do something about maintaining quality control.

We all like to be recognized when we walk into a bank or a store, but even more important, if there's been a problem with your account we need to be able to resolve it quickly and efficiently. If you've got a business deal to close and you're trying to get information about whether something's been posted to your account, you can't wait four days for that information. You need it now. I have to see to it that you can get that information when you need it. If I don't, I may lose your account, and I deserve to.

These are the kinds of things the branch manager has to deal with on a regular basis. He needs to be able to communicate effectively to:

- Establish a relationship with his customers,
- accurately determine their needs, and
- sell to those needs.

It's difficult to overemphasize the importance of really getting to know your customer, sitting down and getting to know the business they're in, doing some homework, and really becoming a salesman in the truest sense of the word. If you're in a steel mill, the branch manager needs to find out something about the business. What's your bottom line for the last five years, what's the economic outlook for the steel industry in this region? In the United States?

Suppose you opened a bakery. How many bakeries are in the area? What kind of background work have you done? What kind of accounts do your employees have and who do they bank with? In addition, the manager should come in and develop a relationship with you and show you that he knows something about your business and that he wants to develop that relationship with you. He should want to get your business account, your personal account, and as many of your employee's accounts as possible. So, the ability to communicate well is critical to one's ability to sell.

Now that the branch manager has these kinds of quotas, he needs to know something about goal setting and planning. What are realistic goals, what does the market look like today? What will the market look like six months or two years from now? If corporate headquarters says that he's got to attain a certain percentage growth in revenue or assets under management, is the goal feasible within the next two years? As manager, determine where your great chance is. If you're in Toms River, New Jersey, there may be many retired people living in retirement communities. You need to offer them services that are significantly different from those which you might offer to a lot of Yuppies living in Summit, New Jersey, who are trying to save money for their kids' college or their retirement. These are two very different clienteles with two different sets of needs.

As a branch manager today, you've really got to be able to evaluate the demographics of your area. For example, according to Ken Dychtwald's book *Age Wave*, 85% of all the people who have their money invested in S&Ls are 65 and older. Seventy percent of all the money, of all the wealth in America today is owned by people 45 to 65 years old. When you look at so much of our market advertising, it's hard to understand why it's directed to the young. In addition, Dychwald points out that the greatest number of people between 55 to 75, are what he calls "brick rich and cash poor;" that is, they own expensive assets such as houses, but have serious cash flow problems. So another important banking question becomes, "How do I come up with some creative technique to utilize that equity in such a way that will enable me to bring new customers to the banking system?" Hence, all the home equity loans available to buy everything from cars to vacation.

Those are just some things of which branch managers should be aware. Who is my market? That comes with goal setting and time management planning. Where's my branch located, who are my customers, where are my new accounts going to come from, etc.? Then, although I may not be involved in day-to-day operations as much, I still have to do the personnel performance reviews at the end of the year. Do I have good motivation and coaching skills? We all know that good managers are made and not born. I can walk into almost any one of our branches and I can tell you by simply sitting down and talking with the branch manager for a half hour, how good that branch is, how cohesive a team they are, and how well they work together.

Motivation, Compensation and Morale

Insurance and securities FCs pay themselves. If they want to take home more money, they need only make more sales. If the branch does well, the branch manager will get a bonus. But what about all of the support staff? How do you motivate them when the chairman comes out and says, "Departmentwide, you've got 5% hourly increase." That means that either everyone gets 5%, or someone gets less so that others can get more. This doesn't give you a whole lot of flexibility, although there's a little bit more flexibility with the nonofficers than with the officers.

Sometimes you'll see some branch managers who get creative and on a Friday night (when everyone's got to work until 6:00 or 7:00), they'll shut down from 4:00 to 5:00 and order pizza or Chinese food and pay for it out of their own pocket. They do little things like that. Perhaps they'll bring in donuts in the morning or take half their staff out to lunch one day and the other half out the next. These managers make their staff feel like human beings. They treat them like people. In most cases they have to do all that out of their own pocket. They have no budget for that. If they do have a budget line, it's not a very big one. They may have some small budget for these kinds of things (kind of a discretionary budget), but it's not a whole lot of money. However, good managers use this budget in little creative ways to communicate to their people that they care about them and that they are important. If you treat your staff like people, you'll get a lot of mileage out of them. For example:

- Remember birthdays.
- When you walk in in the morning, say hello and know your staff by their first names.
- Sit down and joke with people occasionally. The mood of that branch depends upon you.

Summary

Bank branches have changed a great deal over the last 10 years. To succeed now requires communications and selling skills, a genuine interest in your *entire* staff, and an understanding of the market in your area.

Section *VIII*

Domestic and International Community Relations

Your success as a branch manager depends to a large extent upon the reputation of your company and your branch office within your community. At the same time, just what constitutes your community is expanding and changing everyday. Today's domestic and international financial marketplaces are also rapidly evolving, with investors becoming increasingly interested in foreign opportunities. This is true whether you think of domestic investors wishing to invest in another country or foreign investors who are seeking opportunities here.

As a result, it behooves you as manager to become comfortable with the needs and idiosyncracies of your immediate community and the financial services community at large. In these next three chapters, we'll discuss ways to improve your company's image in your local community as well as tips on dealing with international customers.

Chapter 35

Community Relations

When you think about it, one of the most important responsibilities of any branch manager revolves around the relationship between his branch and the community that supports it. As obvious as this is, it is remarkable just how many branch managers appear to take that relationship for granted.

As a manager, your ultimate success depends upon your community's perception of you and your company as represented by your branch and your FCs. To begin with, in many communities, unless yours is a nationally prominent company, most members of your community will really only recognize your company's name from the efforts of your sales force. How do you want them to respond when they hear that name? In this chapter, we will discuss some of the factors that affect your relationship with your community, and some steps that you can take to build a strong foundation in your area.

Factors Effecting Community Relations

There are several important factors that will affect your branch's relationship with the community that supports it.

- Your company's national and local advertising and its name recognition. Do people recognize the name when they hear it? Why? Is it from national media advertising, or the reputation of your FCs? Has the company been involved in any highly publicized legal dispute, either nationally or, especially, locally?

- The demographics of your community. How is your community culturally different from others? What are the local traditions and customs? Are there any significant language, ethnic, racial or religious influences? What is the age and financial breakdown of the community? White collar, blue collar, young, old, retired?

- How involved with the community are your FCs?

- What have you done to find out the needs of the members of your community?

Company Name Recognition

There are almost as many ways to measure your company's name recognition in the community as there are marketing specialists willing to do it. However, regardless of the technique used, when measuring community awareness, it is important to know whether the name recognition was measured using *aided,* or *unaided* awareness techniques.

- *Unaided awareness* is measured through open-ended questions like: "Who do you consider to be the top five financial services institutions in the United States?" The individual then responds with five names, such as Citibank, Prudential Insurance, Merrill Lynch, etc. Questions can also be industry specific, e.g. the top five banks, or the top five brokers, insurance companies, etc.

- *Aided awareness* studies are multiple choice type questions, such as, "Among these regional banks/securities firms/insurance companies (give a list of 10–20, including a few fictional), which do you consider to be the best?" The individual then chooses several, possibly even ranking them.

Aided awareness studies offer the easiest techniques because they measure only name recognition. However, unaided studies require the individuals tested to bring forth your name without prompting, indicating a higher level of impact upon them. Needless to say, if the individual fails to select, much less recognize, your firm's name, you have your work cut out for you in your area.

Demographics and Community Relations

What are the demographics of your community? If you live in southern Florida, you need to be prepared to deal with at least two major populations, the retired and the Hispanic. You will need FCs who speak Spanish and who are familiar with local customers. You will also need FCs who are both familiar and comfortable with older customers. Such things may even affect the placement of your office and your facilities. For example, when working with a large population of retired people, you may wish to make sure that your office is on the first floor, that there are ramps available if there are steps at the entrance, and that there is sufficient room for a walker or a wheel chair to pass easily between desks. You may even wish to provide available parking for the handicapped.

Hence, your demographics should have a tremendous impact upon your recruiting. By recruiting individuals who reflect the make-up of your community, you increase their perception of your branch as being responsive to their needs. For example, Merrill Lynch has recruited individuals who can sign (speak sign language) and use special communications devices for the deaf, to work in areas where there are high concentrations of deaf customers.

How to Enhance Community Relations

Besides the classic technique of national and local media advertising, there are several powerful techniques that can help you to significantly increase your name recognition in the community, as well as your company's image. An added benefit of these techniques is their cost effectiveness.

Media relations can make or break you in a community. Yet, despite this, few branch managers in the financial services industry make any kind of a serious effort to develop a working relationship with the financial editor or the publisher of the local newspaper, radio or television station. Ironically, forming a solid relationship with the media requires very little time, effort, or expense on your part. Here are some ideas for building that relationship.

- As a branch manager, you can give the press access to information that is normally closed to them. Meet regularly with the financial editor(s) of the local press. Find out *significantly in advance* who in finance is coming to town and invite the finance editor to lunch with him. For example, any major figure in your company, a major speaker who is coming to address your sales force, an investment banker, or an analyst who will be in town to meet with various companies. When an analyst comes to town to examine companies in your area, arrange to have him meet with your FCs, then have him speak to the branch's customers. If invited to attend, or provided with a summary, the press will generally cover the event.

- Editors are like everyone else; they have limited resources with which to cover all of the news of interest to their community. Prewrite articles on areas of financial interest to your community, within the area of expertise of your company and submit them. With a little luck, you may be able to develop a regular column. Needless to say, each time you publish such an article, you and your company become identified in the minds of many readers as the experts in that area.

Charities can be an important source of good will for your branch. Try to get every FC in the branch involved in some form of community service. This accomplishes several important things:

- It shows the powers that be in the community that your company is genuinely interested in the community and is not just a boiler room operation.

- It will get your FCs involved and committed to the community, making them more professional and dedicated to the community's well-being. And,

- It may bring in additional business (while it is considered a conflict of interest for an individual to personally solicit business from a charity for himself, it may be considered appropriate for him to solicit it for the branch). In addition, as the individuals who do volunteer work with the FCs see their concern and professionalism, they will be more likely to approach them for business.

For example: many brokerage branches have significant unused watts time available. Each year on Christmas, Merrill Lynch donates that time to the communities where they have branches to call family and loved ones. This costs virtually nothing and is remembered for the rest of the year. Do you have a local college or prep school in your area? The next time they have a fund raising drive, offer to let them come into the office at night to call their alumni. If the media doesn't send a crew to cover it, bring your own video and 35mm still cameras to take pictures for the paper and the local evening news.

Recognition is something that almost everyone both needs and desires. It can also be a great source of enhanced community relations. Without using it to solicit business, show the community an attitude that says, "We at (your firm) like to recognize people who excel." In the end, you'll get plenty of business.

You can sponsor events like athletic contests, walk-a-thons or the Special Olympics. You can also offer scholarships, etc. For example:

- Ask high school seniors to write an essay on a local issue connected with finance (e.g., "Should government pay the costs for all higher education? Why?"). Then have the local paper publish the names of the top 10 (any number depending upon the number of papers submitted), and the actual papers of the top 1–3. Then award a zero coupon bond or CD as a prize.

- Buy a trophy and award it to the top high school or college scholar, athlete, etc. each year. The trophy can be kept in a case at the branch and every year it goes to another student. Publish the names and a two-line summary of the top 50 students who were nominated (you may have to buy space for that in the paper, but you know that those 50 families and their friends are going to remember the name of the company that helped them brag about their child). The next time one of your FCs calls one of those houses about opening an account, at least he'll get a pleasant reception.

The important thing is to recognize the achievements of others. As you do, they will recognize you and your company and it will pay off in increased business. When you think about it, the awards you give are limited only by your imagination. Some more ideas include:

- Best scholar athlete,
- hero awards,
- best public servant (recognize any government worker),
- good neighbor awards (have people nominate people who have been a good neighbor to those in need),
- best teacher,
- most improved anything,
- best boss, worker, secretary, etc., and
- best service (shops, restaurants, service stations, etc. that have consistently given cheerful, helpful service over the last year). Give the names and a line or two about each employee.

> Recognize others and your community will recognize you.

Summary

The art of community relations doesn't require large expense outlays. All that is necessary is a genuine commitment to your community and a little imagination. As you reach out to serve, and to give recognition to members of your community, they will respond in kind and it will pay off in long-term business.

Chapter 36

International Business Considerations

James G. Miller

The Changing World Environment

The world and the financial marketplace are expanding rapidly for today's financial consultant. This is exciting but it can also be danger-ous as FCs try to successfully wind their way through a complex maze of different cultures, regulations, and currencies to both deal with interna-tional clients and to select international opportunities for their domes-tic customers.

In 1990 alone, the demise of Communism appears to have taken place throughout most of the world. Industrial privatization is begin-ning in Eastern Europe. Germany is becoming re-unified. The two Germanies have united and are using the Deutchmark as their curren-cy. The European Economic Community is going to be opened to internal international trading and investing in 1992. Taiwan has decided to allow private commercial banks to be established. The Soviet Union is doing business with Pepsi Cola by bartering with ships and vodka (since the ruble isn't easily converted into hard currency).

Once initiated, it is doubtful that any of the governments involved will be able to stop the process. If these Eastern European leaders truly want to raise their countries to a higher standard of living, they won't even try to stop it.

In 1989, we saw an attempt to open the doors of China. Even though it was unsuccessful, and probably will not be repeated soon, the fact is that the younger people, many of whom have tasted the fruits of privatization and capitalism, are becoming disillusioned with the old systems, and want to join the rest of the world.

There is talk all over Eastern Europe about the privatization of industry, independent banks, and even a stock exchange. We now frequently see magazine advertisements for business opportunities and investments in Eastern Europe and the USSR. The international business possibilities are very exciting and potentially unlimited.

Until recently, most Americans didn't have much of a concept of what was available outside of their own country. Today, more people are realizing that there is a great deal of potential in other parts of the world. In addition, with some of the recent anti-takeover legislation that has been introduced in many states, more Americans will begin investing their capital outside of the United States.

However, privatization is a process. It takes time, money, and expertise. Even though the opportunities are enormous, FCs and their clients need to approach these new situations with caution and forethought. The great American journalist, H. L. Menkin, once said, "Love is the triumph of imagination over intelligence." Before we encourage our customers to invest in the images of untold riches with which both we and they are being tempted, we need to be sure that those images do not triumph over our intelligence and innate caution. The fact is that all that is happening is so new and the world is changing so fast, that even though the potential opportunities are unlimited, so are the potential pitfalls.

I remember once being impressed by a beautiful urn displayed on a podium in the main board room of the New York Stock Exchange. The urn was a gift from Czar Nicholas II of Russia in 1904 for the listing of Imperial Russian Bonds on the exchange, the money from which was to be used for the purchase of railroads. Not long after, the revolution came, and the bonds ended up being completely worthless. The urn is all that's left in memory of the deal. The point is that things in the world are changing so quickly right now that a little caution and forethought should accompany the excitement of unlimited wealth from new international business deals. As the branch manager, your knowledge and understanding of the world market and world political situations will be increasingly important if you are to provide the guidance necessary for your FCs to succeed in this arena.

Fundamental Differences

FCs need to recognize that there are a variety of differences between the way Americans and people from other cultures do business that should be considered before dealing with foreign nationals. This is true whether one is doing business with them in their home country, or within the United States. For example:

- Regulatory differences.
- Cultural differences.
- Public image.
- Currency exchange rate differentials.
- Financial services competition.

Regulatory Differences

When an FC is doing business in countries other than the United States, it is very important to keep in mind that there are many legal, or regulatory, differences throughout the world. While too lengthy to present here, there are different rules and regulations involving prospecting for business, transacting business, and different tax laws which might make certain investments either unattractive or illegal in other countries.

For example, it is *illegal* in some European countries to make a prospecting call without previously sending a solicitation letter. In other countries, one may be prohibited from using certain product lines, or from making certain promises or allegations regarding performance.

In addition, it is important to be aware that there can be different legal interpretations and presuppositions in different countries. Within the United States, a legal contract between two parties is considered to be binding. This is not always the case in other countries. In some countries, a legal contract may be considered only a very strong indication of intent to do business. However, if one party to the contract finds that, due to a change in circumstances, it is now disadvantageous to fulfill the contract, it is understood (and this may be upheld by the local judicial system) that one can escape from the contract.

The main point is to *look before you leap*. When working with an overseas client, you may be playing by a different set of rules than you expect. It is necessary to check the laws, rules, and regulations of the country in which you plan on doing business before setting up operations there. You may even want to check with your company's marketing and legal specialists before doing international business. If nothing else, they may at least help to ensure that you are not violating any major taboos (something that is very easy to do).

Cultural Differences

This is an area that needs to be considered by any FC who wishes to deal effectively in the international marketplace, particularly in the area of financial services. That is, cultural and national interests may influence which stocks or bonds to recommend or to avoid recommending to various international customers.

These differences may also influence how one prospects for business or how one goes about selling various products. In the United States, it may be acceptable to sell or prospect in an aggressive manner. However, in many cultures, such aggressiveness is anything but acceptable. In some countries, it may even be necessary to avoid discussing business at all during the first few meetings, while in others, business before pleasure is the rule.

In many parts of the world, it is important to speak more than one language and to be aware of things like political changes and constantly changing rates of currency exchange. Europeans and Asians tend to be more politically and economically astute and more sophisticated than their American counterparts. American FCs too often tend to take an isolationist view of the world.

The need to meet or exceed the level of sophistication of one's clients is basic to a long-term relationship. This tends to be true whether one is dealing in Europe directly or with European clients within the United States. It is equally true of the more monied people all over the world. Wealthy individuals want to work with other financially sophisticated individuals and certainly wish to be reassured that their FC knows what he is doing.

If they are to deal effectively on an international level, financial consultants need to develop a more knowledgeable view of the world situation than most currently have. They need to have *worldwide political consciousness*. One of the best ways of acquiring this knowledge is by reading journals such as *The Economist*—a weekly financial magazine that is available on most better newsstands and by subscription. It reviews world events and provides excellent commentary on the U.S. economic and political situations from a European point of view. This international awareness will certainly help your FCs to deal both internationally and domestically with a better understanding of world events and of cultural interpretations of those events.

Public Image

Your FCs' effectiveness in doing business in other countries will also be affected by your company's public image. A company's public image abroad may be very different from its public image at home. Many companies which enjoy good name recognition in their own country may be virtually unknown in other parts of the world.

We may have a different image of a certain European company than they have in their own country. This image difference may be based simply on a difference in cultural values and not on business reasons. Such knowledge is important in selecting stocks and bonds to recommend to clients. It is impossible to make broad generalizations. Each situation is unique to the companies and countries involved. Obviously, a good rule of thumb is to *know your territory*.

Exchange Rate Differentials

Cross currency exchanges and financing are very complicated issues of which most Americans have little awareness, much less understanding. The potential difficulties in this area are great. Because of the differences in exchange rates at various times, a product might be overly expensive or inexpensive in other countries. This, of course, would influence the ability to import or export tangible items, and would similarly affect the viability of certain financial products.

Currency risk is an extremely important concern to international investors. This includes both the speculative and hedge uses of various currency options and/or futures contracts. Your FCs should have a good working knowledge of exchange rates, interest rates, financial futures, and commodities in order to effectively compete in the complex world of international financial services. This requires far more training and experience than most FCs have.

Financial Services Competition

Profound changes are taking place in the banking areas. This is due to three recent events:

1. *Deregulation* of the banking industry in the United States and Japan.

2. *Globalization*—a world market wherein economic and currency interdependence is characteristic. One country's economic situation (for example inflation, unemployment, interest rates, and exchange rates) directly affects that of another.

3. *Technology* is making global securities services possible.

The eventual demise of the **Glass-Steagall Act** will certainly lead to merchant banking in both America and Japan. Europe has had universal (merchant) banking for a long time. However, in the United States, the two areas were separated following the stock market crash in 1929.

Right now, the banks are trying to get as involved as they can in the securities side of the business. Over the last few years, banks have begun to sell stocks, bonds, mutual funds, insurance, and financial planning services in addition to their regular fare. This increase in competition will continue to have a significant effect on how securities and financial services are marketed worldwide.

In the United States, investment houses are now getting involved in many areas that previously were exclusive to banks. Investment houses are already supplying insurance and banking services such as deposits, credit, money markets, and checking accounts. Historically, this hasn't really been allowed in America or Japan, but the wall that separates banking from investing will soon come tumbling down. Everyone is getting into everyone else's back yards. Even companies that have nothing to do with financial services are getting involved in the financial services area.

With financial institutions in the United States trying to compete in the international markets, we are now seeing U.S. investment companies becoming involved, for example, in Euromarket issues. We should expect to see this trend continue.

The banking industry is an extremely strong force within the European community. It is associated with an image of safety, honesty, integrity and, as with the Swiss banks, confidentiality. Other financial competitors are not usually considered within the same league.

However, money knows no national boundaries, and will always seek that which will give it the greatest rate of return. Some of the international mutual funds that have enjoyed popularity recently are only harbingers of things to come. Investment will continue to occur on a worldwide basis, and it will be the manager's responsibility to ensure that the financial consultant is able to adequately function on an international basis.

Summary

Both the complexities and the rapid rate of change in today's international financial markets make the involvement of the branch manager even more important than ever before. Cultural, legal, currency, and even language differences can result in serious difficulties for the unprepared. However, for those who are prepared, the rewards can be significant. As the branch manager, it is your responsibility to make sure that your FCs are adequately prepared before allowing them to deal on an international basis.

> Today's branch manager must be familiar with international business ramifications.

Chapter *37*

Selling Cross-Culturally and Cross-Nationally

James D. McLean

The odds of an American businessman doing business with someone from another culture in 1990 are far greater than what they were in 1940. Since World War II, the economic development of other nations has made them greater potential customers, business suppliers, and partners. Advances in communication, ease of travel, and the overall global trend in world economies has created new markets for American business, and a greater likelihood that the American businessman will be doing business with cultures other than his own.

Keys in Doing Business Cross-Culturally

Each individual is a product of a culture, the product of a national and sometimes a regional experience. What is culture? It's essentially a code: A code of appropriateness or inappropriateness, of acceptability

361

or unacceptability, of behavior within a given group of people. It has elements that are almost ritualistic, such as the handshake or the exchange of business cards. Also it has an effect on the way that we view and understand interpersonal and business relationships.

Culture is quite a bit like tying your shoe. It's something that you learn at a very early age, but is difficult to explain verbally. Each person sees the world through the eyes of his culture—cultural rose-colored glasses. The eyes or glasses will be very different for people from different cultures. There are four key words to carefully consider as we think about culture and about doing business with people from other cultures:

- observation,
- open-mindedness,
- avoidance of stereotypes, and
- flexibility.

Observation

Observation is important because most of us do not have the time or the resources to fully research another culture. Observation of the proper manner in which to approach and deal with individuals of a culture is the best way to remain appropriate. Watch the other individual. Listen to the other individual and match your behavior, your mannerisms, and expression to what he does; remembering that what he does is an expression of what is acceptable in his particular culture.

| To establish rapport, observe and match your host. |

Open-mindedness

Open-mindedness is extremely important. We need to avoid assigning the values that our culture attaches to given words, mannerisms or approaches to those of other cultures. For example, Americans doing business with individuals from the Middle East frequently interpret the Middle Eastern people's coming within very close physical proximity during a conversation as a sign of aggressiveness, or desire to

362

dominate. This is not the situation. Within Middle Eastern cultures, it is normally acceptable for people to stand in much closer proximity than Americans would in a normal conversation.

In certain parts of the Far East, the hand shake is very brief and very pressureless. This can be interpreted by an American, who is used to a firm grip handshake, as a sign of disinterest, or coldness, in the individual. This is absolutely not true. Also note that in Asian society a handshake is always offered by the older person to the younger, and from a woman to a man.

Stereotyping

Stereotyping is both a highly natural and highly destructive phenomenon. As human beings, in order to make sense of our world, we lump information into clusters that we can easily handle for efficiency. Thus, we tend to put labels on things and tend to make assumptions (e.g., "That group is arrogant," "Those people are like us," "They think much differently than we do," etc.). All of these are grossly unfair and highly disruptive. Within any culture there is a mix of opinions, feelings, personalities, and attitudes. Culture is a mode of expression, and only a mode of expression. It is the color of the fruit, not the taste. Through observation, open-mindedness, and flexibility, you can adapt to the individual, rather than working with a stereotype.

If you are operating from stereotypes, you are ignoring observation, which is the first rule of doing business cross-culturally. You are also violating the second rule, *open-mindedness.* Look at individuals for what they are and your open-mindedness will be communicated very elegantly, without effort, and will result in a far more favorable relationship between you and your client.

Flexibility

Flexibility is the final key term. Flexibility in your behavior, your beliefs, and, perhaps, in the way you do business. When you match the other individuals' culture, you add to their comfort, build your credibility, and build an ongoing personal and business relationship.

Flexibility can take many forms. The first is flexibility in terms of physical mannerisms and of voice. Americans, who are used to standing and conversing at a fairly good distance from each other, usually find it highly uncomfortable, in most circumstances, working at the shorter physical distances that are appropriate in many cultures. By the same token, Americans tend to speak rapidly and with enthusiasm, particularly in selling situations—whether it is face-to-face or over the phone. Within many cultures, specifically the Korean culture, this may be perceived as lack of good breeding and as an indication of low social status. It may be necessary for you to modulate the level of your voice and slow your rate of speech.

Consider, Asians will eat rather noisily, at least by American standards, as a sign of appreciation of the food. Americans who have been taught that noisy eating habits are poor manners, both insult and are insulted simultaneously. (Note that most Asians who are familiar with Western customs will alter their table manners out of courtesy.)

Flexibility is also important in the way that you present information, the way that you document information, the way you support an agreement, and also in the area of contractual agreements. For example, most Americans tend to respond in a bottom line, bullet point, linear fashion in a business deal. Once the topic has turned to business, we tend to stay on business until the topic has reached a conclusion, preferably, before we go on to the next step and work on future issues. However, in the Middle Eastern culture, rather than a business interface being a linear progression, many times it takes the form of reaching some sort of agreement or understanding on one point of the proposal, then there is an abrupt switch onto a topic of a more personal nature. After that, the discussion moves back into the business area to negotiate another point, and then goes back to the personal. This can be extremely disconcerting for many Americans. Having the personal flexibility to adapt to this can certainly increase the probabilities of success.

> Be prepared for differences in
> speech, thought, and organization.

Culture and Contract Flexibility

Culture even affects our outlook on contracts. As Americans we tend to feel that a contract must be followed to the letter. This view is not shared in many other cultures and is one of the reasons that the Japanese have done better in certain parts of the world, specifically

364

Asia, than Americans. Written contracts were not even used in Japan and Korea until the 1940s. Verbal agreements were the standard and were subject to change as circumstances warranted. Much business in Japan and Korea is still carried on in this way. When contracts are used, the wording is kept simple. A standard, American, detailed proposal made to a Japanese company will be confusing, require the retention of an expert in American law for analysis and counter-proposal, and result in a slow response or a lost opportunity. Proposals and contracts in Asia must be simple, short, understandable, and flexible.

In many cultures the concept of the written contract is that it is a manifestation of the willingness of two partners to enter into a mutually beneficial relationship. The contract is a symbol of the commitment of both parties to the success of the other. As a result, it is likely that the non-American partner company, within certain cultures, will feel very free to ignore or to alter some of the terms. By the same token, the non-American will be highly confused by the American partner's annoyance or insistence to follow the contract to the letter of the original agreement. It also implies a requirement from both parties to maintain flexibility in the administering of that agreement.

Flexibility can also be a willingness to be more patient and to avoid expressing any impatience. Americans are an impatient people. For example, within the Japanese culture a strong way to build rapport and credibility is to respond to questions in very fine detail. The Japanese tend to be detail-oriented, while we are not. Therefore, it is not uncommon for an American company or an American sales representative to lose credibility by his impatience with what might seem like unending requests for detailed information from a potential Japanese customer. This will be discussed in greater detail later in the chapter.

Business and Personal Relationships

In any business relationship there are inevitable elements of business as well as elements of personal chemistry that enter into play before a relationship is built and before a deal is made. Ignoring the timing and sequence between business and personal relationships is often a major cause of misunderstanding. We will refer to this as the *have a nice day syndrome*. This phrase is almost certainly offered to you or offered by you within the course of your normal day. It is generally viewed in a very positive fashion. However, it is used so often that it is considered virtually meaningless.

Interestingly enough, this casual intimacy is a very common element of the stereotypes of Americans. Here is the reason why. Imagine a cross-section of the trunk of a tree. View the concentric growth within that tree. Assume that the bark of that tree is the extreme of formality and the extreme of distance. Assume that the core circle within that three represents the personal intimacy of two good friends.

The most common mistake of many an American businessman is to evidence an ease, openness, and informality with other people upon first meeting them. This is generally very well received by most foreigners during their first experiences in business with Americans. The common complaint then is that as the topic moves to business, the American's manner is very businesslike, abrupt or, sometimes, even inflexible or confrontational. This leaves the other individual with a feeling of confusion—almost a feeling of having been drawn into what appeared to be a close personal relationship and then rebuffed. For this reason, when dealing with people from other cultures, the safest rule of thumb is to proceed initially with a certain degree of formality and, as the relationship builds, peal away the layers of formality in a very gradual fashion.

An American is very likely to say, "If there is anything I can ever do for you, let me know." In many cultures, particularly Asian cultures, this will be interpreted quite literally and it will imply a responsibility on your part to provide, not only business, but personal assistance, upon the request of an individual. It will also imply a responsibility on the part of your client to respond in similar fashion. Familiarity, therefore, should be approached in a very open, yet cautious, dignified and formal fashion. And, it is best to take the lead from your client, to observe and to be flexible in establishing the proper degree of formality or informality within a business dealing and eventually within a business relationship.

> Avoid casual personal commitments.

Americans tend to have a reputation for taking personal relationships extremely lightly. One of the perceptions, occasionally taking the form of humor, is that of Americans as a disposable society; at the top of that list is disposable relationships. Your willingness to adapt to local customs and to take a personal interest in those customs, in those cultures, and in those clients with whom you deal, will break down that stereotype, and will greatly improve not only your business performance, but also your own ability to broaden your horizons as an individual and as a businessman. It's one of the great joys of doing business in the international marketplace.

From a personal standpoint, it is also best to listen to the topics of conversation raised by your client. Generally, it is highly appropriate to ask questions regarding the welfare of family members within Latin cultures. However, within middle Eastern cultures this should be strongly avoided because family life is considered highly private. Thus, a simple question such as, "How has your wife been since I last saw her?" is considered to be highly offensive.

Also to be avoided in many cultures, particularly Asian cultures, are positive remarks on items that may be within your hosts' home; or perhaps making the remark "That is a beautiful tray you have in your home," later on. Such remarks may imply to your host a responsibility to give you that tray (which may have very great financial or emotional value to them).

Other areas that must be carefully monitored by the American businessman and researched are gift giving and visits or invitations to another's home. Within the United States we are comfortable with inviting people or business acquaintances to our home on an informal basis. No particular meaning is attached to this. In Europe, it is very rare to entertain within the home. Generally, this is reserved for relations and only the closest of friends. The invitation of a foreign associate to your home may be seen as an expression of personal commitment and intimacy that may be stronger than you wish to communicate at a given time and within a given negotiation. By the same token, if you are invited to a Europeans' home it is very important that you understand the honor attached to that invitation and the expression of personal trust that the invitation connotes.

Gift giving is another area where you may wish to do specific research on the given culture that you are dealing with. In Europe it is *expected,* upon invitation to another's home, that you will bring flowers. If the invitation is made by the lady of the house, quality chocolates are advised. The appropriateness of flowers is something you should research with the florist in the locality in which you are visiting. In general, red flowers are to be avoided. There may be other local considerations which you should confirm with the florist.

Within the Japanese culture, gift giving has a very important business function. Normally, gifts are given by the visitor. The host may or may not reciprocate, and no inference of intent should be taken in either case. Generally, the gift given is related to the status of the individual and to the degree of the relationship. Giving a gift that is either inappropriately expensive or inexpensive can get you in trouble. Hence, in doing business in the Japanese culture it is best to discuss the intended gift in advance with a local expert. In general, the Japanese are very interested in, and appreciative of, gifts that are an expression of American culture, history, or sports for which they have great interest. For an extremely high level gift, high quality pens such as a Cross pen are very well received, as are quality leather products, such as Bally. The Japanese always appreciate designer goods with a recognized brand name.

It is also important to realize that there is a tendency within English speaking cultures to develop the business relationship first, and the personal relationship afterward. However, in non-English speaking countries, the opposite is generally the case. The personal relationship and a sense of trust must be built before even entertaining any thought of developing an ongoing business relationship.

Schedule Some Extra Time

A common mistake made by many American businessmen is to schedule overseas trips too tightly; that is, they do not allow enough time for the visits of prospective overseas clients. It is almost always best to allow a certain degree of extra time on any overseas trip. I would very strongly advise arriving a day early in any unfamiliar culture. In addition, be sure that you have informed your host that you will need to have a little time to sleep and to adjust to the time change on the day of your arrival. This is valuable for several reasons:

1. It allows you to enter your negotiations with a clear head.

2. You can acclimate yourself to the culture, walk around, observe, visit shops, and see the pace of business and the way business is done.

3. To acclimate your body to time change, and your mind and attitudes to the local culture.

Don't Be a Know-It-All

Avoid impatience to get to the heart of your business discussion. Key off your host. In Latin cultures you will probably be taken on a sightseeing tour of the area. Your host will probably attempt to explain something about his culture and the way his people deal with each other (all of which may be expressed in a very subtle fashion). At the same time, he will be making an evaluation of you to decide whether you are trustworthy and if you are an individual with whom he is personally comfortable. If that personal comfort is achieved, the business negotiations will go much smoother and result in a long-term relationship.

During this type of activity, avoid trying to establish yourself as an authority on the local culture. This is a major mistake. If taken to an exhibition on Picasso paintings, it is both wiser and far more politically correct to ask your host questions about their perception of the Picasso paintings, than to display your own knowledge or interpretation of them. This is an important rapport builder.

Never try to exhibit your understanding of your host's culture. This could be viewed as presumptive. It is far better from both a personal and a business standpoint to allow your host to explain his culture through his own eyes. In addition, your interest and questions will be greatly appreciated, far more than the verbalization of your observations.

> Don't be a know-it-all!

Avoid Ethnocentrism

Another habit to avoid is comparing what you see in the host's country to what we have in the United States. There is an important term called, *ethnocentrism*. Ethnocentrism is a natural tendency that almost everyone has, to feel that their culture is superior to any other in many ways. The word *China*, for example, is derived from the Chinese word *Chung Ku* which means "Middle Kingdom." Middle Kingdom expresses the cultural feeling of China being the center of the world.

Each culture feels a pride in its culture that is akin to that of the Chinese naming of their country *Chung Ku*. Appreciation of another's culture is a precondition for success in dealing with people from other cultures. Expression of interest in that culture is very well received and is an excellent rapport builder.

It is also advisable to fly to the host country on that country's national airline. Many American travelers have noted that one of the very first questions their host often asks is, "Which airline did you fly?" Flying the host country's airline, such as Cathay-Pacific or Iberia, builds more respect than does arriving on Pan Am or TWA. It shows a willingness to accept the possibility that the host culture offers a superior service, or at least a service equal to that offered by an American company.

For the same reason, I also suggest that, when dining, you allow your host to select your meal and that you indicate an interest in trying their local cuisine. Americans are also stereotyped as being inflexible and overly ethnocentric. By adapting to the habits and the culture of your host country you can establish credibility and go a long way toward breaking this stereotype.

> Avoid Ethnocentrism!

Dress for Success

Proper business attire will vary from country to country. In general, avoid brown or cordovan-colored shoes in any country outside the United States. These colors are generally reserved for sportswear. Also, avoid any type of loafer or slip-on in any area other than the Mediterranean area of Europe. Outside of these areas they are considered to be too casual for business wear.

When traveling on business within the United Kingdom, a white shirt with a 2⅞-inch collar spread is strongly suggested. This is generally the only acceptable business shirt there. Striped shirts are worn by certain elements within the publishing industry, among doctors, and within the financial industry. However, when meeting with corporate clients a white shirt should definitely be worn. The most acceptable suit—the only acceptable suit—is dark gray or navy and preferably pin-striped.

Pant legs outside the United States, including Great Britain, are generally worn slightly longer. Coat sleeves are worn slightly shorter and show a good ¼ inch of cuff. When traveling on the European continent, a dark gray, solid suit, double-vested worn with a solid tie and a white or pastel shirt would be most advisable.

Anywhere in Europe, avoid wearing the boldly striped American rep tie (they resemble military regimental ties). You are far better off with a solid colored tie or with a muted, nondirectional, neat pattern or a paisley. It's very important that the tie not be overly loud, and that it blend well with the suit.

Generally, the Mediterranean and Nordic countries are somewhat less formal than the rest of Europe. Here, under given circumstances a navy sport jacket and gray slacks may be totally acceptable for business. In many situations in Norway or in Finland, a nice sweater and slacks may be preferable to a business suit or a jacket and slacks combination when doing business in a rural area.

In Japan, it is advisable to wear a solid blue or dark gray suit, white shirt, and a conservative tie. Japan is the one country where a button-down shirt is acceptable under virtually all circumstances. Also, Japan, and perhaps Thailand and Korea, are the only countries in which you might wish to wear the standard, American oxford cloth shirt. In most parts of Europe they are considered much too informal to wear as business attire.

While traveling in Australia, you will find that in the areas of Sydney or Brisbane, standard American business attire is acceptable. However, should you be doing business in Melbourne it is advisable to follow the recommendation for attire within the United Kingdom. This is also true for Hong Kong and Eastern Europe.

In South Africa, light browns or tans are acceptable dress. In general, dress tends to be somewhat monochromatic, that is, brown suit, brown shoes, tan or cream shirt. Here also, a light, gray suit is to be advised given the climate. However, brightly striped American ties should be avoided. A solid tie or a simple neat tie in the same general color areas of the suit is generally most effective.

In Singapore a pair of well-pressed, lightweight slacks, a light colored shirt and a subdued, striped tie is the most effective business combination. People from Singapore rarely wear jackets. They are relatively informal in their attire, but impeccably neat.

Organizational Structures

If you are selling to a foreign institution it is important to realize that they may not work in quite the same way as we do. In the United States there is usually little distance between levels of management and communication tends to be relatively easy. In addition, we have a tradition of inner communication, building political alliances between various levels within an organization. Finally, we have a top-down leadership style where strategy is directed from the top and delegated down through the organization. When working with international clientele, you will often find organizational structures that are significantly different.

Of typical interest is the Japanese organization. Unlike the United States, where promotion to top levels tends to be based on a number of factors including competence and political connection, in a Japanese organization level tends to be based upon seniority. By the same token, where American organizations tend to work from the top down, Japanese organizations usually work from the bottom up. For example, if you were to look at the organization as a triangle, leading to the apex of the chairman, proposals in a Japanese company would be made from the bottom level of the corporation. A consensus would have to be agreed upon wherein everyone supported the recommendation. This recommendation would then be forwarded to the next level within the organization (where agreement has to be made in a very formal fashion) and continue at each step up the ladder until it reaches the chairman. At that point, there is little likelihood of the recommendation being sent back since it is the consensus of the organization. This has great impact in terms of business meetings. Hence, when you are addressing the chairman of a Japanese organization, you can expect to hear the chairman indicate a desire to consult with the members of his team. "We would be willing to take this under advisement," or "We will discuss it and will get back to you," are responses which should be expected.

To us, at some point eager to make a deal, it may seem strange that this attitude is taken. It is because of this bottom up structure that the decision process within a Japanese organization tends to take longer than in an American organization. However, once a decision is made, its implementation tends to be very rapid because everyone is already familiar with it, and implementation comes easily. If your expectations for negotiations with a Japanese firm are based upon your experience in dealing with domestic corporations, you will probably be frustrated with the slowness of the Japanese decision-making process. Ironically, your Japanese counterpart will probably be just as frustrated by the speed of implementation within the American process once a decision has been made.

In other cultures, notably the United Kingdom, you will find that responsibilities within an organization are very tightly defined. Contrast the typical sales representative dealing with an American organization; he is very likely to seek friends or allies at any layer of the organization and then sell outwards to others within that company to create a deal. In the United Kingdom, it is highly out of place to proceed in this manner. Organizations in the U.K. tend to be highly compartmentalized in terms of responsibility. A specific individual will have responsibility for a specific task and your goal must be to identify this individual and to work with him within the parameters of his responsibility. Permutations of these arrangements occur in the various countries in which we do business.

Another way in which we may perceive a difference in the way we do business is in the area of price. American companies often offer certain trial advantages, free services, or samples of services in order for the customer to experience the benefits of these services. After this trial period, both parties understand that the price may go up. However, in many other cultures, introduction to service is generally performed at a *higher* price. The customers are willing to pay the higher price because they recognize that it generally involves a smaller volume and is also a trial situation. Price is then negotiated downward from the initial offering. It can be highly disturbing for a Chinese or a Thai businessman to be given an initial offer and then, having agreed to use the service, to be put in the position by his American counterpart of seeing the price of that good or service increase. Hence, as a general rule of thumb, avoid the use of the trial offer when dealing with other cultures. Instead, start with a higher price than you intend for your ongoing business.

Summary

With the growing climate of global economic change, more and more foreign investors and companies are opening accounts with firms within the United States. Hence, whether your branch specializes in bank services, brokerage, insurance, or all three, every day increases your chances of doing business with some form of foreign investor or company. If you are to work effectively with them, you must be prepared to recognize and adapt to the differences in personal and business culture which they represent.

Appendixes

Appendix 1

Answers to Mastery Exercises

Exercise 1: Personality Traits (See Chapter 8)

"We all know just how important it is to perform exactly what is expected of you—no more and no less. A company ought to get what it pays for and it doesn't pay us to make up new company policies."

- *Bureaucrat* because of the need to perform exactly what is expected and not to modify policies.

"A department is run efficiently if all of the people are working in accord with one another. This virtually ensures that the company is getting optimal performance."

- *Socialite* because of the emphasis on interpersonal relationships as the primary determinant of effectiveness.

"The company requires that you pay attention to both the needs of the individual and the objectives of the department. Neither is always right."

- *Executive* because of the realization that there are two sides to the issue.

"There can be one captain of a ship and one captain only. When I want your opinion I'll ask for it. Till then just do what I told you. After all, I've been through these types of situations before."

- *Dictator* because of the need for individualized command.

This person's office has pictures of various teams that he has participated in, family pictures, and mementoes of every office party ever attended. The placement of the seat is designed for easy, casual conversation.

- *Socialite* because of the emphasis on group activities.

This person's office is rather stark and bare. The seat probably has a high back and is arranged opposite you and slightly above the visitor's.

- *Dictator* because of the control implications of the seating arrangement.

This person's office is somewhat stark but has company-oriented mementoes and plaques and awards placed throughout. It seems to be utilitarian.

- Probably an *executive*, although it is too vague to tell. Remember, that people do not always fall into an easy-to-see category.

This person's office is stuffed to the gills with papers which are so scattered and messy as to be unbelievable. The person's organizational system is to remember approximately which side of the office something is located.

- Again, the information is too vague to categorize this person.

378

"I wonder where all of the competent people went to?" he asks. "The only way to get something done right is to do it yourself."

- *Dictator* due to the insistence that he is the only competent person.

"I know that management and the union are seemingly on opposite sides of the fence. Let's get everybody together to see how we can resolve the situation for our mutual benefit."

- *Executive* because of the realization that there are two sides which deserve attention.

Exercise 2: Sensory Modes (See Chapter 12)

"Let's take a LOOK at all sides of the proposal and decide which avenue is most ATTRACTIVE."

- Obviously, visual.

"What we have here is a failure to COMMUNICATE. Everyone's always just TALKING about what they want, but they never seem to GET IT DOWN ON PAPER. TALK is cheap, but let me have some time to LOOK AT THE FIGURES. Then I'll know whether or not I'm interested."

- This person has both an auditory and visual orientation. It is interesting that the need to see it is a dominant theme.

"Did you ever get the SENSE that they don't know exactly what's COMING DOWN? They MOVE THEIR MOUTHS, but seem to be MISSING the entire idea."

- Kinesthetic.

"I THINK that we should CONSIDER the proposal very carefully. There are numerous points that need to be PONDERED."

- Unspecified.

Exercise 3: Accurate Responses to Sensory Modes (See Chapter 12)

"After I look over the literature, I want to speak with a few people who already own the product. Based upon how satisfied they are, I'll know whether the literature is telling the truth."

1. Let me show you some information which you should find interesting. Then I'll relate some comments from satisfied customers which should help.

2. I'm sure that you'll get a good feeling once you read over the literature. There are a lot of excellent things that people are saying.

3. After you get a sense of what is going on I'll show you a few things that will make you feel even better.

4. I can see that once you read some of the literature, you'll be able to make a decision based on a positive gut reaction.

Exercise 4: Predicates and Criteria for Personality Types (See Chapter 12)

"I want to get a SENSE for the proposal to ensure it doesn't diverge too significantly from standard operating procedure. I know that this has been important to you, but I don't want too much decentralization. You know what happened to our arch rival. He let things get out of control and subsequently lost significant market share to me, I mean us. It made me laugh for weeks. But, there's no way that'll happen here. I'll personally attend to that if I have to make them TOE THE LINE myself."

• This person is a *dictator* because of the emphasis on me/myself/I. The need to take control and the disregard for other people further reinforce this. Kinesthetic words/phrases have been capitalized. Key motivations have been underlined. In this situation the person doesn't want other people to diverge from the standard operating procedures which HE initiated. Control and the fear of decentralization (giving up some control) reinforce this point.

"Most of us have decided that it would be a good idea to attend the lecture on stress management. You know how it's important to the company that we learn as much as we can about it. Anyway, it will be a good chance to get together."

- Socialite.

Numerous factors have led to the creation of this new administration. The people have decided that they want to have the control necessary to positively affect their destinies.

- Possibly a socialite, but could also be an *executive*. Control is the key motivation with the positive influencing of the future a major point. You would probably sell to this person by emphasizing both the fulfillment of a future wish and the people orientation.

I chose this company because of its reputation for reliability. I've HEARD many good things about it over the years and it seems that it warrants those COMMENTS. Over time, I've become more familiar with it and find that the assistance that I've received conforms to the level of service that should be provided.

- Auditory predicates. Note that in the key motivations, reliability and overtime tend to go together. Reliability is partly a function of quality over a time period. Assistance and service are also similar concepts.

My friends know that this is the right place to go. This is where it's at and you can just TELL FROM THE VIBES. It's like where everyone else HANGS OUT and, you know, I have to maintain my image.

- This poor, mostly kinethetic, socialite is a groupie.

Exercise 5: Key Motivations (See Chapter 14)

Read the next three paragraphs and decide which themes have the greatest frequency.

- I chose this company to work for because it has an excellent <u>reputation for quality</u>. Everything they do indicates that. The fact that it offers me <u>many career paths</u> is also important to someone like me who is <u>upwardly mobile</u>. It's also the most <u>well known</u> company of its kind in the world.

- There's a great restaurant <u>down the street</u> which I'm sure you'll enjoy. It has a <u>large menu</u> which always gets <u>rave reviews</u> from those of us who <u>know about it</u>.

- I like people who have <u>a lot of different interests</u> because it makes them interesting to talk to. But, more than anything, I must know that I can <u>turn my back on them</u> without fear.

This person has variety (multiple career paths, large menu, many interests) as a key motivation. In addition, the issue of trust is evident (good reputation, rave reviews, turn my back). Although "down the street" may indicate a location issue, it only is evident once.

Appendix 2

Predicates/Sensory-Oriented Words and Phrases

Visual	Auditory	Kinesthetic	Unspecified
See	Sound	Feel	Think
Picture	Hear	Grasp	Decide
Appear	Mention	Firm	Motivate
Outlook	Inquire	Pressure	Understand
Imagine	Scream	Grip	Plan
Focus	Tune	Moves	Know
Perception	Shrill	Flow	Consider
Foresee	Oral	Stress	Advise
Vista	Earful	Callous	Deliberate
Looks	Listen	Moves	Develop
Clear	Ring	Warm	Create
Observe	Resonate	Numb	Manage

Visual	Auditory	Kinesthetic	Unspecified
Horizon	Loud	Dull	Repeat
Scope	Vocal	Hold	Anticipate
Notice	Remark	Affected	Indicate
Show	Discuss	Emotional	Admonish
Scene	Articulate	Solid	Activate
Watch	Say	Soft	Prepare
Aim	Announce	Active	Allow
Angle	Audible	Bearable	Permit
Aspect	Boisterous	Charge	Direct
Clarity	Communicate	Concrete	Discover
Cognizant	Converse	Foundation	Ponder
Conspicuous	Dissonant	Hanging	Determine
Examine	Divulge	Hassle	Resolve
Glance	Earshot	Heated	Meditate
Hindsight	Enunciate	Hunch	Believe
Illusion	Interview	Hustle	Cogitate
Illustrate	Noise	Intuition	Judge
Image	Proclaim	Lukewarm	Evaluate
Inspect	Pronounce	Motion	Reckon
Obscure	Report	Muddled	Imagine
Obvious	Roar	Panicky	Contemplate
Perspective	Rumor	Rush	Assume
Pinpoint	Screech	Sensitive	Conceptualize
Scrutinize	Silence	Set	Conceive
Sight	Speak	Shallow	Influence
Sketchy	Speechless	Shift	Accept
Survey	Squeal	Softly	Prove
Vague	State	Stir	Depend
View	Tell	Structured	Communicate
Vision	Tone	Support	Comprehend

Sensory Word-Oriented/Predicate Phrases.

Visual	Auditory	Kinesthetic
An eyeful	Blabber mouth	All washed up
Appears to be	Clear as a bell	Boils down to
Bird's eye view	Clearly expressed	Chip off the old block

Visual	Auditory	Kinesthetic
Catch a glimpse of	Call on	Come to grips with
Clear-cut	Describe in detail	Cool/Calm/Collected
Dim view	Earful	Firm foundation
Eye to eye	Express yourself	Floating on thin air
Flashed on	Give an account of	Get a handle on
Get a perspective on	Give me your ear	Get a load of this
Get a scope on	Hear voices	Get the drift of
Hazy idea	Hidden message	Get your goat
In light of	Hold your tongue	Hand-in-hand
In person	Idle talk	Hang in there
In view of	Idle talk/tongue	Heated argument
Looks like	Inquire into	Hold it
Make a scene	Keynote speaker	Hold on
Mental image/picture	Loud and clear	Hot-head
Mind's eye	Power of speech	Keep your shirt on
Naked eye	Purrs like a kitten	Lay cards on the table
Paint a picture	Outspoken	Light-headed
Photographic memory	Rap session	Moment of panic
Plainly see	Rings a bell	Not following you
Pretty as a picture	State your purpose	Pull some strings
See to it	Tattletale	Sharp as a tack
Short-sighted	To tell the truth	Slipped my mind
Showing off	Tongue-tied	Smooth operator
Sight for sore eyes	Tuned in/out	So-so
Staring off into space	Unheard of	Start from scratch
Take a peek	Utterly	Stiff upper lip
Tunnel vision	Voiced an opinion	Stuffed shirt
Up front	Within hearing range	Topsy-turvy
Well-defined	Word for Word	Underhanded

Motivational Criteria and Equivalencies

Buying Motivations Equivalencies

Although people tend to use consistent themes to make decisions, it is rare that one would describe these themes using the same words all the time. Someone may go to a particular gas station because of the *large product line*; a particular clothing store because of its *good selection*; a restaurant because of the *variety* of cuisine; and have *diversity* of interests as a requirement of friendship. In each case, the theme of available alternatives (words in italics) was dominant. To sell to such a person, you should emphasize the concept of multiplicity of choices and use synonyms that indicate choice in your presentation.

Listed below are some of the more common, or dominant, buying motivations/themes and some synonyms that can be used to describe them. The list is not exhaustive, but should help to give you an idea of how synonyms can be used in the sales process. However, remember that while the denotation, or dictionary definition, of a word is the same for everyone, the connotation, or meaning, of the word will differ from individual to individual. For example, *safety* means entirely different things to different investors; so does *risk* or *service*.

Equivalencies.

Advertising	Reputation	Name recognition	Familiarity
Alternatives	Variety	Selection	Product line
Appearance	Looks	Atmosphere	Ambiance
Cleanliness	Looks	Neatness	Sanitary
Convenience	Location	Help	Service
Courtesy	Consideration	Service	Respect
Credit	Cash Flow	Bargain	Discount
Dependability	Reliability	Reputation	Confidence
Extras	Incentives	Bonuses	Gifts
Habit	Tradition	Familiarity	Sentimental
Image	Style	Status	Prestige
Integrity	Honesty	Trustworthy	Honor/Trust
Money	Price	Cost	Discount
Performance	Durability	Standards	Quality
Prestige	Class	Peer pressure	Status
Professional	Competent	Expert	Authority
Prompt	Quick	Speed	Dependable
Quality	Value	Craftsmanship	Reliable
Relationship	Loyalty	Friendly	Affiliation
Reputation	Referral	Popularity	Prestige
Safety	Security	Guarantee	Warrantee
Service	Help	Assistance	Courtesy
Status	Prestige	Authority	Pre-eminence
Suitability	Appropriateness	Applicability	Relevance
Times Open	Convenience	Hours	Availability

Appendix 4

Stress

Early Signs of Stress

As you examine your own behavior and that of your employees, look for emotional, behavioral, and physical symptoms of stress. If you find them, take steps to reduce the stress before they cost you a productive member of your staff.

Emotional Signs

1. *Apathy*–Can't seem to get your motor started.

2. *Anxiety*–Worrying about what will go wrong next.

3. *Irritability*–Short temper with family, employees, and peers.

4. *Mental fatigue*–Sometimes it's just hard to think.

5. *Overcompensation or denial*–What problems?

6. *Feelings of helplessness*–What can I do?

7. *Hopelessness*–What's the use?

8. *Self-castigation*–I never do anything right.

9. *Confusion*–I just don't know what to do.

Behavioral Signs

1. *Avoiding things*–Not making sales calls; not dealing with a problem FC.

2. *Doing things to extremes*–Making more calls than you can follow-up on.

3. *Difficulty solving even simple administrative problems*–Even simple work becomes overwhelming.

4. *Legal problems*–The temptation to take shortcuts.

5. *Loss of productivity*

Physical Signs

1. Excessive worry about, or denial of, illness.

2. Frequent illness—you've always got a cold.

3. Physical exhaustion—You're always tired.

4. Reliance on self-medication—Alcohol, and other over-the-counter medications.

5. Ailments—Frequently not feeling good.

6. Sleeplessness.

7. Loss of appetite or weight—Food becomes tasteless.

8. Chronic muscular aches—Frequent back pain.

9. Accelerated heart rate—Palpitations.

10. Accelerated respiration—Can't catch your breath.

11. Tightness in the joints and muscles.

12. Headaches.

13. Stomach disorders—Diarrhea, constipation, nausea.

The Cost of Stress

The biggest cost of stress is loss of effective production. This may occur because an FC is no longer doing the things necessary to succeed, because of an increase in errors, or because he leaves the branch for another firm. In extreme cases, it occurs because of legal problems (e.g., compliance problems or substance abuse). In addition, stress is a primary cause of the following health problems:

- Skin problems: hives, lichen simplex, or shingles.
- Cardiovascular difficulties: high blood pressure, migraine, heart attack, or stroke.
- Gastro-intestinal problems: ulcers, ulcerative colitis, constipation, or diarrhea.
- Genitourinary problems: difficulty urinating, impotence, or frigidity.
- Psychological problems: depression, anxiety, etc.

Physiological Responses to Stress

Immediate Threat: The Alarm Response

When we first perceive a challenge as a threat to either our physical well-being, our control, or our self-esteem, we become alarmed and our body enters a defensive mode. Dr. Hans Selye, the father of modern stress medicine, called this the *alarm stage* or mode. In this mode, we tend to respond actively, by becoming angry or aggressive and adrenaline is released into our blood stream, causing the following changes.

1. The heart beats faster and stronger, resulting in a rapid rise in blood pressure.

2. The blood is shunted away from the stomach and skin to the muscles.

3. Cholesterol is released into the blood stream to provide energy.

4. The blood thickens to enable it to clot more easily in case of injury.

5. The pupils dilate to enable you to see better.

6. Hearing becomes more acute.

7. Touch is enhanced by the hairs on the body standing up (like the fur of an alerted animal).

8. The senses of taste and smell are enhanced.

9. The skin sweats to cool the underlying muscles.

10. The facial muscles tense and the face flushes.

11. The nostrils flare, the throat dilates, all of the air passages in the lungs dilate, and breathing quickens and blood sugar rises.

12. Endorphins are released from the hypothalamus to block pain.

13. Sex hormones are reduced. You are now ready to fight or flee.

The problem is that, unlike our forefathers who were faced with such threats only a few times a year, we often face them many times a day. For example, when an FC is rejected 50 times a day while prospecting, or an angry client calls with a complaint. In addition, while our forefathers usually did fight or flee, thus burning off the adrenaline, we cannot, and the amount of these chemicals in the blood can rise to alarming levels.

Long-Term Threat: Resistance and Exhaustion

When we feel threatened over a long period of time, our defenses enter what Dr. Selye called a *maintenance mode*. In this mode our defenses keep us vigilant, and hyper-alert to any additional threat to body or ego. Continued too long, we begin to feel that we've lost control of our lives. This sense of having lost control makes us feel passive, helpless to remove the threat, and hopeless of gaining any improvement. After awhile, we begin to develop self-doubt and question our self-worth, becoming anxious and depressed. During this hyper-alert period, cortisol is released and moves slowly through the body causing the following changes.

1. The blood pressure rises slowly. If maintained too high, too long, this can lead to essential hypertension.

2. The body tissues retain vital body chemicals, such as salt.

3. Cholesterol and clotting agents are released into the blood, making it harder for the heart to pump.

4. Production of sex hormones, like testosterone in the male and progesterone in the female, is repressed.

5. Production of gastric acid is increased to maximize digestion.

6. The immune system's defenses against disease are impaired.

7. The body's alertness is chronically aroused.

If we remain out-of-control and threatened too long, we will reach what D. Selye called the *state of exhaustion* in which we become totally unable to cope. This can result in mental breakdown, physical illness, or even death.

Substances to Avoid

Tobacco

Of 50 million people who smoke, one-half to two-thirds will die simply because they smoke.

If you could distill all of the nicotine, arsenic, strychnine, and tar from a single cigarette and inject it into your veins you would be dead before you could reach the door to call for help. Ninety-eight percent of all smokers are addicted to nicotine.

Nicotine plus carbon monoxide make a deadly pair. The nicotine speeds up the heart and makes it work harder while the carbon monoxide from the cigarette robs the heart of the oxygen it needs, slowly strangling it.

When the body becomes stressed, the air sacks in the lungs expand to increase the amount of oxygen to the body. If you smoke when you are under stress, you can cause almost 10 times the damage to your lungs as you would smoking when you are relaxed.

Women who smoke while on birth control pills run even higher risks of developing or aggravating hardening of the arteries, blood clotting (which can lead to stroke or heart attack), and heart disease.

Alcohol

Among the many damaging side effects caused by alcohol, the following are some of the most serious.

- It stimulates production of the stress hormone, cortisol.
- It is a diuretic—it dries you out—enhancing the body's clotting mechanisms.
- It directly damages heart fibers; over time it causes the heart to become weak and flabby.
- It *kills brain cells.*
- It causes cirrhosis of the liver, the fourth-largest killer of middle-aged men.
- It causes alcoholic hypertension.
- It causes temporary, reversible damage to the bone marrow.
- It puts pregnant women at special risk and can result in *fetal alcohol syndrome.*
- It significantly increases the chance of breast cancer in women.
- It contains empty calories.

Caffeine

Coffee and tea, two popular *safe* drinks which contain the stimulant caffeine actually have harmful side effects. These include:

- releasing adrenaline,
- aggravating stress,
- causing irritability and anxiety attacks, and
- hindering restful sleep.

> Keep yourself fit to cope with stress.

Index

Bureaucrat
  as customer, 72–73
  as financial consultant, 70–72
  as manager, 61–63
  need for power in, 131
  as personality type, 56, 71
Burnout
  causes of, 186–188
  recognizing process of, 192
  stress-related, 148, 149
Business attire, 370–371
Business units, interaction among, 312
Buyer's remorse, 83
Buying motivations, 124

C

Career sample training, 278–280
Case studies, 322
Catalytic leadership, 255, 257, 258–260
Central information file, 339–340
CEO training, 312–313
Certified Financial Planner (CFP), 325, 329–330
Character
  attributes of, 10–11
  development of, 9–10
  habit and, 12–13
  importance of, 7–9
  setting goals for development of, 11–12
Character traits
  development through habit, 12–13
  list of beneficial, 13–14
Charities, 350–351
Chartered Financial Consultant (ChFC), 276, 280, 328–330
Chartered Life Underwriter (CLU), 276, 280, 328–330
Checklists, for meeting preparation, 47
China, 354
Chunking
  explanation of, 141
  of long-range goals, 20–21
Churchill, Winston, 26
CLAPing technique, 200–206

Clarification, 200–201
Clark, Robert, 275
Client-centered market, 3–5
Clients. See Customers
Coaching
  for employees with substandard performance, 212–215
  setting goals in, 215–216
Cold calls. See also Prospecting techniques; Sales techniques
  contacts from, 27, 178
  developing scripts for, 178–179
  in down market, 10
  fear of, 176–179, 290
  providing lists for, 41
  rejection from, 60, 174–176
College for Financial Planning, 325, 330–331
College of Insurance, 325
Comfort, at meetings, 47
Comfort zones, 292–293
Communication
  branch, 267–274. See also Branch communications distance during, 363–364
  establishing rapport needed for, 94
  patterns in, 85
  in positive terms, 115–117
  posture as form of, 91–96
  problems regarding, 181–194
  sensory orientation and, 103–109
  speed of, 99–101
Communication skills
  of branch manager, 49–50, 340
  and leadership, 87
  steps toward effective, 183
Community activity, 274
Community relations
  demographics and, 349
  factors effecting, 348–349
  importance of, 347
  methods of enhancing, 349–352
Compensation, 4
Competition
  changing nature of, 3–4
  effecting banking industry, 337–338
  and international business, 358–359
Complementary relationship style, 83

Ehre, Victor T., Jr., 267
Eliot, Robert, 150–153
Emotional people, 141–142
Employee transfer, 210, 211
Employee turnover
    due to failure to share goals and objectives,
        273
    high cost of, 211, 212, 248–249
    minority, 248–249
Employment interviews, 142–143
Environmental factors
    impact on performance of, 210
    and internal branch communications,
        273–274
Equal Employment Opportunity (EEO)
    goals, 244
    quotas, 245
Ethnocentrism, 369–370
Europe. See Cross-cultural business;
    International business
European Economic Community, 300,
    353–354
Examinations, prehire, 277
Exchange rate differentials, 357–358
Executive
    as customer, 77–78
    as financial consultant, 76–77
    as manager, 59, 64–65, 83–85
    as personality type, 57, 76
Exercise, to reduce stress, 169
Expectations
    and fear of failure, 25
    and performance, 209
External motivation, 142–143

F

Failure
    among financial consultants, 284–287
    overcoming fear of, 25–27
Family
    impact of career changes on, 161–164
    job as rival to, 164–165
    need for support from, 289–290
    relationships in different cultures, 367

role in reducing stress, 165–166
    as source of stress, 160
Family council, 165
Fear of failure, 25–27
Feelings, control of, 158–159
Female financial consultants. See Minority
    financial consultants
Financial consultants (FCs)
    assessing cost of goals on, 17–18
    bureaucrat as, 70–72
    challenge of managing, 3, 4
    dealing with problems of, 33
    dictator as, 67–68
    differing levels of, 283–284
    educational requirements for, 331
    executive as, 76–77
    intermediate-level, 286, 291–294
    job needs of, 257–260
    managers as former, 8–9, 60
    messages appealing to, 257
    minority, 243–252. See also Minority
        financial consultants
    reasons for failure among, 284–287
    responsibilities of, 319–320
    selection and training of, 277–282. See also
        Recruitment; Training
    socialite as, 74
    stress in, 148, 150–153
    submissive, 83
    as threat to manager, 60
    top-performing, 295–296
    trainees. See Trainees
    winning characteristics for, 8
Financial planner certification, 325, 329–331
Financial Satellite Network, 333
Financial services industry
    awareness of commitment to minority
        issues, 250–251
    changes in, 3–5, 299–300, 335–336
    criminal activity in, 9
    impact of changing world environment on,
        353–355
    need for continuing education in, 326–328
Finland, 371
Flexibility
    in international relationships, 363–365
    in relating to personality types, 82

International business
    changing environment for, 353–355
    cultural differences in, 356–357
    and exchange rate differentials, 357–358
    financial services competition and,
        358–359
    impact of public image of company on, 357
    regulatory differences in, 355–356
Interviews, preemployment, 277–278

J

Japan
    changing financial industry in, 358
    contract use in, 365
    dressing for business in, 371
    gift-giving in, 367–368
    organizational structure in, 372
Job responsibilities
    redefining, 210, 211
    understanding of one's own, 270–271
Judgmental statements, 214

K

Kaiser, Henry J., 26
Kinesthetic orientation, 104, 105
Korea, 364, 365

L

Lag time, 24
Language patterns, 183, 184
Leadership
    catalytic, 255, 258–260
    conceptual, 254, 257–259
    grid presentation of, 54–57
    importance of, 87–88
    management and, 254
    matching predicates aiding in, 109
    motivation and, 119, 256–257
    as personality type, 52–53
    and rapport, 96
    relational, 255, 258–260

    structural, 255, 258–260
Leadership message model, 254–255
Leading
    changing states through, 96
    to deal with angry people, 196
    test for rapport through, 94–95, 101
Lee, Ivy, 34–35
Life Underwriter Training Council (LUTC),
    280
Linear thinking, 140
Litigation, 326, 327
Logical people, 141, 142
Long-term goals
    attainable, 157
    chunking down, 20–21
    example of, 22
    setting time frame for, 21–22
Lose/win orientation, 144
Loving Trust (Esperti and Peterson), 322
Lying, 13

M

Magazine articles, 322
Management
    as element of measuring, 19
    leadership and, 254
    of sales and operations, 253
    training of senior, 312–313
Managers. See Branch managers
Marketing meetings, 45–46. See also Meetings
Marketing specialists, 45–46
Marketing territory, 276–277
Matched body posture, 91–93
Matched breathing, 97
McLean, James D., 361
Media relations, 349–350
Mediocrity, 19
Meetings
    determining purpose of, 39–40
    for educational purposes, 321–322
    making plan for, 40–41
    marketing, 45–46
    preparation necessary for, 46–47
    preparing agenda for, 43–44
    using agenda for, 41–43

402

Training (*cont.*)
    centralized, 323–324
    for employees with substandard
        performance, 212
    and legal difficulties, 326, 327
    for middle agents, 280–281
    for minority financial consultants, 246–248
    for new agents, 280, 285
    product. *See* Product presentation program
    value of, 275–276
Training meetings, 41–43
Transfer of employees, 210, 211
Tuition assistance, 324–325
Tuition refund programs, 324–326
Type A personality, 152
Type B personality, 152

U

Unaided awareness studies, 348–349
Unconscious motivations, 121–124
United Kingdom
    dressing for business in, 370
    organizational structure in, 373
Unscheduled appointments, 33
Unspecified words, 109
U.S. Army, 46

V

Visual aids
    for branch manager training, 316
    for presentations, 46–47
Visual orientation, 104–105

W

Warmth, 89
"We"-oriented people, 142
Win/lose orientation, 144
Women, recruitment of, 244. *See also*
    Minority financial consultants
Words
    denotation vs. connotation of, 184
    subject to individual interpretation, 188
Work environment, 167–168
Work force, 243
Work schedule, 36–37
Written goals, 12–13, 18–19

Y

Yeager, Joseph, 150